NIANTIC JEWEL

Seaburn

Graham Griffith

Niantic Jewel.
Copyright © 2009 by Graham Griffith.
All Rights Reserved including the right of
Reproduction in whole or in part.
For permission please write to the publisher:

Seaburn
P.O. Box 2085
Astoria NY 11102

ISBN: 1-59232-219-0

Library of Congress Cat. Num.-in-Pub.-Data

2009 Griffith, G.
Niantic Jewel.

Ref. CSO.1010S10-Sta2

Printed in the United States of America

NIANTIC JEWEL

Graham Griffith

Graham Griffith

Acknowledgment

This book would not have been possible without the work of modern historians, ethnohistorians and archeologists in replacing the nationalistic perspective of earlier writers with a factual appreciation of Native American cultural history, particularly the 17th Century in New England. Thanks also to the Narragansett Indian Nation for courtesies extended, and to my wife Linda for her unflagging encouragement and unwavering belief in the project.

CHAPTER 1

THE OUTSIDER

But to see her was to love her,
Love but her, and love forever.
ROBERT BURNS

Low tide at Quonnie Cove is the best time to gather blue mussels from the two rocky points anchoring the crescent of sand where land meets the ocean. There, on the undersides of boulders in the intertidal zone, the dark grottos exposed only when the water recedes, is where the largest specimens of the tasty bivalve mollusk Mytilus edulis are found. Such is the bounty of life even at the margins.

And Nature knew no bounds today: a glorious late-July morning on Block Island Sound with the island 9 miles offshore barely discernible in the fair-weather haze. The sparkling sun approached its zenith in a cornflower-blue sky dotted with woolly puffs of Cumulus humilis that looked like grazing sheep. The placid ocean mirrored the lush color field above, save for shimmering teal blue patches where terminal moraine poked through the sandy bottom.

The only sound was the lapping of the enervated tide and an occasional gurgling when it ebbed between the rocks enclosing a tide pool. Now the salty air carried an extra tang of seaweed and a whiff of the sun-ripened shells left at high-water mark by the last tide.

Here and there, herring gulls and one or two black-backed gulls picked among the detritus for crab and lobster parts and the few intact clam and horse mussel shells they could fly off with to drop onto flat-topped rocks, whereby to crack open the prize.

Colin soon had enough mussels for his lunch. Pail in hand, he jumped from one dry rock to another near the shoreline, trying to avoid the wet, slippery ones or stepping onto the damp, sticky sand. It was a game, and he felt like a child again – unselfconscious and free – until time caught up with him.

Reflexively, he found himself glancing around to be sure no one was watching. The rocky shoreline and dunes to the west were deserted. In front of him, he was screened by the massive glacial boulders rising up to 15 feet out of the sand that defined the western tip of Quonnie Cove. The game ended where the moraine formed an impassable barrier. But he had the urge to press on. In the week since arriving from Boston, he had explored neither the point nor the cove beyond, although he could see them from the upstairs windows of the small saltwater farm he was minding for the owner.

He surveyed the sheer face for handholds, but in vain. Picking his way among the smaller boulders, he followed the central mass beyond the high tide line where the sand was dry, looking for a way over. Just as it seemed he'd have to detour into the dunes to bypass the rampart, he noticed a fissure 10 feet up where the outcrop had begun to split apart.

Putting down his pail, he began jumping with arms outstretched until he got a fingerhold in the base of the cleft, enough to pull himself up by one arm until he gained a foothold. From there, doubled up precariously, he inched his hands up the crevice by pressing hard against its sides. It took all his strength to defy gravity, but soon he was standing upright in the opening.

Patches of map lichen caught his eye, their yellow-green crusts tracing delicate patterns on the dark conglomerate of gneiss and quartz that geologists call graywacke. On one large colony, someone had scratched out a heart enclosing the barely legible initials TM and JP. Above it was a narrow ledge he was able to

NIANTIC JEWEL

climb to, and from there he had only to pivot on his stomach to swing himself onto the broad flat summit.

He sat up, not daring to stand yet, and took in the vista from his high perch. To his right, the shoreline of sand and rocks stretched half a mile to the headland at Sunset Beach, where a breachway linked the ocean to Quonochontaug Pond. Across the channel, a mile of barrier dunes and pristine beach gave way to rocky cliffs at Weekapaug Point, leading to the blue-collar state beach at Misquamicut and then the blue-blood enclave of Watch Hill at the western tip of the Sound. To his left, the Cove curved to the next rocky point at Orient Beach. Arching beyond, as far the eye could see, lay the dunes and beaches of Ninigret Conservation Area, Charlestown, Green Hill, Matunuck and 12 miles away, out of sight in the haze, Jerusalem, Galilee and the Sound's eastern tip at Point Judith.

Suddenly, before he saw anything, his brain registered it. The start threw him momentarily off balance, and he dropped to his knees to steady himself. She wasn't more then 20 feet away, sunbathing on a secluded pocket of sand ringed entirely by the high boulders on which he sat, except for a narrow, sandy opening to the water.

She lay on her stomach facing him, propped up on her elbows, her head in a book, a yellow pail at her side. The chestnut hair curled onto tanned shoulders and a broad back tapering to the flare of her hips. The burnt-orange bikini bottom was only a shade darker than the beach towel she was half on and half off, so that her shapely golden thighs and calves were on the wet sand at the shoreline and her feet were in the water. A glowing aureole of ocher sand encircled her, fading into shadow cast by the brown boulders framing the scene.

His eyes roamed the curves of her body to the red-brown hair gleaming in the sunlight – and the white stripes on her back and shoulders where, it struck him perversely, her bikini straps should be. The orange top was just visible on the amber towel under her elbows, but it was the deep, though mostly obscured, cleavage below her collarbones, that captured his gaze – until a pang of guilt diverted it to her face. From this elevated angle, all he could make out was a short rounded nose.

And then she moved. Her head snapped back. She glanced quickly to each side, as if aware of a presence. Closing the book, she dropped onto her stomach. Her hands reached for the bikini top, deftly pulling the two straps across her back and hooking them. He felt like a voyeur exposed. The flight response propelled him back into the fissure and down the boulder. Behind its brow, he descended carefully and quietly. The only sound he heard was his heart pounding in his chest. He tried to calm down, reassuring himself that his innocent peek had gone undetected.

*   *   *

Back on the sand, he retrieved his pail and retreated into the cover of the dunes, picking his way between dense clumps of marram grass and beach plums until emerging on the other side of the point. He stopped to rest on a driftwood tree trunk cast up on the sand and bleached silver in the salty air. Stretching out his legs, he gathered his thoughts and looked around him.

It was a different world in the cove. In the distance, a raucous gaggle of small children built castles in the silky sand and splashed in the water, watched by mothers and the occasional father and mother's helper in their beach chairs. The territory in front of the dunes where the boardwalk cut through to the parking lot was the hangout of pubescents loath to be seen with their parents but still within sight of them, and, more important, in a prime location to be seen with one another.

The older teenagers who didn't have summer jobs or whose shifts hadn't yet begun worked on their tans and planned their late-night beach parties in another enclave 100 yards to the east, back near the dunes but with a clear run to the water whenever they needed to cool off their hot bodies. Out in the Sound, a lobsterman was pulling traps half a mile offshore and the sails of a few small sloops tried to catch what breeze there was.

Then, out of the corner of his eye, he saw her emerge from the smaller boulders of the point at water's edge 20 yards away,

NIANTIC JEWEL

headed straight for him, The yellow pail hung from one arm while the other cradled the book and towel. She was looking along the shoreline, and he seized the chance to stare.

Now he could see the moon-shaped face highlighted by cascading curls and bangs of auburn hair scintillating in the sunlight. And, now too, upright and in motion, there was confirmation of her voluptuous figure. To male eyes, the fetching bikini erred only in its nod to modesty. She seemed to be in her early 20s, 5' 7", 130 pounds. She turned her head toward him, and their eyes met briefly until he dropped his gaze to the yellow bucket, trying to look deep in thought, as if he had barely noticed her. When she was almost upon him, he looked into her open face again and renewed contact with her blue eyes.

"Salacia! Good morning! You came from nowhere! Are you a mermaid from the ocean, or an angel from the sky?"

Surprised, she stopped in front of him, her full lips parting in a winsome smile.

"Sorry to disappoint you. I came around the point. There's a way through at low tide. You must be new here. I don't think we've met... Anyway, who's Salacia?"

"A Roman goddess of the ocean. Neptune saw her one day and was smitten by her grace and beauty. He wanted to marry her, but she ran off and hid in the Atlantic so he sent a dolphin to bring her back. She agreed to marry him, and they lived happily ever after."

"Well, dream on...."

Desperate to engage her longer, he could only manage a feeble "It's a lovely day."

"Isn't it just?..." She swung her pail toward his. "... Unless you're a mussel."

She bent over to peer at his pickings, giving him a close-up of her ample breasts.

"I see you're a connoisseur too, and you know where to find the big ones. But keep it quiet; we don't want everyone knowing, do we?"

He was at eye level with her navel, which lay in the center of a gently rounded stomach curving to the bikini bottom. Beneath the fabric was the unmistakable rise of her mound of Venus. He fought off the thrill of arousal and looked up at her, again grasping for words.

"Do you have a special recipe?"

"I'll tell you mine if you tell me yours."

He smiled, encouraged by her playfulness.

"That's fair, but it's not really my recipe. I picked it up from a friend's wife. She said it's called Moules a la Quonnie. You add a cup of white wine to the water you're steaming the mussels in. When they're open, you set aside the largest third of the shells and discard the empty halves. Then you add the smaller mussels to those in the bigger shells – so there are three to a shell...."

She rolled her eyes and giggled.

"What is this – a recipe or a math quiz? We just steam and eat them with melted butter and Greek seasoning."

"Patience is a virtue, you know."

She tossed her head and pursed her coral pink lips in mock defiance.

"Not when I crave mussels. But do go on."

"... Let's see: Next, you cream 3 tablespoons of butter, mince 3 garlic cloves, chop 1 cup of parsley and mix it all up. Put a dab in each shell. Place the shells on a toaster oven tray and broil for 2-3 minutes. That's it. Oh, and this way, you don't get butter dripping on you. You pick up the shell by the neck and slurp it onto your tongue."

He waited for her appraisal, but instead heard a shout from behind. He turned to see a young man in tennis whites waving vigorously as he ran toward them from the boardwalk. She waved back and started to leave.

"Have to run. I lost track of the time and I'm late for tennis. Nice talking to you. 'Bye."

He could only blurt "Me too. Cheerio then."

And she was gone before he realized to his dismay that he'd failed to get her name.

He could only watch in frustration while she strode hurriedly toward the intruder, the muscles of her thighs and buttocks rippling with the effort. He caught only snatches of the exchange when they met. "Your mom... down here... waiting." She handed

NIANTIC JEWEL

him the pail as they stepped onto the boardwalk and disappeared into the dunes.

*   *   *

Rather than return to the farmhouse the way he'd come, he felt like exploring more of this new world he'd entered. After a decent interval, he followed them off the beach, through the gantlet of listless adolescents at the boardwalk, and into the parking lot for the short hike home.

The small summer community of Quonochontaug Cove was a maze of narrow, tarred-gravel lanes, hedged by thickets overrun with beach roses, brambles, wild honeysuckle and bittersweet vines. Every 100 feet or so, a dirt driveway with a mailbox indicated a cottage tucked away somewhere behind the riot of vegetation.

He knew that if he took Ninigret Avenue outside the parking lot and followed it along the back of the dunes it would curve away and link up with Sunset Beach Road, the asphalt state highway that ran north to south down the western side of Quonochontaug Neck from Route 1 to Sunset Point. By turning left at this road, he would come eventually upon Niantic Drive, whose grand loop, enclosing its own labyrinth of lanes, reached down to and along the shore of the great salt pond before arcing back.

Beside the pond, at the drive's southern bend, a mailbox with the name Quaiapen Farm stood at the foot of a bare track with fieldstone walls on either side. The trail cut through pasture in which, on the land sloping to the pond, some Jersey cows and a calf grazed. On the ground rising away from the track, a small flock of sheep lay in the shade of a broad white oak.

The shingled, $1^{1/2}$-story farmhouse with a wraparound veranda sat on a rise facing the water. Its most prominent feature was a big gambrel roof, whose side view from the street gave the appearance of an upturned keel with a stone chimney poking through. Chickens and ducks pecked in the farmyard behind, near the open doors of a barn parallel to the house and forming a horseshoe with a long, open-fronted shed containing a car, a tractor and farm equipment.

It should have been a simple matter of heading northwest from the beach, but with intoxicating visions of the red-haired beauty saturating his mind, Colin took a wrong turn at an unmarked fork where the road veered off from the dunes. The daydream evaporated when he came to an intersection and realized his mistake. Unwilling to double back, he took a left along a lane that soon curved right and led to another crossroads.

Disheartened, he complained aloud to himself:

"Damn it all, Why can't they mark these lanes? Now I'm totally lost."

While he pondered his options and switched hands on the pail, which grew heavier by the minute, a car approached. It slowed for the intersection and he was eye-to-eye with the driver through the open window.

"Sorry to bother you, but I do believe I'm, well, lost.,,,"

Before he could finish, the slim, middle-aged woman with short black hair shot back:

"By Jove! I'd say you're off course by 3,000 miles, judging by that accent. You're in the Colonies; Rhode Island to be exact."

He frowned in exasperation.

"Yes, I'm trying to find Sunset Beach Road. I'm staying on Niantic Drive."

She lowered her shades and peered into his pail.

"And you've been gathering mussels at the point. You'd better get them home and out of the sun before they spoil. I can drop you off if you like. My daughter's been musseling too. I had to run to the store for butter and a few other things. Hop in"

She motioned him around to the passenger side of the maroon Prius V hatchback. Accepting what seemed a fait accompli, and glad at the prospect of shade from the sun, he complied. He put his pail on the floor between his legs and grappled with the seatbelt, taking the opportunity to scrutinize his Samaritan while her eyes were on the road. She wore khaki shorts with a navy T-shirt. Her seatbelt lay flat across a tight, slender frame, which with

NIANTIC JEWEL

the severity of her short, straight hair and lack of makeup lent her an austere aspect despite the delicate profile of her face.

"This is awfully kind of you. I'm really grateful."

She glanced at him, allowing a better view of her face with its thin lips, angular cheekbones and narrow nose. It seemed improbable that the redhead on the beach could be her daughter.

"You're welcome. You looked like a lost puppy. What brings you all the way to Quonnie?"

"Oh, I'm minding Mr. Stanton's place while he's away."

"The farm?"

"Yes."

"He's a such an old dear. I always buy my lobsters from him when I can. I've often wondered what age he is. He's been here forever. He looked old and weather-beaten when we came 10 years ago. He's not sick, is he?"

"No, it's his brother in New Hampshire. He had heart surgery last week. He's a widower too, with no family close by to help him at home. So Joe's gone up there with the border collie, and I'm here until Labor Day."

"You don't look like a farmer."

"No, I just grew up on one."

"In England."

"Yes, near Chester in Cheshire."

"Where the cheese comes from – and the Cheshire Cat?"

"That's it. Have you been over there?"

"No, but my son's in London with the State Department. He loves it there."

Preoccupied with the conversation, Colin was unprepared when the dashboard pitched upward for a second and he bounced in his seat while grabbing to steady his pail. A loud thump and an unnerving scraping noise quickly followed, then another bounce. His driver nodded and smiled knowingly.

"I forgot that speed bump – but it didn't forget me."

He glanced backward as they passed a sign reading "Quonochontaug Cove Association. 15 mph. Private Roads. Residents and Guests Only. Hidden Driveways. Please Drive

Slowly." Then they turned onto Sunset Beach Road and he had his bearings again

"There's a sign like that at the end of my street. How far does the association property go?"

"Oh, about half a mile through here between the ocean and the pond. I suppose there are about 80 cottages: two-thirds on our side of the road; the rest on yours. Originally it was three farms – yours was one of them – until it was developed as a summer colony in the 1930s."

"Are they all just summer homes?"

"For the most part. At least, there aren't many people here year-round. Even the few retirees go to Florida in the winter. When we started coming, not many cottages were winterized, but most are now. So people come out of season for Thanksgiving or Christmas, but it's really quiet between Labor Day and Memorial Day."

He laughed politely.

"Seems hard to imagine it any quieter than it is now."

"That's what makes Quonnie so special. It can't be developed the way Cape Cod was."

"Why's that?"

"Under the association covenant, the 1- and 2-acre lots can't be subdivided. There's a 30-foot height restriction on improvements. You won't see any telephone poles and power lines here; everything's underground. And the thickets you see either side of the lanes are 20-foot-deep registered wildlife preserves."

Warming to what was apparently a topic close to her heart, she went on:

"They're part of the bigger sanctuary starting at the dunes and ending at the reed beds of the pond, with reverted farmland and salt marshes in between. You're not a birdwatcher by any chance, are you? I love it. This is bird heaven. We have 310 species recorded here, though I'm only up to 85."

"That's jolly good. I was keen on birds, growing up on the farm. I'm ashamed to say I even had an egg collection. And when I was a teenager I shot game birds – but always ate what I'd bagged. That makes it permissible, wouldn't you say?"

NIANTIC JEWEL

She gave a sigh of resignation.

"Well, I eat chicken, and someone has to kill it. Hopefully, it's instant death, so the bird doesn't feel pain. There can be no moral justification for that. I couldn't eat anything knowing it had suffered: I'd be an accessory. But then there's still the problem of ending its life prematurely so that I might eat meat, when I could be a vegetarian.

"You can argue that the food chain is necessary for life to exist – part of the balance of Nature – but that doesn't help ethically, nowadays, when meat-eating is a matter of choice, not of survival. The human condition makes hypocrites of us all, don't you think?'

Aware from his hesitation that her bluntness had caught him off guard, she retracted the question.

"You don't have to answer that! I can't help philosophizing, even on vacation... So, how do you know Joe Stanton?"

"I don't really. I spent Monday with him while he showed me the ropes. Then he left for New Hampshire. He's due to call tomorrow. It all came about through his neighbor down here, Lloyd Forbes. He's a friend at work and we live close by in Boston."

"What do you do?"

"I work part-time on the wire desk at the Boston Gazette – while I'm getting a master's at UMass."

"Really. How interesting. We get the Gazette. At least I do. My husband can't stand it – too liberal. We're from Boston too – Wellesley... So you're here alone?

"Yes.... "

"Damn! Sorry, we're here already. Should I drop you at the house or here by the mailbox."

"Here's fine. The turnaround in the yard can be a tight squeeze."

"Oh, I'm Alise Palmer. I'm so glad we met."

She offered her hand.

"Colin Grosvenor. The pleasure is mine. And thanks again for your kindness."

He began to get out.

15

"Maybe you'd like to... I mean, we'll see you on the beach won't we? Don't be a stranger; come over and we'll talk some more.... And enjoy your mussels."

"I'd love to, and yes I will. 'Bye-bye."

They waved and he walked back up the rutted track, kicking loose stones and feeling more alive than he had in a long time.

NIANTIC JEWEL

CHAPTER 2

PAPER TIGER

Beneath the rule of men entirely great,
The pen is sometimes mightier than the sword.
EDWARD GEORGE BULWER-LYTTON

The newsroom of the Boston Gazette was quiet at 7:30 on a Saturday night, in contrast to the noise and bustle preceding the first edition deadline half an hour earlier. The two horseshoes of the Metro and Wire desks formed an incomplete oval with center access on both sides. In the middle of each arch sat a slotperson, who assigned stories on the daily budget to four or five copy editors on the rim, checked their work and sent the edited copy, headlines and any accompanying photo captions to the electronic typesetter.

The copy editors sat at video display terminals and worked from a queue containing the slugs, or taglines, of their stories. They clicked the slugs to open the files and begin editing. An inquiring as well as a creative mind was needed to be a good copy editor. It required almost a sixth sense, as well as broad general knowledge, to spot factual errors missed or created by the reporter or the story editor earlier in the process.

But their real craft was the English language: vocabulary, grammar, syntax and usage as laid out in the Gazette Stylebook. Though many were fine writers, often having been reporters themselves, they kept the reporter's or columnist's own writing style intact while editing. Improvements to structure or

17

phraseology were encouraged but were to be cleared with the writer, story editor or slotperson.

The edited story had to conform to a specified length, measured in agate lines (in hot metal days, the name of $5^{1/2}$ point type). This was computed by the word processing system and displayed to the copy editor, who then artfully trimmed an over-length story to fit by employing shorter synonyms, deleting adjectives or discarding a nonessential idea. News stories were rarely cut (though reporters upset when their work was not printed in its entirety tended to disagree). In editorialese, cutting denotes lopping from the bottom, and since the final paragraphs of a concise, crisply written story are as indispensable as the first, the practice sacrifices quality to expediency. If a story was too short, the copy editor entered a command and the software program imperceptibly increased the space between lines and paragraphs until a fit was accomplished.

Finally, came the headlines and captions, in separate files. Headline writing was more a gift than a skill – a form of haiku that condensed the story into a given number of lines (or decks) of a certain breadth (from one to six columns wide) and in a specified type size (usually from 18 to 48 points). The hed might also have a drophed beneath it, or overlines above it. So the headline writer could have as few as three words with which to catch the reader's eye or more than a dozen.

Within these strict confines there was, theoretically, a perfect headline for every story, but the copy editors did not have the poet's luxury of time in which to find it. Instead, they had to think quickly under deadline pressure – a few minutes at the most, The perfect headline might elude them, but a close approximation rarely did. When inspiration faltered, the slotperson, always a seasoned practitioner of the art, offered guidance or, if deadlines dictated, assumed the task.

Each desk also had a pagination editor, identifiable by the second, larger screen beside them. This displayed the dummies, or schematics of pages to be laid out. In addition to the literary virtuosity of their journalistic calling, these editors practiced the graphic arts to design visually appealing pages while conjuring

NIANTIC JEWEL

stories of varying lengths to fit their allotted space – give or take a few lines of type. They determined the headline specifications and typography (in accordance with the newspaper's style), placed, sized and cropped photos electronically and established how many lines of caption were needed. For them, each of the paper's three editions was a new challenge as pages were rejigged for later and more newsworthy content.

But the heaviest responsibility rested with two people at a parallel line of desks: the Page One editor, who designed the front page and minute by minute late into the night monitored the pulse of the city, region, nation and world for major news events; and the night editor, who coordinated editorial content and production. Beside them was a photo editor, who selected staff and wire service images from the display on another large screen.

At this time of night, the rows of cluttered reporters' desks stretching as far as you could pitch a morning paper were unoccupied, save for a couple of scribes click-clacking on their keyboards. The walls of this cavernous rectangle were lined on three sides with darkened editorial offices separated from the hoi polloi by a perimeter aisle and banks of brown filing cabinets.

But the dominant presence was a sleeping monster that awoke every night, and often in the day – the giant, high-speed presses that created thunder in the Pressroom and shock waves of energy throughout the building as they printed 200,000 newspapers an hour. They were attached by myriad tentacles of conveyor strips to the distribution floor above, where the sections were combined, advertising supplements inserted and the fully assembled newspapers bundled off to delivery trucks waiting in covered bays below. From there, the bundles sped to news dealers and finally to home delivery agents who worked the cold predawn hours to have the paper on subscribers' doorsteps (or at least at the end of their driveways) by 7:30 a.m. (8 on Sunday) 365 days a year, Nor'easters and blizzards notwithstanding.

This colossus of information and commerce was located on filled land beside Boston Harbor, backed up against the Southeast Expressway in Dorchester. On one side, commercial buildings lined the boulevard to the boundary with South Boston and the

19

towering downtown skyline 2 miles away. The other side looked much as it did 100 years ago: a tidal creek, now a small park, meandered below the middle-class enclave of Savin Hill whose slopes retained a fringe of Victorian architecture along with two- and three-deckers and a couple of apartment buildings popular with single Gazeteers for its proximity to work and the diversions of the city.

It was from one of these complexes that Colin took the short walk to the Gazette's back gate, across the immense parking lot, up the ramp to the rooftop parking lot, passing beneath the helipad and the array of radio masts and microwave dishes that fed the Muse her lifeblood of information, to a back door and into the womb of Mother Gazette.

*   *   *

"Paper's up," shouted the copy boy (nowadays a male or female co-op intern from Northeastern University) as he pulled a dolly loaded with first edition papers from the Pressroom and handed them out. Colin checked the clock. Fifteen minutes to the end of his shift. Just enough time to eyeball his stories for mistakes that could slip by in the rush to deadline. But the bulk of his work had been on the main lead – an exclusive by a staff writer who had tracked down the notorious fugitive Sean "Bulldog" O'Malley in Ireland.

And because this was one of those rare scoops, an exclusive story in an age of instant communication, the copy had been pored over and proofed by half a dozen news executives from the Editor on down before it reached Colin. Even so, he felt a tingle of excitement at seeing his banner headline that had been chosen above those of his superiors: "'Bulldog' slips collar again". And the drophed "Fugitive found hiding out in Irish village, tipped off, dodges FBI".

As if reading his mind, Colin's slotman and mentor, Lloyd Forbes, leaned over to him.

"Nice job. Too bad the bastard got away again. Have you seen tomorrow's follow-up?"

NIANTIC JEWEL

"No, but Moira's over there. She's probably finishing it now."

He pointed to one of the few occupied reporter's desks, where a young woman in frayed blue cutoffs and a green tank top sat perusing the first edition. A mop of unruly, carrot-red hair proclaimed her Celtic heritage while a cigarette held high in her left hand characterized her rebel ethos. She knew smoking was prohibited, but also that by having procured a scoop, she could get away with it, and reveled in the fact.

Moira O'Neill had known she was not meant to live a conventional life while still in parochial school; long before she graduated from Boston College Law School with dreams of advocating for the underprivileged and changing society; even before she became openly gay and married her partner. Her fiery, forthright idealism had made her anathema in the polite, cozy legal circles she needed to infiltrate – and that was alright with her, because she soon realized that justice was readily attainable in theory atop the red-brick towers of The Heights and a dozen other law schools around the city, but less so in practice on the streets, where social justice was determined by the privileged.

So, marshalling her Celtic powers of imagination, observation, language, esthetics and intellect, she had turned herself into a photojournalist. Usually, photographers and journalists embodied discrete and mutually exclusive sensibilities: visual versus verbal. But Moira had them both – and a law degree to boot, which came in handy with the edgy, provocative pieces she was known for, whether shadowing a public official whose office was the golf course or exposing the tenement houses of a politically connected landlord. And so she had thrived at the Gazette, where she found a comfort level unknown to her before in the fellowship of social misfits who make up the ranks of the Fourth Estate.

She sputtered in mid-puff on her cigarette, dropped it and yelled "Jesus Christ!" before grabbing the paper and marching to the Wire Desk, where, with arms crossed menacingly, she buttonholed the slotman.

"Lloyd, where did this crap about "Bulldog's" tattoo come from? Is it right? Nobody cleared it with me."

The slotman covered as best he could.

"You weren't here earlier, or we would have mentioned it. But don't worry. It's been verified and cleared. Colin spotted it. He can tell you all about it."

She nodded to her Savin Hill neighbor, friend and frequent Scrabble opponent.

"Oh hi Colin. So you're doing the honors, traitor."

Now she declaimed sarcastically to the desk in general:

"He's moved out of our building, you know. Deserted us. Gone to the luxury accommodations on the other side of the hill. Couldn't take the drubbings I gave him at Scrabble."

Aware of the audience demanding a riposte, he teased back:

"I couldn't take the cheating anymore. You're not supposed to look up words in the dictionary. And she sulks when she loses.... Yes, I moved to get away from her. It has nothing to do with English cars not starting in Boston winters and that the new place has a covered garage."

Murmurs of approval put her on the defensive. She retorted with a raised finger.

"I'm immune to your disdain, you bastards."

She eyeballed Colin with a withering look.

"OK limey. You can beguile them, but you don't fool me.... Tell me why a Virgin Mary tattoo turns into St. Bridget."

Pausing to call up a library file on his screen, Colin motioned her to him. She mussed his hair and leaned over his shoulder.

"You remember when 'Bulldog's' brother Brendan, then the Port Authority director, was subpoenaed by the congressional panel to testify about how the FBI let 'Bulldog' skip town?"

"Yes, but Brendan swore he hadn't seen him in years. And took the Fifth a lot, as I recall."

"Except when he was portraying 'Bulldog' as an innocent lamb gone astray. You're right that everyone thought 'Bulldog' had a Virgin Mary tattoo on his right forearm — as well as the Marine Corps bulldog on his bicep. All the clippings say so. But here's the testimony Brendan gave: He says he and his brother were choirboys at St. Bridget's in Southie and, as a mark of his devotion to the church, 'Bulldog' carries a tattoo of St. Bridget on his arm."

She reached in to scroll the text.

NIANTIC JEWEL

"That's weird. It sure looked like the Virgin Mary to me. The photos I took in the pub at Inveran show the tattoos quite clearly. How do you tell a Virgin Mary from a St. Bridget?"

"It is a Virgin Mary."

"Whaaat? You've lost me."

"When he got it, after he'd been kicked out of the Marines and was serving 6 years for manslaughter in California, the jailhouse tattooist used a generic Virgin Mary template and added St. Bridget's name beneath. But small print smudges, and it was practically illegible – so no one knew. Not even his cohorts who later cooperated with the FBI. In fact, your photos are so sharp they provide the first corroboration of what Brendan claimed – now that we know what to look for in the smudging. You can't see it in the newsprint reproduction, unfortunately, but in the digital image it definitely says St. Bridget… Mystery solved!"

She gave a whistle of wonderment.

"How did you know about those few lines of testimony? It happened long before you got here."

"Just luck. I was checking your reference about him and his girlfriend Mary meeting up in Bridgetown, Barbados, after leaving town separately. And the keyword Bridgetown brought up Bridget."

She punched his arm and quickly stepped out of reach.

"I knew it had to be pure luck. I'm surprised you could add two and two together. Well done, Colin… I hope you'll be handling the follow-up tomorrow night because I won't be here. I'm bushed."

He logged off his terminal and reached for his bag.

"Probably, but right now I have to get back to Rhode Island to milk the cows."

"Oh that's right. You're helping out Lloyd's neighbor down there. When do you move into your new place? Where's all your stuff?"

"There's only a carload. It's in Lloyd's garage until September. You and Tara will have to help me pick out new rental furniture."

She rubbed her hands with glee.

"You'll live to regret that Colin. But who do we beat at Scrabble until you come back?"

He slung his bag on his shoulder, made his farewells and walked her back to her desk.

"Why don't you both come down to the beach? We'll swim, gather mussels and play Scrabble. I'm dying to hear about your adventures in Ireland."

"Will I get to milk a cow?"

"There are machines to do that. But, yes, I'll show you how."

"It's a deal. I'll check with Tara and call you."

She gave him a peck on the cheek.

"Thanks for everything. See you soon, daaarling."

… *NIANTIC JEWEL*

CHAPTER 3

SAVED BY THE BELLE

It is the very error of the Moon;
She comes more near the earth than she was wont,
And makes men mad.
WILLIAM SHAKESPEARE

After a week at the farm, Colin had settled into a routine. Molly, the black cat, and the rest of the animals had become comfortable with him – except for the rooster, a big Rhode Island Red, which squawked threats with flapping wings, fanned tail and puffed feathers whenever Colin went near his harem to collect eggs from the coop beside the barn. At other times when he saw Colin in the yard, he would charge with feathers ruffled, then stop after a few feet and screech indignantly. Colin christened him Eric, after Eric the Red, the 10th Century Viking warlord who colonized Greenland.

Conversely, the 2-month-old calf, which he named Angel, saw him as a surrogate parent. She spent her days in the pasture with her mother and the rest of the herd, but slept in a pen of baled straw inside the barn, since the cold night air induces pneumonia in developing lungs. Daytime suckling at her mother's udder was augmented by morning and evening feedings from a pail on which Colin had to keep a firm grip to avoid getting soaked.

Such was Angel's prodigious appetite that when the pail was empty she would glom onto his fingers as surrogate teats and try to force them apart with her sandpaper tongue. Fascinated by the force of the sucking reflex, he always offered her four bunched fingers for a few seconds, which gave him time to exit the pen without being butted. A hand covered in warm slobber was a small price, he rationalized, if it saved the world from another neurotic Jersey cow.

He rose at 7, microwaved a cup of instant coffee and carried it to the pasture gate, where the 12 cows, creatures of habit that they were, waited patiently for him to let them through to the barn and their breakfast of crushed grain. With three milking machines at 5 minutes per animal, the operation was over in less than an hour – even with the stripping, or hand-milking, that enticed the last 10 percent of the milk their udders withheld from the antique rubber-cupped contraptions.

When the neck chain keeping each cow in its paired stall was removed, the beast continued to drink from its water bowl or tongue its salt lick until all 12 were untied. It was only when Colin slapped the rump of the animal nearest the open barn doors that each in its turn backed up a few steps, gracefully pivoted about and followed its leader Indian file back to the pasture. Here they grazed and ruminated, extending themselves only to trudge to the water trough, until at 4 p.m. without fail they gathered by the gate for their next milking.

After breakfast, the routine was for Colin to clean out their stalls and lay fresh straw, then to scrub and sterilize the milking units in hypochlorite. He scattered a few handfuls of corn near the chicken coop and, while the little flock was feeding, went inside to collect the half dozen eggs they laid each day.

The 20 Cheviot sheep required no care other than to check the ball valve on their water trough and to count them to be sure none was sick, injured or absent. By 10 a.m., he was free until milking time to read history texts for the degree he hoped would spring him from the fast-declining newspaper business.

Every Wednesday, a truck from the farmers' cooperative came to pump 200 gallons of milk from the refrigerated tank and pick up a few trays of eggs. On Thursdays, he drove his Jaguar XK8 convertible to the Wal-Mart 3 miles away at Dunn's Corners. And punctually at noon on Fridays, Joe Stanton called from New Hampshire to engage in long conversations that had more to do

NIANTIC JEWEL

with their mutual passion for history than with the farm. Weekends, Colin earned his meal ticket at the Gazette: noon to 8 Saturday; 6 p.m. Sunday to 2 a.m. Monday. These were the narrow confines of his world – until the rooster intervened.

* * *

He was stretched out in the swing chair on the veranda with Molly on his lap, reading Roger Williams' 1643 "Key Into the Language of America," when he took a break to let the serenity of his surroundings wash over him. The front pasture sloped down to the great salt pond and the small dock with the old man's faded-blue lobster boat, Old Queen, moored alongside. A pair of mute swans with three cygnets glided by. In the distance, sport fishermen in their outboards plied the channel to and from the breachway, past thicketed islands and a scattering of rock outcrops, some towering high above the water. These were the basking places of cormorants, gulls and terns, while long-legged egrets, herons and bitterns fed in the tidal mud flats close to shore.

He wondered if the Seeker clergyman who founded Rhode Island in 1636 and based the book chiefly on his knowledge of the local Narragansett Indians, might have stood on this very spot. After being tried for advocating separation of church and state, liberty of conscience and the equally heretical notion that Indian land must be purchased not expropriated under an illegal royal charter, the Calvinist intellectual was banished by the Puritans of Massachusetts Bay Colony in January 1636.

To them, the church was the highest authority and the state was its civil arm, a man could be punished for "sinning against his conscience" and the Indians didn't own their land, so they shouldn't be paid for it. The rationalization used was that the aboriginal peoples didn't enclose the land or "improve" it through agriculture.

By the same reasoning, an English lord's hunting park would have been ripe for the taking. More to the point, the Bay's 1629 patent from Charles I instructed that land be purchased from the natives.

Four-time governor John Winthrop Sr. explained the Puritan philosophy like this: "[The Indians] have no other but a natural right to these countries. So if we leave them sufficient for their use we may lawfully take the rest." He believed the English coming to be divinely inspired since "God consumed the natives with a great plague." This accounted for the empty land the Pilgrims found at Plymouth after the 1615-18 plague epidemic that wiped out the Patuxets there. And the doctrine of vacuum domicilium in international law gave anyone the right to move into a vacant area.

The rhetoric of justification also cited Genesis 28: "Be fruitful, and multiply, and replenish the earth, and subdue it: and have dominion over the fish of the sea, and over the fowl of the air, and over every living thing that moveth upon the earth" – as the Israelites had done in subduing the Canaanites and occupying their land. No matter that the king's patent adhered to English monopoly and corporation law, which stated that colonized land was held subject to the possessory rights of the natives.

So, leaving his wife Mary and two infant daughters at Salem, where he was the minister and ran a trading business, Williams fled into the winter wilderness (probably with his servant boy, Thomas Angell) just before he was to be seized and shipped back to England.

It had long been his plan to establish a mission among the Indians. His trading activities brought him into contact with Massasoit, the Wampanoag sachem in southeastern Massachusetts, and Canonicus and Miantonomi co-sachems of the Narragansett confederacy, whose authority at its zenith stretched from eastern Long Island and southeastern Connecticut through their Rhode Island homeland and deep into eastern and central Massachusetts.

Until the English contained their expansion around 1640, the Narragansett were the most powerful nation in southern New England with 5,000 warriors and a population of 20,000, according to Daniel Gookin, superintendent of Indians for Massachusetts Bay at the time (and author in 1677 of "An Historical Account of the Doings and Sufferings of the Christian Indians in New

NIANTIC JEWEL

England'). Richard Smith Jr., who ran a trading post among them near Wickford, put their numbers at 30,000. Modern estimates suggest 40,000 before 1633 and 10,000 in the 1640s. Smallpox epidemics in 1633-4 and 1649-50, each claiming many hundreds of lives, make the figures for any given time just a guess.

*   *   *

Williams quickly learned both tribes' Algonquian languages and became their interpreter and agent to the English. Because of his gift for public speaking, the Indians held him to be a sachem. As early as 1634 he had made a verbal treaty with the three chiefs for land beside Narragansett Bay on which to plant his mission. Now, he trudged south through the snow from Salem almost 60 miles to Massasoit's winter quarters at Sowams (Warren, R.I.).

While there he settled a dispute between his host and Canonicus. In return he was given land nearby on the east bank of the Seekonk River, which he and three other outcasts from the Bay Colony began planting in the spring. The seeds were barely in the ground when Williams received a letter from Gov. Edward Winslow of Plymouth Colony telling him to move across the river. The land was inside the Plymouth patent and the colony could not harbor those expelled from Boston.

It was while Williams was scouting for a new home on the far bank that a romantic legend came about: He and his little band of outcasts were in full flight across the Seekonk River when they ran into Canonicus, who greeted Williams with the words "What cheer, netop [friend]?" and made them welcome.

What really happened will never be known, except that two other versions seem more plausible. However, the greeting is accepted by all, since "What cheer?" was a standard salutation of the time corresponding to "What's happening?"

According to James Ernst's 1932 biography, Williams canoed across the river alone on his scouting trip and was hailed by some natives on a high rock. Ola Elizabeth Winslow's 1957 life prefers an account that has Williams and his companions hailing the

Indians and then coming ashore beside a large rock. The Providence city seal depicts this version.

Even the rock holds its share of confusion. It was known both as What Cheer Rock and Slate Rock until being buried under made land. A monument at the corner of Williams and Gano streets in Providence stands nearby. As with the site itself, the exact date of the landing in April 1636 is also uncertain, although Benedict Arnold (great-grandfather of the Revolutionary War traitor) held it to be April 20.

In any event, the trip resulted in Williams relocating to a spring beside the Mooshassuc River (The site is now the Roger Williams National Memorial). For his many services, Canonicus and Miantonomi gave him the land that became Providence, where, in addition to founding the colony, he ran a trading post. In 1645, he opened a second post at Cocumscussoc (Wickford Point), near the Smith family who had arrived between 1640 and 1643 to become the first permanent English settlers in Narragansett Country. Wickford was a prime location. It lay on the Pequot Path, a major Indian thoroughfare, and had water access, allowing goods to be shipped in and out.

Williams often journeyed to the winter village of the Eastern Niantic at Chemunganock/Shumuncanuc (the modern village of Shannock 8 miles inland) and the summer village at Weekapaug, the spit of land Colin could see 3 miles away at the western end of Quonochontaug Pond. His quickest route would have taken him down the Pequot Trail to Fort Ninigret, the Niantic stronghold and trading post 4 miles to the east, then, depending on the season, west to Shannock or by canoe across Ninigret Pond to Quonochontaug (Quawnecontaukit as he wrote it). After portage across the Neck, he could have launched his canoe for the last leg to Weekapaug from the shore below, where the Old Queen now bobbed,

The reasons for the visits were threefold:

1) To trade with Ninigret, the Niantic sachem, whom he described as "proud and fierce," and gather intelligence before the 1637 war with the neighboring Pequot of southeastern

NIANTIC JEWEL

Connecticut, common enemies of the Niantic, Narragansett and English.

2) To ally Ninigret with the English against the Dutch, whose influence reached from New Amsterdam (New York City) up the Hudson and Connecticut rivers and along Long Island Sound. They had opened a trading post at Manhattan in 1613, established Fort Orange (Albany) in 1624 and built the short-lived Fort New Hope (at Hartford) in 1632. The English soon displaced them from the Connecticut River with the founding of Saybrook, Wethersfield, Windsor and Hartford all in 1635. By mid-1636, there were 800 English on the river and increasing numbers around New Haven, settled in 1638 at the mouth of the Quinnipiac River. The New Haven Colony joined Connecticut when the latter obtained its royal charter in 1662. Until then, New Haven was a full member of the United Colonies of New England, the loose defensive alliance formed in 1643. Meanwhile, the Dutch continued to trade up the rivers by ship, but they were more interested in the Hudson River and its access to the rich beaver lands of the north. New Netherlands was peacefully surrendered to the British in 1664 with the takeover formalized three years later in the Treaty of Breda.

3) After 1644, when Rhode Island obtained its charter, Williams needed Ninigret's support to counter territorial claims by Plymouth, Massachusetts Bay and Connecticut. The sachem was recognized by the English as an "alliance chief" wielding influence beyond his Niantic homeland. So close were the kinship ties between the Niantic and Narragansett, they have been called Southern Narragansett. Sometimes Ninigret was empowered to speak for the whole Narragansett confederacy, yet the bond didn't preclude him from often being independent of it.

Devout Christian that Williams was, he wouldn't have proselytized to the Niantic unless they first sought out the word of God. And Narragansett Country was particularly barren ground for the Gospel. When Thomas Mayhew Jr., who made hundreds of conversions on Martha's Vineyard, asked if he could preach at Weekapaug, Ninigret replied, "Go and make the English good first."

Graham Griffith

*   *   *

According to Joe Stanton, whose ancestors were the first European settlers in the area, the farm was the site of a trading post in Colonial days, exchanging metal tools, glass bottles, beads and cloth for furs, food and wampum (the shell currency of the day), which were shipped in and out through an impermanent channel between the pond and the ocean that had preceded the 20th Century breachway. No trace of the post remained and how long it lasted, until a hurricane or Nor'easter may have closed the channel, was unknown.

Part of the farmhouse dated to the 1740s, but how long it had been Quaiapen Farm was also a mystery, and a vexing one, because it was an illustrious name. Quaiapen, or the Old Queen, was a sister of Ninigret, who ruled these coastal lands subject to his kinsman Canonicus. She married his son Mixanno in 1649 and played a leadership role in Metacom's War, the conflagration that annihilated Indian power in southern New England, until being slain at North Smithfield July 2, 1676.

At the time, she was one of the six Narragansett sachems. Also known as Squaw Sachem, Sunck Squaw, Magnus and Matantuck, she had three children: two sons, Scuttup and Quequaquenuet (aka Gideon), who became sachems, and a daughter, Quinemiquet.

Sidney S. Rider's 1904 "The Lands of Rhode Island" records that William Harris, a member of Roger Williams' original band, knew her as "a great woman; yea ye greatest yt ther was; ye sd woman, called ye old Queene." And in his 1677 "A Narrative of the Troubles with the Indians in New England," Rev. William Hubbard of Ipswich (Mass.) described her as "a woman of great power." She was a sachem and the daughter, sister, wife and mother of sachems.

Thinking of this woman brought Colin's mind back to the redhead on the beach, particularly the vision of her sunbathing topless in her secluded nook. She had become a fantasy object of his loneliness, the goddess Salacia incarnate, and he rued the

NIANTIC JEWEL

missed opportunity that could have opened the door to more than a fleeting encounter. Instead he'd brought a nagging frustration upon himself. Was she Alise Palmer's daughter? Was the tennis partner her boyfriend? And how could he meet her again to at least find out?

Joe Stanton and Lloyd Forbes were no help. Both knew the Palmers by sight, but not their children. Joe was better acquainted with Alise Palmer, who, as Colin already knew, bought lobsters from him periodically. From their brief chats, she struck Joe as friendly and down-to-earth. He thought the husband did something in telephones. He'd been on the Association's board of governors a few years back when the state environmental busybodies complained about the cows having access to the pond.

Colin had pored over the Cove Association wall map in the living room. It demystified the baffling street layout and had a key to the plots and their owners. And next to the phone, he'd found a Cove directory with numbers, summer and winter addresses and e-mail addresses. Some entries even listed children, but not the Palmers'.

Now he knew his way around, but nothing more about her. He thought of stopping by the Palmers, or calling on some pretext. That might answer one question, but subterfuge was dishonorable. He could spend time at the beach, hoping to get lucky, but he couldn't study there. And what if he met someone else, someone who filled the void but fell short of his idealized image of her, and then he met her again?

His angst was interrupted by a commotion in the farmyard. There he found the rooster comically attempting to mount one of the Aylesbury ducks, which resisted noisily amid a flurry of flapping wings. The allegory to his own situation registered in his subconscious: The object of his desire eluded him.

Impulsively, he picked up a stone and threw it at the unseemly spectacle 20 feet away. By sheer chance, it hit the aggressor in the back of the head, bowling Eric over momentarily and allowing the duck to flee. The enraged rooster came at him, but he retreated onto the veranda and remained there until milking time.

Graham Griffith

*   *   *

Eric had sensed his fear, and during milking time he came into the barn. Colin was stripping a cow, seated on a stool with a pail between his legs, when the bird strutted up the center aisle, stopped a few inches behind the Jersey and began squawking. The cow turned its head, let out a bellow and kicked out with both hind legs. The agile rooster flew 2 feet into the air, evading the hooves and making more racket, which unsettled the rest of the herd. The cow's explosive movement sent Colin sprawling beneath it. The stool went one way and the pail another. He was spread-eagled beneath the half-ton beast, drenched in milk, when its back legs came down.

How the nearest leg missed landing square on his right ankle was due only to the animal's quick reflexes. As it was, he felt a jolt of pain as the hoof glanced the instep of his canvas shoe and the Jersey regained its footing. Dazed and disoriented, he carefully extricated himself, gathered the stool and pail and hobbled to the aisle. He stretched the throbbing foot, tested it with his full weight, then knelt down to examine it. There was a swollen, red contusion, but the skin was unbroken. The throbbing subsided. although a bruise was forming and the area was painfully tender. Grateful for small mercies, he patted the cow's rump and told her "Nice footwork princess, but I wish you'd kicked Eric, not me."

He got through the milking chores by limping around, pivoting on the right heel to immobilize the instep. He let the cows back into the pasture and returned to the house to rest and take stock. A few minutes off the foot revived his spirits, and after dinner he got the idea that saltwater therapy and a good night's rest would cure the injury. It was only 7 o'clock – still time to drive to the beach and soak the foot. He checked the tide chart: high tide at 5. Not the best time to swim, but outside the kitchen window the pond lay calm and streaked with silver as the sun began its descent into the western sky.

*   *   *

NIANTIC JEWEL

There were still a few cars and golf carts in the beach parking lot when he drove up to the boardwalk. He climbed out gingerly. Using his foot on the gas pedal had been painful. But once he could hobble on his heel, the ache subsided. He headed for the bathers loosely grouped in the water in front of their watchers (for no one swam unaccompanied on an ebb tide with its undertow and chance of riptides). Placid as the ocean was, low rollers broke with resounding booms and cascades of spray in the trough below the shoreline, followed by a whoosh and a maelstrom of churning foam as the water was sucked back on itself.

The trek across the soft sand was more of an effort than Colin anticipated and he was glad when he could drop his shirt and towel on the ledge above the shoreline and stumble down the slope into the ocean. He ducked under a couple of 3-foot rollers until he was beyond the breakers, 30 feet out, in chest-deep water. From this angle, the surface shimmered silver and pink all the way to Block Island as the setting sun painted bands of low-lying cirrus clouds.

The warm water felt good against his skin, and when he swam a few strokes its buoyancy allowed the sore foot to move freely without pain. He turned onto his back and began floating, becoming one with the ocean, his weightless body rising and falling with the ebb and flow, his freightless mind in harmony with the universe.

It was a feeling of utter tranquillity – until a whitecap crested over his face and abruptly ended his reverie. Sputtering and coughing to clear his airways, he dropped his legs to feel for the bottom – and found only roiling water. His gut clenched as he realized a riptide had carried him out of his depth.

He began to breast-stroke in an effort to gain the few feet needed for a footing, but made no progress, and his frantic kicking sent jolts of pain through the entire leg. It was futile to fight a riptide even with two good legs. He knew that. The rule was to go with the current sweeping you away from the beach; to wait until it spat you out. With only one good leg he couldn't even stay afloat, let alone swim back to shore. Nausea punched his stomach and panic jabbed his brain.

He gasped for air and told himself to keep his head even as he felt the current taking him. Desperate, he tried to crawl free, but his lame foot refused to move and with his body unbalanced he swallowed more water. All he could do was fight the pain and try to dog paddle while he looked around for help.

Fifty feet to his left, the last two bathers were leaving the water. To his right, he saw only breakers. Then, out of the spindrift nearby, a head emerged swimming his way. He shouted, hoping to be heard above the pounding surf yet trying to appear calm at the expense of sounding ludicrous.

"Excuse me! Sorry to bother you. I can't make it back to shore. Can you help me?"

The swimmer increased her stroke and was soon beside him. She held out a straight-arm.

"Grab hold and swim with me."

The exertion set his foot on fire again leaving his rescuer to pluck him from the current and drag him into the shallows. She turned to him, gasping:

"You should be able to put your feet down now?"

"Yes, I can! Thank you so much."

But he stumbled in agony on the first step and she had to help him up. Their eyes met. It was her.

"Let's get you out of the water. Are you alright?"

"Just a sore foot. I thought the saltwater would help it, but I made it worse thrashing around."

She hooked his arm over her shoulder and with her free hand around his waist steered him to shore, then up the ledge, where she eased him to the sand.

"Sit here and catch your breath. I'll get a towel. You're Colin aren't you? We talked by the rocks last week. Salacia, remember? And Mother mentioned you. Stay right there."

She turned to go, but Alise Palmer came running over with towels.

"What happened? Oh, it is you Colin. I thought that blond hair looked familiar. Are you alright? I see you've met Juliana. You picked the best swimmer on the beach to get into trouble near."

NIANTIC JEWEL

He went to stand up, but she motioned him down and knelt in front of him.

"Hello again Mrs. Palmer. Yes, Juliana rescued me. I would have drowned without her."

He looked up at his savior.

"You're a lifesaver. Thank you Juliana."

She shook her head and gave him a warm smile he would never forget, then dropped to her knees beside her mother.

"Nonsense. Is that your way of meeting girls?"

He protested and recounted the tale of the rooster while Alise Palmer examined his foot with her delicate hands.

"The bruise seems to be gone. Maybe the saltwater did help. And what a handsome foot. Look at that high arch! And the toes are so straight. Even the half-moons on the nails are flawless... Forgive me. I love feet – toe-tally!"

She chuckled at her pun, while her daughter groaned. Then, rocking back on her knees, she engaged him with intense, green eyes – the whimsy gone.

"You seem to be saying that Eric planned his revenge. But birds aren't capable of cognitive thought. They exist only in the present. Their lives are one long moment. They can't imagine a future. Eric's actions would follow the theory of determinism, which holds that all events are totally determined by cause and effect. He doesn't have the ability to choose future actions. That's confined to the animals that have evolved complex sensory systems. In roosters, there's stimulus and reflexive response. In higher brains, the stimulus detours through more advanced circuitry. The delay allows a considered, voluntary response to override the reflex...."

She was cut off by her daughter:

Mother! You're sounding like a philosophy professor. Birds have consciousness, and time passes through it, so they're aware of their past. They learn from experience. It's a hard-wired survival mechanism. They're capable of voluntary action because they have memory. They have perception. They experience qualities, feelings and sensations, from which free will emerges. Humans aren't the only animals to have it, because it has nothing to do with intelligence – only memory.

"Now you're sounding like a psychology major, Juliana."

Colin caught himself surveying the contours of the violet swimsuit below the captivating face and red hair. He realized there was an opportunity to ingratiate himself.

"I agree with Juliana. One thing leads to another. The way I see it, I'm a stranger to Eric; therefore a threat. I go into the coop and take eggs, displacing him as cock of the walk. I hit him with a rock, arousing primitive rage. He sees me in the barn and instinctively obtains release in an assertive display. He knows the cow will kick when he squawks near her because that's been his experience. But he didn't have a conscious understanding that the kick would affect me. It was just coincidence that I was with the cow at the time. Two discrete events converged."

The mother brushed sand from her slim legs and got up.

"I can tell you're no stranger to philosophy or psychology. You've managed to agree with a determinist and an existentialist. What a diplomat! But the way you tell it leaves room for doubt, despite the prevailing wisdom. Maybe we're underestimating Eric after all. Is he a chicken Machiavelli, an avian Aristotle, a feathered Faust? So you see, daughter dear, I'm open to soft determinism that would allow Eric free will – but only as a mutant majesty!… Anyway, it's getting chilly. Can you walk Colin? We can drive you home…."

When they got up he found he could limp along in the soft sand without much trouble. He assured them he was fine and repeated his gratitude. They separated to pick up their things and met up to head for the parking lot. His mind was reeling with the euphoria of this lucky turn of events, but he knew he must act quickly or the gain would be lost. It took him by surprise when Alise Palmer put her hand on his shoulder.

"You're such an interesting person, Colin. You must come to dinner. My husband would love to meet you, wouldn't he Juliana?'

He thought he sensed a moment's hesitation, but maybe the question had taken her unawares. Before she could answer, he stepped in:

NIANTIC JEWEL

"You're very kind, but I owe Juliana the best dinner in town first."

He looked pleadingly into her eyes.

"You must let me repay you in some small way. Will you allow me to do that?"

She gave him a bemused look.

"It's not necessary, really."

There was an awkward silence accompanied by a hollow feeling in his stomach, until he heard:

"Oh, don't be so coy Juliana. I'll go if you don't want to."

At that moment they reached the end of the boardwalk. The Jaguar and a purple Yamaha golf cart were the only vehicles remaining. The older woman whistled.

"So this is yours Colin. I noticed it when we arrived. I knew I hadn't seen it here before. What a great color. What is it?"

"It's a Jaguar. The color's British racing green. I came by it in Maine when I worked there. They're quite useless for most of the year in northern Maine – like a fish out of water."

"Well, you had a good catch."

She patted the rear panel.

"Will a ride in this help you make up your mind Juliana?"

There was a look of exasperation on the daughter's face.

"Mother! I only said it wasn't necessary."

Then turning to Colin and smiling

"If you really feel you must."

His exhilaration was muted by the obvious dilemma.

"I'd love to take you both to dinner. What is the best restaurant in town?"

The two women exchanged glances until the mother tapped her index finger to her lips.

"Thank you Colin, but I'll take a rain check... Shelter Harbor Inn is always excellent. Wilcox Tavern is the closest, Weekapaug Inn the prettiest, but there's a new chef at the General Stanton Inn. You haven't eaten there since he came have you Juliana?"

"No I haven't. That would be fun to try."

Mildly relieved, he pressed on.

"Is Friday good for you?"

"Friday's fine."
"Pick you up at 7?"
"OK."
Her mother broke in:
"Come early Colin, and you can meet Ben, my husband."
"I'd love to. Until Friday then."
He got in his car and waved goodbye.
"Cheerio then."
Alise Palmer called after him.
"Cheerio! And rest, that foot."

CHAPTER 4

HEART-TO-HEART

No, there's nothing half so sweet in life
As love's young dream.
THOMAS MOORE

The two days to Friday seemed like two weeks. She was all he could think of. That afternoon he made the reservation and went up to Hoxsie's Nursery on Route 1 to cut some dahlias, gladioli, zinnias and cosmos, which he split into two posies and left outside in a pail on the veranda. After the farm chores, he showered, shaved and splashed on Essenza di Zegna. He picked out a lightweight tan suit with a pale-blue cotton sports shirt, gave his long blond hair a last brush, and at 6:30 headed out on tenterhooks, flowers at his side.

A scarlet Audi R8 coupe with a darkly tanned young woman at the wheel sped out of the Palmers' narrow drive as he was about to turn in. He braked sharply and remembered the posted warning about hidden driveways as he passed through the entrance thicket.

The postmodern gray-shingled house with white trim stood at the far end of a circular gravel track. Momentarily confused whether he should enter from the right (as in a US traffic circle) or the left (as in an English roundabout), he chose the right, then realized that closed circles universally flow clockwise.

He hoped no one had seen him through the island of wild pin cherry trees that screened the house and grew among boulders, rhododendrons and neatly trimmed grass. The track took him past the porticoed front entrance with its planters and hanging baskets of scarlet impatiens to an equally colorful parking area, where he pulled up beside the maroon Prius, the purple golf cart, a silver Mercedes CLS coupe and a yellow Mini Cooper S convertible.

A hallway with a gleaming hardwood floor leading to a central staircase lay beyond the screen door. Broad, shallow arches on both sides allowed views of large, open rooms. A formal dining area and a display case filled with silver trophies was visible to the right, a U-shaped sectional sofa surrounding a large, glass-topped coffee table to the left.

Alise Palmer answered the door chime with a breezy welcome. She inquired about his foot as they exchanged pleasantries and accepted her flowers while unaccountably calling upstairs "The blue one, dear." He followed her past the sofas, through French windows to a patio with white wooden rails bearing planters filled with more impatiens. A giant of a man with silver hair sat at a table reading The Wall Street Journal. He put down the paper when they approached, placed his cigar in an ashtray and took a sip of his martini.

"Ben, I'd like you to meet Colin. Colin, this is Ben, my husband... and Juliana's father."

The crunching handshake that accompanied the how-do-you-do's unnerved Colin, but he offered no resistance.

"I thought maybe you were from FTD with all those flowers. Why don't you put them on the table for now. Sit with me and have a drink, Colin. What would you like?"

"A glass of water please, if there's time."

He glanced at Alise Palmer, who nodded.

"I'll put my flowers in water and bring you a glass. Juliana will be a few minutes. She wasn't sure what to wear – casual or dressy – until you arrived. I suggested she call because you didn't ask the address, but she said it would be a good test of your resourcefulness. How did you find us?"

He explained about the wall map and she excused herself.

Her husband reached over his broad potbelly to tap the newspaper, and gruffly announce:

"I hear you're with the Gazette, but I won't hold that against you. The Journal's my paper. Even if the Gazette had decent

NIANTIC JEWEL

business coverage, I don't need its liberal bias. Of course, I'm outvoted by the women of the house, so I have to pay for it anyway."

He sighed, and while Colin was deciding how to respond, Alise Palmer returned to hand him a glass. She pulled up a chair and changed the subject.

"You know I teach philosophy. There's a moral dilemma I'd like your take on, if you're willing."

"I'll try my best."

Ben Palmer chuckled as if he'd heard it all before, and returned to his newspaper.

"You're at a job interview with a CEO. He asks what you'd do if you were driving by a bus stop on a stormy night and saw three people waiting:

"1) An old lady having a heart attack.

"2) A long-lost friend you've never repaid for saving your life.

"3) The girl of your dreams.

"Which would you offer a ride to if you could take only one?"

Colin sensed something amiss, an undercurrent he couldn't fathom. But it would be discourteous not to go along with it. The solution that came to him in a few seconds confirmed his misgivings.

"I think I'd give the car keys to my friend and let him take the old lady to the hospital while I stay behind and wait for the bus with dream girl."

Alise Palmer's grin turned to a frown.

"That's quite good… but no job for you in corporate America. The correct answer is to run the old lady over and put her out of her misery, screw dream girl on the hood of the car, then drive off with the friend for a few beers."

Colin was speechless, until Ben Palmer winked at him.

"It's one of my wife's cruel jokes, Colin. You're wise not to laugh."

Now he felt he'd been rude. He glanced at Alise Palmer for a sign of disappointment.

"I'm sorry. American humor's still new to me, and I'm not very quick on the uptake."

She waved him off and smiled.

"Ben's right. It's a sick joke... What do you hear from Joe Stanton?"

"He called earlier as a matter of fact. He's well, but misses the cows, and lobstering. His brother's doing well, too."

"That's good to hear. Did you know that the General Stanton Inn is named for his family?"

"He did mention it when I told him about tonight. And he said he was grateful for Mr. Palmer's help with the environmental people a few years ago."

"Ah! You've been checking up...."

He shook his head then hesitated, afraid that denial would be disingenuous, until Ben Palmer saved him again.

"The farm's part of the Association, and I was on the board of governors at the time. The clean-water bureaucrats came to us moaning that the cows were fouling the pond. We told them to come back after they'd dealt with boat exhausts, not to mention birds, fish and deer. Can you believe it? A few cows! We sent them packing."

He emphasized the point with a sweep of his hefty arm, which sent his glass skidding over the edge of the table. Colin stabbed out his left hand, caught the glass in midair and returned it to the table, almost empty but intact."

The big man's eyes popped.

"Thanks. You're quick!"

Colin shrugged.

"It's from wicket-keeping in my cricket days."

Alise Palmer threw her head back and laughed.

"I know they serve drinks to the players during matches, but martinis? What else do you play?"

Her sharp eyes darted over to the house.

"Oh, some other time. Here's Juliana."

Colin sprang up, took the flowers and watched transfixed as she approached, the red tresses swaying to her movement. The short, cobalt-blue cocktail dress hugged her body, tapering above the swell of the bust line to a narrow crescent, which tied behind the neck, baring her golden shoulders and half her back. Her full lips parted in a wide smile.

"Hello Colin. Sorry to keep you waiting."

"It was well worth it."

He offered the flowers, which she accepted with her left hand.

"You look breathtakingly beautiful."

She grinned self-consciously.

"Thank you – and for the flowers, too. It's nice to dress up a little for a change."

He gestured to the planters.

"Bringing flowers to your home is like taking coals to Newcastle."

He caught Alise Palmer's eye.

"I love your house; the way it fits into the landscape. It's so peaceful here. Idyllic."

She nodded approvingly and reached for the flowers.

"Let me take these, dear. You should really be going."

She stood up and hugged her daughter, who then leaned down and kissed her father. He squeezed her hand.

"Have a good time – the two of you... I hope to see you again Colin."

He reciprocated and left with the bewitching beauty at his side, under the spell of her mesmerizing presence and intoxicating perfume.

*   *   *

No words passed until he opened the car door for her and she sank into the leather bucket seat.

"This is great! How fast does it go?"

"Zero to 60 in 6 seconds. But don't worry, I never go above the speed limit."

She buckled her seatbelt while he backed out of the parking area and took the arc to his left, continuing his mistake coming in.

'I'm glad to hear it, but do you always drive on the wrong side? I noticed it when I heard you come in."

"Sorry. I'm always doing things backwards... counter-intuitively. But I promise you'll be safe!"

She listened to his embarrassed explanation with a trace of amusement. It was bad start, he thought, and he scrambled to change the subject.

"This is a wonderful place to spend the summer. How long have you been coming here?"

"Almost as long as I can remember. I always wish that summer will last forever, especially this year because I didn't have to get a real summer job. No more waitressing, camp counseling or child care."

"What are you doing?"

"Mother's writing a chapter for a philosophy textbook. She's a professor at Wellesley College. She `hired' me to annotate the footnotes and be her gofer in general."

"Like a graduate assistant."

"Exactly, except I don't graduate until next year, and psychology's really my thing. Philosophy's too bloodless for me. The old German masters are awfully stodgy, decidedly Germanic, although Hegel was pretty funny when he said philosophy is the world turned upside down."

"And where do you go to school?"

"Wellesley. We live in town too – about 2 miles from the college – but I'm in a dorm. I almost grew up on campus, and never wanted to go anywhere else. It's perfect. No male distractions – though I don't have anything against men. How about you? Mother said you're with the Gazette, and getting a master's at UMass. What in?"

"Colonial History. I fell into journalism by accident at 16. My family knew the editor of the local paper so I free-lanced for pocket money, then kept it up while I was at Liverpool University. Afterward, it seemed natural to make a career of it. I did that for a year, then got wanderlust and, through an English acquaintance over here, happened upon a job at the Rockwood Herald, way `down east' in Maine. They wanted someone with experience but willing to work for virtually nothing to fill in for a Reservist sent to Afghanistan.

NIANTIC JEWEL

"By pulling some political strings they wangled a Green Card, and I came. Just weeks later, the Reservist was badly wounded. He spent a few months recuperating and then needed his job back. So I hitched a ride on a newsprint train going straight to the Gazette, where the Scottish managing editor took pity on me and offered a part-time job. The Herald publisher was overjoyed to get rid of me and threw in the Jag, which he also wanted to ditch.

"Then last winter, I realized that journalism's not for me – history's my thing – but it's a meal ticket until I can change horses. I live on Savin Hill, next to the Gazette, and the Umass Harbor Campus is just across the street. My classmates think I'm a foreign student, but the Green Card gives me permanent status – and the privilege to work. It's going well, so far, although I couldn't afford tuition or an apartment without my trust fund...."

She shifted in her seat, causing the dress to ride immodestly up her slightly parted thighs until she noticed his interest and quickly covered up.

"We're both trust fund brats! I can't touch mine until I graduate. Daddy set them up for my brother and me. How did you get yours?"

"My parents died."

"I'm sorry. I didn't mean to pry."

"No, you're not... My mother was killed in a car accident when I was 17. My father was devastated and had an accident cleaning his hunting rifle a year later... But the family money comes from my great-grandfather. He was a cotton broker in Liverpool and bought the farm as a country retreat. Then my grandfather and later my father made it their lives, in the days of gentleman farmers. Now my brother and sister make it theirs."

"You never wanted to be a farmer, too?"

He laughed, flattered by the curiosity in her radiant face.

"Three's a crowd. They're 8 and 10 years older. I was a surprise. I learned about farming growing up, of course. Then I got interested in writing for the newspaper. Farming's too uncertain for me – too much at the mercy of the English weather. So after university, when I went into journalism, they bought out my share. It's a complicated arrangement over time. As a result, there are two trust funds. The family solicitor handles it all.... Now you know everything about me!"

She pursed her lips.

"I doubt that! There's something about you I can't quite put my finger on – something vaguely familiar."

They pulled into the General Stanton and he hopped out to open her door, but she beat him to it.

"Sorry. American men don't normally do that. Call it a downside of liberation. But I appreciate the gesture."

She accepted his hand, then, once on her feet, broke contact.

*   *   *

They were shown to a table he'd asked for on the patio. She had a glass of Jonathan Edwards pinot grigio and he Ty Nant, partly for the blue bottle that matched her dress, but mostly because Welsh mineral water tasted to him of romantic causes and druidic orgies. Now that she faced him across the table, he felt the full exhilaration of her sensuality. She sipped her wine, and, looking up from the menu, asked:

"You don't drink?"

"No, I'm allergic."

"Just to alcohol, or other things as well?"

"Just alcohol. It's poison to me."

"Even beer?"

"Even NyQuil."

"I have allergies, too. I was a preemie. My immune system didn't have time to develop fully. I get sick if I eat strawberries or cantaloupe. It comes right back out through my pores – the odor that is. But staph bacteria are the worst. They're everywhere; so if I eat shellfish, especially shrimp, that's not totally fresh, or anything with mayonnaise that's been left out awhile, my lips and tongue swell up. Then I can't breathe. It's really dangerous. Insect bites and cuts get infected if I don't clean and medicate them right away. Plus, I'm allergic to penicillin, so I have to take tetracycline.

"And I'm O-, which makes me a universal donor but means I can receive only O- blood, and just 7% of people have it. Luckily,

NIANTIC JEWEL

Mother has it, too. We give blood once a year in hopes they'll have some if we ever need it – in case we're not around to help each other. As if it's really going to make a difference. Call it illogical or superstitious but it makes us feel better."

He took the opportunity she'd inadvertently provided to survey her stunning upper body longer than was polite, until their eyes met.

"No, you're wonderful to do that. I'm O- too, but giving blood never crossed my mind... The allergies and the staph must be a nuisance, but may I say you look very well-developed now. I admire your structural integrity – as well as your humanitarian principles."

She gave him a knowing smile and returned to the menu.

"Have you decided what you're having?"

"Calamari Diablo and the Osso Bucco. And you?"

"The duck liver pate. And the Caribbean Cod 'served over roasted sweet potatoes and a drunken tropical fruit salsa.' I love blackened fish."

She put the menu aside and studied the tablemat, which described the inn's history.

"I should show you the inside before we leave. Three of the dining rooms are more than 300 years old. It says here that the original Stanton, Thomas, was only 20 when he came over from England and started a trading post around 1647 near the mouth of the Pawcatuck River. Then in 1655 an Indian sachem gave him a tract of land in Charlestown 'over 4 miles wide and 2 miles long' in reward for arranging a princess's ransom!"

She sipped her wine and sighed wistfully.

"History's so romantic – not like psychology at all!"

He nodded.

"Nor newspapers. But I wouldn't have wanted to live back then. There was constant warfare, especially after Europeans established the fur trade, which led to power politics and territorial disputes over the fur-bearing lands.... Joe Stanton told me how the ransom came about.

"The Manisses from Block Island, who were Pequot allies at the time, attacked the Niantic village at Weekapaug, took one of sachem Ninigret's three daughters hostage and demanded a ransom in wampum. He must have been short of cash, because he had to borrow from Thomas, who had the trading post at Pawcatuck Falls and kept plenty of wampum on hand. Also, he spoke the language and had a reputation for fairness, so both sides trusted him to broker the deal. The tract he received probably included Quonochontaug.

"I didn't tell Joe this, but it's a bit of a mystery: Ninigret should have had more wampum than he knew what to do with. The Niantic actually made the stuff in large quantities, and had grown rich from it... Maybe they'd just shipped a big order and were low on inventory. Another thing: Why didn't Ninigret just repay the loan in wampum? Could it be that land was to be the 'reward' from the outset? Maybe not, but I'll get to that....

"If it truly was a reward, Ninigret must have had a poor memory because Thomas owed him a favor from 10 years earlier for getting him in trouble with the English. They'd sent a debt collector from Boston to threaten him. Thomas was the translator and didn't like the highhandedness; his business depended on peaceful relations.

"He wrote a letter urging more respect for the sachem in future and reported Ninigret as saying 'No Englishmen should step out of his doore to pisse, but he should be killed.' His good intentions backfired though. The English were incensed and made ready to invade. Ninigret had to apologize. He said he lost his temper when the messenger provoked him.

"At first, I thought Joe's ransom story was just a family folktale, but the historical sources mention it. In fact, Thomas helped rescue two princesses. Both events happened within two years of each other, and the gift of land may belong to this earlier kidnapping.

"In 1653, Ninigret sought revenge after the Montauk sachem Wyandanch and his sub-sachem Mandush of the Shinnecock burned the body of an agent Ninigret supposedly sent to kill Mandush. The Long Islanders had been subject to the Pequot across the Sound until the Pequot War of 1637 almost obliterated the tribe. Afterward, Ninigret moved in to fill the power vacuum, but now Wyandanch wanted to ally with the English in

NIANTIC JEWEL

Connecticut. Ninigret was bound by a treaty with the Bay Colony not to go to war without permission, so he went to Boston, claimed innocence in the Mandush plot and got the green light to retaliate.

"He chose the time of the Green Corn Festival in late summer when the Montauks would be off their guard and their leaders gathered in one spot. The village was pillaged, 30 men slain and 14 captured, including two sachems and Wyandanch's daughter Quashawem – the princess. Before leaving, the Niantic burned a warrior to avenge their man.

"A second raid followed, then Ninigret sent a woman (possibly his sister Quaiapen) to negotiate peace terms. The ransom was arranged, but Thomas 'intercepted' it in transit. How the wampum came into his hands is unknown. Whatever the circumstances, he turned it over to Ninigret, who was grateful enough to give him the 8 square miles in Charlestown.

"That makes two gifts of land when we know there was only one. So it seems he wasn't as hard-headed about Ninigret's daughter's ransom as I suggested, and let Ninigret replace the wampum after all.

"Another version of the story is told by the Gardiner family, descendants of Lion Gardiner, the military engineer and power broker who built Fort Saybrook at the mouth of the Connecticut River for a group of aristocratic English investors in 1635. When the River Colony was founded a few months later, Saybrook Colony became part of it. As the fort's commander, Lion opposed the Pequot War despite heroically surviving a months-long Pequot siege in summer 1636.

"He protested to the Bay Colony, which sought to crush the Pequot and take their land, that it was easy to order hostilities from a safe distance while his people paid the price. 'You come hither to raise these wasps about my cars, and then you will take wing and flee away,' he wrote.

"Disgusted with the Puritans after the war, he started looking for a new home, and in 1639 his friend Wyandanch gave him Gardiners Island, the 5-square mile estate still owned by the family in Gardiners Bay at the eastern tip of Long Island.

"That made him the original English settler in the whole of what would become New York state. He always had cordial relations with Native Americans, yet he paid them trinkets for the vast amount of land he accumulated. His brief `Relation of the Pequot Warres' was written in 1660 though not published until 1833. He died in 1663 at the age of 64 – and a very rich man.

"The Gardiner family's twist to the story is that Ninigret captured the princess during her wedding, and killed the bridegroom. Lion was the go-between trying to disengage the Montauks from Ninigret and ally them with the English, and it was he who arranged Quashawem's ransom.

"The truth may lie somewhere in between. Lion didn't speak Algonquian and had used Thomas as a translator for 16 years. He helped negotiate the sale of 31,000 acres of Montauk land that became East Hampton in 1648. Maybe both men arranged the ransom and Thomas was to deliver it to Ninigret. Five years later, Wyandanch rewarded Lion for this and other services with a 47-square-mile gift of land – compared to the 8 square miles Ninigret gave Thomas!

"Interestingly, in September 1653, Wyandanch complained about the abductions to the commissioners of the United Colonies. This was a compact formed by Plymouth, Massachusetts Bay, Connecticut and New Haven in 1643 to present a common diplomatic and military front to the Indians, who were equally as adept at the realpolitik of playing one colony off the other as the English were with them.

"He hoped the commissioners would force Ninigret to free his daughter without a ransom. Connecticut was all for invading the Niantic, since Wyandanch was an ally, but Massachusetts vetoed the idea because it had permitted Ninigret's raid. Hartford had to do something, so Thomas was sent to demand that Ninigret return the captives. When a Niantic brave insulted Thomas, he impetuously took a swipe with his sword at the wolf's tail on the warrior's head. Then Ninigret asked what the English were going to do, because he wasn't about to yield to the demand. There was a heated discussion during which the Niantic surrounded Thomas and made a show of loading and priming their guns.

NIANTIC JEWEL

"That was Thomas' story anyway. My theory is that it was all a masquerade, which Thomas reported to Hartford with a straight face. Quaiapen and Wyandanch had already negotiated the ransom. Lion and Thomas were facilitating the deal, but knew Hartford would be outraged if a ransom was paid. The interception ruse allowed everyone to be happy: Wyandanch would get back a token amount of wampum plus his daughter and the rest of the captives; Ninigret would get his ransom; Hartford would have cowed Ninigret; and Lion and Thomas would get their reward.

"Thomas was quite a man. He and his wife Anne were living at Hartford when they married in 1637. Their 10 children account for the myriad descendants, including members of the Narragansett nation. Two sons went to Harvard, paid for by the Society for the Propagation of the Gospel. In addition to being a founder of Stonington, where he and William Cheesebrough bartered for beaver skins from their trading post, Thomas was an interpreter at all the major negotiations with the Niantic, Pequot, Mohegan, Montauk and Shinecook for 40 years. As the foremost linguist in the colonies, he was appointed Interpreter for Connecticut in 1638 and later Interpreter General of New England at a salary of 25 pounds a year.

"More than once, he risked his life acting as an intermediary in times of conflict. Take the Pequot War for instance. The sachem Sassacus tried to expel the English from Pequot-controlled territory between the Connecticut and Thames rivers by killing traders and attacking settlers and their families. He wanted his neighbors, the Narragansett, Eastern Niantic and Mohegan to join him, but Thomas and Roger Williams helped dissuade them. They were all traditional rivals of the Pequot but also had plenty of beefs with the English, so it was quite a diplomatic coup getting them to join the Connecticut-Massachusetts alliance.

"In hindsight, things might have turned out better for Native Americans if they'd united to drive out the English right then. They could have obtained the European goods they wanted from the French or the Dutch, and possibly held onto their land and their independence.

53

"By 50 years later, the English had taken everything. Even the Mohegan sachem Uncas, who built a mini empire out the wreckage of the Pequot War, his friendship with the English and marriage alliances formed from his having seven wives, died a disillusioned old man in 1683-4. The Mohegans of the Thames River Valley had been part of the Pequot confederation. Uncas' failed attempts to break free left him with about 400 people and a fraction of his former territory by 1636. Forty years later, he was collecting tribute (i.e. protection money) over a wide area. Then after Metacom's War, the River Colony no longer needed him, and stole his land.

"But back to Thomas. On May 25, 1637, the Pequot fort at Mystic, Conn., was burned in a punitive massacre that killed 600-700 mostly women and children; seven escaped and seven were captured. Pilgrim Father William Bradford wrote at the time: 'It was a fearfull sight to see them thus frying in the fyre, and the streams of blood quenching the same, and horrible was the stinck and sente ther of.' Those trying to flee 'were slaine with the sword, some hewed to peeces, others rune throw with ther rapiers, so as they were quickly dispatchte, and very few escaped.'

"Sassacus and his main force of warriors weren't there, as the English well knew, but that didn't matter. They eventually cornered him, or so they thought, in a swamp at Unquowa (Fairfield) on July 13. Thomas was sent in to parley and returned with some 200 old men, women and children seeking safe conduct, among them the family of Mononotto, the Pequot's second in command. He also brought back a challenge to fight to the death.

"Under the circumstances, Thomas may have had to be asked twice to return to the swamp, but he did. This time he carried a surrender ultimatum, which so incensed the warriors that he had to flee for his life amid a hail of arrows. His cries for help were heard by soldiers guarding the perimeter, who rescued him in the nick of time. So much for 'Don't blame the messenger'.

"When the English entered the swamp the next morning, they found only a few dead warriors. Sassacus may or may not have been among the 70 who slipped away in the night. In any case, his

NIANTIC JEWEL

luck had run out. He and 20-30 warriors ended up with the Mohawk, hoping to enlist their support. It could never be. They had commercial and political ties with the Narragansett, at whose behest he was killed and his head sent to Hartford.

"Sassacus probably wasn't at Fairfield at all. He and Mononotto would have been leading separate groups to make it harder for the tribe to be hunted down. He was probably on his way to the Mohawk at the time. Sadly, 180 of the women and children who surrendered became war booty consigned to perpetual servitude in Connecticut and Massachusetts; two women and 15 boys were shipped away to be sold as slaves.

"By the end of July, about 2,000 Pequot had been slain or captured. Indians were aghast at the scale of the slaughter. They had never seen anything like it. Traditional Algonquian warfare spared women and children. Narragansett co-sachem Miantonomi even obtained a pledge that noncombatants would be well treated before agreeing to join the campaign.

"When his men saw the Pequot fort being torched, they protested that it was evil, then turned around and went home appalled and disgusted. Many tribes promptly submitted to the English and began hunting down Pequot survivors. Rather than face torture and death at Indian hands, the fugitives surrendered to the English.

"Captives were parceled out in the 1638 Treaty of Hartford by which the River Colony abolished the tribe and took its land: 80 prisoners were given to the Mohegan, 80 to the Narragansett and 20 to the Eastern Niantic. In return (as if their military aid hadn't been enough) the Indian allies were required to pay Connecticut an annual tribute in wampum for each slave and to send four children as hostages until 200 fathoms (66,000 beads) were delivered. Thomas was designated a collector of these payments.

"It was a thankless task. The Indians entered the alliance as partners and felt betrayed when they didn't get equal spoils. Ninigret repeatedly refused to pony up (hence the debt collector's visit). According to Roger Williams, Miantonomi complained, 'Did ever friends deal so with friends?' The Bay Colony was also upset: Connecticut had shut it out, too.

55

"By the 1650s, many of the slaves had died or escaped and the tribes stopped paying the tribute completely. Connecticut retaliated by removing the remaining Pequot and setting them up in four towns, which ran their own affairs except for a court of appeals. Thomas was one of the three magistrates whose job included settling disputes with English neighbors.

"In his official dealings with Uncas, Ninigret and Miantonomi, it's ironic that Thomas had the least trouble with Uncas, whom he thoroughly disliked. Since the English used the Mohegan sachem as their ears and eyes among the Indians and depended on his military aid, they gave him what he wanted, so Thomas was usually the bearer of good news.

"But he had more in common with Ninigret and Miantonomi who were independent-minded and unpredictable. The English viewed them as potential threats, so he was often delivering lectures from the authorities in Hartford.

"Cultural differences were a major source of frustration. The English viewed sachems as kings and held them accountable for their people. That was how the European political hierarchy worked. In reality, sachems ruled loosely by consensus. They were intermediaries to the outside world as the powwows, or medicine men, were to the spirit world. No one had to obey them, except in wartime.

"People were bound only to their kinship group or clan and were free to switch tribes. They could vote with their feet. Each clan had its own allotted area in the village designated by a symbolic totem, usually an animal. Its members were as brothers and sisters. Intermarriage was taboo. Nor could a clansman testify against another. To harm one was to harm all: Insults never went unavenged except by those too weak to obtain redress. So the English air of superiority was a sore point that festered and spread over the years.

"The individual was paramount in a closely knit democracy of equals.

"Land was inseparable from Nature and therefore couldn't be owned. Sachems assigned usage rights within their tribes and even 'sold' them to the English, but the notion of exclusive private

NIANTIC JEWEL

ownership in perpetuity was outside their conceptual framework. The legal documents in a foreign language to which sachems affixed their marks were beyond their comprehension.

"They understood the idea of 'usufruct' as a kind of tenancy, but 'alienation,' the legal term for selling property, was inconceivable. It was also beyond the sachem's power. When boundary disputes were settled by negotiation, rather than war, the whole tribe had to approve the terms, or any other major decision.

"It was obvious that the English 'sachems' with all their laws couldn't control their own people, so how could Ninigret with only custom and tradition to call upon be expected to control his?

"One time, when there were fears of an Indian conspiracy, Thomas actually arrested Ninigret. The Pequot sub-sachem Robin Cassacinamon at Noank on the Mystic River was hosting hundreds of Indians at what appeared to be a war dance lasting several days. There was information that Robin had taken wampum to the Mohawk to enlist their aid. Thomas and a band of militia showed up at the dance and proceeded to break it up. Ninigret tried to stop them and was arrested. A tense standoff ensued until Robin convinced Thomas it was just a wild party and gave him some wampum to forget the whole thing.

"During the first Anglo-Dutch War of 1652-4, Thomas was a go-between in another close call that was to have lasting consequences. The Dutch offered goods at half price to any tribe who'd join them. The Mohegan and Montauk told the English that their Narragansett and Niantic rivals had gone over. Ninigret and the Narragansett co-sachems Pessicus and Mixanno denied the allegations.

"They asked Thomas to 'inform the Sachems in the Bay that the child that is now born or to bear shall see no war made by us against the English.' His report fell on deaf ears, and only the war's end forestalled an invasion.

"To add injury to insult, the English levied heavy fines to recoup the costs of their planned invasion. Together with previous fines for warring with the Mohegan and Montauk without English permission, the burden forced the Narragansett to mortgage their territory to the Atherton Company of land speculators in 1662.

"These Narragansett Proprietors, as they became known, were the original Boston Brahmins. They included Governors John Winthrop Jr. of Connecticut and Josiah Winslow of Plymouth, Richard Smith Sr. and Jr. of Wickford and Thomas Stanton Sr. and Jr. of Stonington.

"The deed was obtained under another threat of invasion. Rhode Island rejected its validity, as did a 1664 royal commission that gave Narragansett Country crown protection as King's Province.

"But the Bay Colony's rabid Puritans asserted that they, not the king, had supreme authority in New England, and persecuted anyone who challenged them. Their victims, including many of their own people, Rhode Islanders, the Narragansett, and settlers in what would become New Hampshire and Maine, petitioned King Charles II to cancel the charter, which was held at his pleasure.

"The royal commission, with a flotilla of warships, was sent to annex New Netherlands into the British Empire as the Province of New York. Its other task was to bring Massachusetts to heel. As well as abusing Indians and its own dissidents alike, the Bay was flouting the king's Navigation Acts, which gave Britain a monopoly on trade with its colonies, whereas the Puritans preferred to sell their products to the highest bidder and to buy from the cheapest supplier, while evading customs and excise duties.

"This secondary objective proved to be more difficult than dealing with the Dutch. They were being devastated in raids by Indians they had antagonized and could obtain no military aid from Holland. Consequently, they were happy to accept English protection.

"Following the Restoration of the monarchy in 1660, Charles II confirmed the Bay's charter in 1662, noting that its "principal end & foundation" was "freedom & liberty of conscience" for all. Not surprisingly, the commissioners found that the Bay government "is both against the honor of God and the justice of the King." But

NIANTIC JEWEL

events in England conspired to bury their report. And sadly for Native Americans the damage had already been done.

"The Puritan mindset of subjugating the Indians, rather than coexisting as equals in an interracial symbiosis, prevailed. For the 20-30 years the English depended on their neighbors' generosity, know-how and trade, they were happy to recognize them as sovereign nations. When they were no longer useful, they became subject peoples.

"Plymouth and Connecticut colonies followed Boston's lead for another decade until the cataclysm of 1675-6, despite the efforts of good men like Thomas Stanton. As late as Jan. 8, 1676, he wrote to the United Colonies vouching for Ninigret's allegiance at a time when all Narragansett were being hunted down. Ninigret was one of their six senior sachems, so he might have been a goner without Thomas' letter.

"He spent his life in public service and was a representative to the Connecticut General Court 1666-75. Uncas trusted him to write his will in 1670. When Thomas died in 1677 aged 68, he owned several farms or plantations covering 20,000 acres hereabouts. The trading post grew into an international import-export business with a branch office run by his son Daniel in Barbados. Using their own ships, they traded smoked and salted fish, corn and flour to West Indies plantations for sugar, molasses and rum. The company thrived for 100 years.

"He's an unsung hero laying forgotten under the shroud of collective guilt that hides – and continues to deny – the ethnocide of Native Americans that he did his best to prevent. It's true that he got mixed up with the Atherton Company, but no one's perfect.

"You would have liked him. He had scruples and wasn't shy about voicing them, particularly on English policy toward the Indians. It got him in trouble with colonial officials in Hartford, but he was so invaluable that all they could do was fine him. It's not a stretch to wonder if the tenuous English foothold here in those days could have been sustained without him. Then American history would be entirely different....

"There's a funny story about his irreverence. Rev. John Eliot of Roxbury, Mass., the Apostle to the Indians, sought his help while translating a catechism into the unwritten Massachusetts dialect around 1654. (This was before Eliot's Indian Bible came out in 1663, crowning a 14-year effort that was herculean in its sweep despite being a crude interpretation rather than a translation.)

"The Puritan ministers in Boston who were supervising Eliot wanted to be sure that Thomas was a good Christian, so they summoned him for an interview. It seems that Thomas didn't have much time for religion. His outspokenness so offended the pious elders that they left the room and vowed never to be in his presence again. But, like the Hartford bigwigs, they couldn't do without him, so Eliot was left to consult him unofficially. Rev. Abraham Pierson of Connecticut did the same in compiling his 1658 bilingual catechism."

She shook her head in disbelief.

"How do you remember all those dates?"

"It's history. I'm like a sponge for it. I bet you're the same with psychology."

CHAPTER 5

BEYOND THE CALL

The meeting of two personalities
Is like the contact of two chemical substances:
If there is any reaction, both are transformed.
CARL JUNG

After the food came, they shared bites as they ate and he steered the conversation toward her,

"Your parents seem really nice. What does your dad do?"

"He owns Synegenys, a telecom in Wellesley. The name's a palindrome he made up. He seems intimidating when you first meet him, or so I've been told, but he's really just a big, lovable teddy bear."

"And your mum's smashing – so friendly. She must be really bright, too. Is she easy to work for?"

She wiggled her fork while swallowing a bite of fish.

"Mostly she is, although we have our differences. We're both analytical, so we think alike. Too much alike! She seems to know what I'm thinking. She doesn't let me get away with much! Daddy's more sentimental – and temperamental. More passionate. I can always go to him and he'll understand. They're both still adjusting to the fact that I'm 21 and can make my own decisions. Sometimes I think they're overly protective."

"In what way?"

"It's difficult taking friends home – boys that is. They tend to get scared off. If Daddy doesn't browbeat them, Mother embarrasses them...."

"But she seems so considerate."

"At first, yes… You see, she has this mission. It's not that she's a militant feminist. She just feels there's a certain amount of hypocrisy in male perceptions of women – a double standard. Men can sow their wild oats, but if women do the same, they're called whores. They want women to be chaste and virtuous, but they're excused! She's convinced that men are the biggest whores of all. So she tries to lure them into behaving badly. She says she can tell a lot about a man by how he reacts. It's a rotten trick, but maybe they deserve it!"

"I agree. It's a riot. How does she do that?"

"She tells off-color jokes to see if they bite. Or she traps them into male chauvinist postures. Sometimes she even flirts with them; you'd be surprised how many respond. She says 'Give men enough rope and they'll hang themselves'."

Suddenly it came to him.

"Wow! I think your mum gave me the third degree on the patio, and I didn't even know it."

"Oh nooo! She's too much. Tell me what happened."

"She quizzed me about a moral dilemma, except it seemed to be a joke I didn't get. Your dad had to save me."

"I know that one. Your choice doesn't matter. The point is to lull you into the punch line and gauge your response to that. If you laugh politely or, in your case, not at all, you pass. But some guys think it's really funny – those who've been desensitized by the prevailing misogynist culture… She goes way too far, though I agree with her that there can't be equality of the sexes while women are held to a different standard."

He smiled while admiring the conformation of her bare arms and shoulders: how the firm, tanned flesh moved over the strong bone structure as she ate.

"Your mum's right. Men are easily tempted. But isn't that our biological and evolutionary destiny? We're genetic vehicles propelled by our hormones. The genes convey the imperative to procreate and the hormones compel its actualization…."

She interrupted with raised eyebrows and a scornful laugh.

NIANTIC JEWEL

"So that gives you carte blanche? Men aren't responsible for their behavior toward women? Isn't that what free will is all about: the ability to make morally responsible decisions?"

He struggled to extricate himself.

"Yes, of course. Free will enables us to choose between right and wrong actions according to one's moral compass. But determinism plays a role, too: a cause will follow the path of least resistance to an effect; it takes willpower to arrest it.

"I'm suggesting it's harder for men to restrain their natural urge to impregnate women than it is for women to control their desire to get pregnant. The male libido is aroused in the blink of a woman's eye. The female brain runs through an automatic checklist before mating occurs, or doesn't occur."

"You're still giving men an excuse to be jerks. Granted, most aren't, but that only proves that men can be gentlemen – if they so choose. And I wouldn't agree that it's any easier for women... What is this checklist anyway?"

"It's Darwin's 'survival of the fittest.' Ideally, the woman wants a strong, healthy father, a good provider for her child, plus a good husband and lover for herself. But sexual attraction is strongest toward the physical dynamic. Hence the maxim that 'nice guys finish last'."

She shook her head disapprovingly, causing the flowing red curls on each side to sway in unison.

"That's not true nowadays. Working women can be economically independent. They can have a child and a career. Now that we have access to education and labor-saving inventions like washing machines, permanent press clothing, vacuum cleaners and prepared food from supermarkets, as well as child care, we're not tied to the home anymore. Relations with men are irrelevant to motherhood. They contribute one cell, and we can get that from a sperm bank!

"Equal rights aren't a claim, they're a concession. Men can't stomach the fact that women are no longer subservient to them, so we have to put up with their displays of machismo – like spiteful little boys who've had their toys taken away... I'm sorry. That's a sweeping generalization. It just bugs me."

The bluntness jolted him, but her mild self-reproach took the edge off.

"Well, 'little boys' is right! Men in general are physically stronger, but emotionally weaker – immature by comparison. The emotional complexity of women makes it easier for them to overcome 'desires of the flesh.' They're emotionally three-dimensional – lovers, wives, mothers – in equal parts. Men may be lovers, husbands, fathers, but the latter roles are mere shadows of the first. Men are simple, id-driven creatures who do daily battle with their primal instincts. Women only have to do that once a month – or the few days they're in estrus. The cycles are different. So it's probably unrealistic to want men to be more like women… That's how it strikes me, anyway."

She finished eating, dabbed her lips with the napkin and sat back in her chair, frowning skeptically, as if he'd made only half an argument. His mind went blank. He took a mouthful of food, hoping to disguise his failure.

"Sorry. I've been talking too much and eating too little. You're way ahead of me."

There was that disarming smile again, stretching clear across her face, revealing perfect teeth.

"I'm a fast eater! Don't rush on my account… You mount an unusual defense of the indefensible. Tell me more."

He fell back on a historical point of view, since it was all he could think of.

"I'm just looking at things in the broader context of history. While women's lib has largely swept away male domination, I wouldn't say that it alone has caused a chauvinistic backlash. Men have always feared women because of their superior generative powers, and sought to subjugate them. That's been the eternal 'the battle of the sexes' back to the time of the Earth Mother/Goddess in the Mesolithic period more than 10,000 years ago when the female capacity for nurturing was extended to domesticated plants.

"The previous nomadic hunter/gatherer cultures based on brute force would have been male-dominated. But horticulture, the settled communities it required and the advent of pottery for

NIANTIC JEWEL

better food storage changed all that. The female principle came to be regarded as magical and divine - for thousands of years – until the increased food supplies themselves, plus competition for fertile land, led to renewed warfare and the last cycle of male domination."

As he finished, she looked up from the blue scarab bracelet she'd been toying with on her right wrist.

"Sounds as if you've been taking women's studies courses as well as history. And while that should be obligatory for all men, the Earth Goddess is only myth after all – even though it's feminist doctrine. There's no real proof is there."

He met her quizzical gaze and couldn't help but smile admiringly at her contrariness.

"Skepticism is the measure of a discriminating mind.... But what kind of proof are we looking for? Most of what passes for history is subjective interpretation. History is written by the victors. And you're right that male archeologists and mythologists tend to dismiss the Earth Goddess.

"But it seems to me there are too many surviving pictographs, petroglyphs, cave paintings and figurines of a Paleolithic Venus fertility symbol – from all over the world – for us to accept the orthodox view that they hold no special significance. So I side with the revisionists, whether or not they have a feminist agenda, because it's good science – as far as history can be scientific without absolute proof. It's not reproducible after all."

The busboy came to clear the plates. She finished her second glass of wine while he drank in the fetching glow on her rounded cheeks and the warm sparkle in her blue eyes. He looked over the dessert menu and then handed it to her. He was about to say he was addicted to Indian pudding, but she waved off the menu.

"Not for me. I'm not getting enough exercise and can't afford the calories."

"But you swim and play tennis."

"Not as much tennis as I'd like. I play for the college in the spring and used to be on the Quonnie club team, until this summer...."

"Oh, your job prevents it?"

Graham Griffith

"Well, that's my excuse, but really the crowd I grew up playing with has changed since we went off to college. It's complicated.... Now I just play with them if someone drops out and I'm free."

"That's why you dashed off with the jock in whites when we first talked?"

She rolled her eyes.

"I was hoping he wouldn't find me and I could show up late, but that wouldn't have been right...."

"I thought he must be your boyfriend."

A pensive look came over her face.

"That was Tom Morton. I've known him forever. Our parents are friends. We're both jocks. He was the only boy who could beat me at tennis. We were always doubles champions – until last year. We had a thing going after our senior year in high school.

"Then he went to Wesleyan and got in with the party slackers. We dated during the summer, and visited each other at college in the winter, but the drinking and drugs got worse. I tried to talk him out of it because I truly cared for him, but I couldn't get through.

"By last summer, it was obvious we had nothing in common anymore. So we broke up. He wouldn't accept it at first. He kept coming over, and calling. It was a miserable way to spend the summer. Now he's mostly over it. I feel badly for him. It's hard to lose a childhood friend, but he's become obnoxious. He even gave me grief about talking to you at the beach. I just hope he comes to his senses before he blows his chance for an education."

A picture of the heart on the rock came into Colin's mind: TM and JP. He wanted to be open about having seen it, but not now.

"You did your best. You can't help someone until they want help."

There was a sniffle, then the sadness passed from her face and her eyes lit up again.

"Maybe we could have coffee in the Night Watch Tavern. There's live music and dancing on weekends."

"That's a splendid idea. I'm glad you thought of it."

*   *   *

NIANTIC JEWEL

He paid the check and they walked into the inn, through low-ceilinged rooms with hand-hewn timbers. She stopped by the ladies room.

"You go ahead and grab a table. I shan't be long."

The tavern was crowded and noisy, but he found a corner table for two. He sat down and moved the other chair to his side so they both faced the band. He felt like an O'Doul's Amber and wondered if she'd like an Irish coffee, then feared it would be presumptuous to order. But while she was in his mind's eye, a waitress appeared and he went ahead anyway.

He saw her enter the room and look around for him. He stood and waved, unable to take his eyes off her. She spotted him and walked quickly toward him with a puzzled expression.

"Sorry, did I take too long? Did you change your mind?"

Now he was confused.

"No, I ordered you an Irish coffee. Is that alright?"

She moved the chair closer and sat down beside him.

"That's my favorite... But why were you calling?"

"I wasn't calling!"

She cast him a disbelieving glance.

"I heard you call my name in the ladies room. I'm sure it was you. It was so clear."

"No, I've been here the whole time. I was thinking about you though."

She sipped her coffee, taking care to dab the cream from her upper lip, before teasing him.

"That's pretty powerful thinking for me to hear you! What exactly were you thinking?"

He didn't want to belabor the inexplicable.

"I was wondering if we could play tennis. Joe Stanton said I could use the courts as his guest, so I brought my gear just in case. Of course, I don't know anyone to play with! But if your mum keeps you too busy – or if you have other partners – I understand. It was kind of you to come out tonight. You don't have to.... "

She stopped him with a finger on his lips.

"... see you again? You're sweet to give me an easy out, but Mother wants you! That is, she wants to have you over for dinner on Monday – providing I give you a passing grade tonight, and you're not spooked by what I've told you about my parents!"

"I'm not spooked, so far. But how many passes do I need to make to get a passing grade?"

She groaned and shook her head in feigned exasperation.

"Not that kind of pass. Your puns are worse than Mother's."

As the band started into "Stay (Just a Little Bit Longer)" she got to her feet and tugged his arm.

"I want to see how well you dance. C'mon. I love this song."

He took off his jacket and followed her among the half-dozen couples on the small dance floor in front of the band. Watching her uninhibited shimmies, twirls and sensual gyrations at close quarters stirred his blood. He let the pounding bass line wash over him and became part of it, moving spontaneously and ecstatically to a primal rhythm. They were laughing with sheer joy, enthralled in magic moments that went on and on as the band segued into "Take It to the Limit" and "You Can't Always Get What You Want."

When the set-closer began with the slow progressions of "A Whiter Shade of Pale," it seemed entirely natural for their arms to fold around each other and for their bodies to come together. She laid her head on his shoulder, and the scent of her hair made him weak at the knees. The exhilaration of the next 5 minutes was overwhelming. And then it was over. They disengaged, their minds still connected by unspoken words, and walked hand in hand back to the table.

He held the chair for her and pulled his even closer, unwilling to let go of the intimacy.

"Thank you. You're an amazing dancer."

"I love to dance. It makes me happy! But it takes two to tango, and a lot of men have two left feet. You're pretty good!"

"I was feeding off your energy."

"So that's why I'm exhausted. But it was good exercise, as well as fun. More than I've had in a long time."

"Me too. I don't want it to end... but I've kept you out longer than I should have. It must be 11, and I have a feeling your parents are getting concerned right about now. I could be a degenerate for all they know."

She checked her watch.

"It's exactly 11. You don't have a watch. And you couldn't have read mine...."

She looked at the bar and around the walls for a clock, then shrugged it off.

*　　　*　　　*

He resisted the urge to take her hand as they left, but she accepted an assist into the car. The cool night air gave him an excuse to put the top up and be cocooned, alone with her in private for the first time. Her electrifying nearness rendered him speechless until she pointed to the dashboard clock.

"What was that trick with the time then? Where was the clock? It was a lucky guess, wasn't it?"

He ventured to pat her hand in mock indulgence.

"You don't need a timepiece to tell the time. There's a clock in your brain."

"Well, yes, to regulate biological processes, and there's inner, psychological time, but that doesn't help keep track of external real time in our consciousness. We can count intervals of seconds and assign them numbers in space as long as we concentrate on just that. But we can't think of two things at once! So why don't you wear a watch? It's un-American not to! Anyway, you haven't answered the question."

"The answer's a bore."

"Because you'd have to 'fess up?"

"OK. Watches, rings, neck chains are dangerous around farm machinery – the same as loose clothing and long hair. I've had a couple of close calls with watch straps. One got caught in the intake drum of a combine harvester. I was almost pulled in and shredded to bits. Then, after not wearing one for a while, I found I didn't miss it. Who wants to wake up to a blaring alarm if you don't have to?"

She chuckled dismissively.

"Now you're going too far. That's impossible, unless you habitually get up at the same time every single day, and nobody does that. Stop teasing me!"

He took her hand, cupped it around the clock display and left it there.

"Tell me when the minute turns. I'll recite 60 seconds of poetry for you, and stop."

She returned her hand to her lap in a gesture of mild annoyance.

"I'm not falling for that ploy. You have a piece of poetry that lasts 60 seconds. Is this like your pretending-to-drown ruse?"

For the second time, her sharpness surprised him, but he laughed it off.

"I haven't thought of a piece yet, but it'll be longer than a minute. Would that be a sufficient condition for you to suspend your endearing disbelief?"

She gave him an impish glance of contrition.

"I'm sorry. I didn't mean to be... mean. Go ahead, but make it 90 seconds. And I'm going by the second hand on my watch. Just to be sure."

She covered the clock display with her palm. Impulsively, he placed his hand over hers.

"Not so fast Ms. Juliana Palmer! Now, it's going to cost you! If I win, you have to play tennis with me Sunday morning."

"And if I win?"

"You'll know I'm a dishonorable cad; a disreputable charlatan."

He returned his hand to the steering wheel.

"When you're ready."

She sighed apprehensively.

"Alright, I'll give you 5 seconds either side... Go!"

> "I want you when the shades of eve are falling
> And purpling shadows drift across the land;
> When sleepy birds to loving mates are calling –
> I want the soothing softness of your hand.

NIANTIC JEWEL

" I want you when the stars shine up above me,
  And Heaven's flooded with the bright moonlight;
I want you with your arms and lips to love me
  Throughout the wonder watches of the night.

"I want you when in dreams I still remember
The ling'ring of your kiss – for old times' sake –
  With all your gentle ways, so sweetly tender,
I want you in the morning when I wake.

"I want you when the day is at its noontime,
  Sun-steeped and quiet, or drenched with sheets of rain;
I want you when the roses bloom in June-time;
  I want you when the violets come again.

"I want you when my soul is filled with passion;
  I want you when I'm weary and depressed;
I want you when in lazy, slumbrous fashion
  My senses need the haven of your breast.

"I want you when through field and wood I'm roaming;
  I want you when I'm standing on the shore;
I want you when the summer birds are homing –
  And when they've flown – I want you more and more."

He stopped and caught his breath.
"There is 'more and more,' but that's 90 seconds."
She whistled in astonishment.
"Good Heavens! I don't believe it! That was exactly 90. Well done!
But finish it, please. It's beautiful. So poignant – the pleasure and
pain of love and longing."

"I want you, dear, through every changing season;
  I want you with a tear or with a smile;
I want you more than any rhyme or reason –
  I want you, want you – all the while."

"Is that an English Romantic poet – Byron, Shelley?"

"American. Arthur Gillom. `I Want You'. The strange thing is, no one knows who he was or of anything else he wrote. Just that one work in `Best Loved Poems of the American People'."

"And what made you choose that one?"

He pulled back from the precipice of exposing his naked feelings.

"I didn't choose. Poetry is of the soul – a `magical evocation.' Anyway, Mallarme said to name an object is to kill the joy of a poem, which is made to be divined little by little. To suggest the object is the dream."

She shifted position to observe him better.

"How many poems can you recall entirely?"

"All I've read twice and made mental pictures of."

"You don't mean you remember everything you read twice?"

"No, thank goodness! Just things that resonate emotionally – like literature and history. I'm hopeless at math, and anything abstract – like physics and chemistry equations. It works with anything I enjoy, if I concentrate on preserving it."

"Not whole books!"

"Only the odd page if I need it, but then I'm drained and need to rest for 20 minutes – to replenish the neurochemicals, I guess."

She backed off into the corner of her seat.

"Now you're really scaring me."

"I'm sorry. I shouldn't have said anything. I never mention this stuff because it upsets people, but I thought with you being into psychology... That's why it's hard to make friends, especially girlfriends – to get really close to people. They think I'm pretending for effect, or bonkers, and drop me like the plague. Unless I keep it hidden. And then I can't be myself. It's a curse."

He dropped his head in dejection, and she edged a little closer.

"Have you had it checked out by a psychologist or a psychometrist? Not that I think you can objectively measure a subjective state of consciousness. Those who say we can are frauds. Associationist psychologists reduce mind to brain and try to make quantative notations of qualitative states. That would make us mechanistic automatons without the free will, which we

NIANTIC JEWEL

obviously have, to substitute voluntary responses for programmed reactions.

"You can't explain mental operations mechanically, as if the mind were a machine with the laws of physics governing how it works. They can measure the superficial self that deals with our conventional social lives, but they can't touch the passionate self where feelings and ideas coalesce and can't be mapped out."

Her clinical analysis took him aback.

"I never thought of it that way! I did see a professional, when it started after my parents died. I was entirely mediocre until the watch thing began and my grades shot up. I was seeing a psychiatrist for depression. She said photographic memory or total recall were unusual but not extraordinary; that heightened perception was often associated with the psychic disturbance of grief, and would pass – to enjoy it while it lasted.

"The movie 'Rain Man' was inspired by Kim Peek, who memorized 11,000 books. St. Thomas Aquinas wrote Summa Theologica in his head and dictated it mostly from memory. Seneca the Elder repeated 2,000 names in order, but he used mnemonic devices developed to facilitate the art of memory – like those used in learning the Talmud and the Koran.

"Anyway, according to her, there are two kinds of memory, which work together. The first is the automatic memory of the body: the motor habit of rote learning carried out by the brain. The second is the image memory of the mind: a memory of imagination carried out by the spirit, which registers all the events of our daily lives as they occur.

"Both kinds pass into the unconscious mind, from where they can be recalled into the conscious mind to serve our needs. But most image memories don't serve our needs – because of their totality. They resurrect themselves spontaneously only when we dream.

"Her idea was that the psychic disturbance of grief was enabling me to activate these dream images while I'm awake.

"Actually, she was more concerned with treating the negative aspects of my depression. That was six years ago, and although the depression lifted after a few months, its psychic symptom remains.... But enough of that!"

Partly to emphasize the closure and partly out of audacity, he squeezed her bare knee for a brief instant, then immediately regretted it when he felt her leg tense.

"I'm so sorry! I took a liberty. It was entirely inappropriate."

"That's OK. It was I who made you uncomfortable to begin with... Your psychiatrist's explanation is intriguing. You wouldn't get an answer like that here – at least not on the East Coast. You'd be lucky if you got an answer!

"Short-term memory is pretty straightforward. Sensory input becomes a pattern of connections between neurons in the outer cortex, which organizes the pattern and places it briefly on hold in the frontal lobe. But you're talking about the long-term memory that develops from this.

"Current orthodoxy refers to the two types of memory systems as explicit and implicit: things we know we remember, which the hippocampus encodes and sends to the cortex for storage; and things we know without having to consciously remember, which require additional processing elsewhere – perceptual learning in the neocortex, habits and skills in the cerebellum and basal ganglia – before being stored in the cortex.

"Memories with emotional content get special treatment. They're plugged in to the amygdala, part of the limbic system in the forebrain, where primal instincts lie... If I were a psychologist, I'd say your amygdala, your primitive essence, is compensating for the loss of your parents.

"Like a blind person's other senses being heightened?"

"Sort of. Except with you, it's metaphysical. You're being compensated as a person as opposed to you as an organism, as would be the case with a sensory loss. Deep in your psyche, the photographic memory has become a manifestation of your parents, a way for you to maintain symbolic contact with them. Possibly, a major impression they made on your limbic system was their high academic expectations of you. That engenders a heavy filial obligation and a powerful emotional connection... D'you see what I mean?"

NIANTIC JEWEL

"I think so. Same conclusion my shrink came to, but in precise terminology. And how did you know my parents were always badgering me to do better in school? You're brilliant!"

As they turned into the Palmers' driveway he noticed they'd triggered a security beam that activated small pedestal lights around the circle's perimeter. She waved him to the right fork.

"Take your favorite route. Then I can hop out on the doorstep."

He stopped beside the portico and, feeling the awkwardness of the moment, turned on the dome light. Her radiance engulfed him, but he also felt a tinge of sadness.

"I've imposed upon you with my baggage. I'm sorry. The bet's void. You didn't know... when I forced you into it. And you can say to your mum I'm just another eccentric Englishman... not worth feeding."

A frown of regret creased her brow.

"That's nonsense. You can't just throw in the towel like that. If anyone did any forcing, it was me... Actually, Sunday morning isn't the best tennis time for me. I make late breakfast and we loaf around reading the papers. How about 2 o'clock? I'd really love to play."

His spirits were buoyed by her irresistible smile.

"I'd love it, too."

"It's settled then. I'll sign us up."

"You're on my way to the courts. Can I pick you up?"

"That would be nice. But I should warn you, I always play to win!"

He shrugged, hoping a gesture of nonchalance would hide the misgivings her challenge had stirred.

"No problem! I have just enough time to practice."

She squeezed his thigh in an emphatic tit-for-tat while opening her door. Once outside, she ducked her head back in.

"Thanks. I really did have a wonderful time. Goodnight Colin. Oh, and can I tell Mother you'll come? There's something we should let you in on that you might find mildly interesting."

"Sounds mysterious. I'm hooked. Sweet dreams Juliana."

He watched the sway of her hips as she walked to the door. She turned to wave and went inside.

Graham Griffith

CHAPTER 6

BLOODBATH

War. The hell where youth and laughter go.
SIEGFRIED SASSOON

The clear skies and golden sun of a perfect week in late-July gave way to the haze of high cirrus clouds as Colin counted the sheep Saturday morning. A tropical storm was meandering up the coast off North Carolina, headed northeast, but so far out to sea that heavy surf was the only impact expected on New England.

Colin chalked a net line on the side of the barn, scratched out a service line and got in an hour's practice before it was time to leave for his shift at the Gazette. He wondered if he was even in her league. He'd never been up against a club player, and worried that he'd disgrace himself. Then he considered his weapons: height, power, ambidexterity, agility, topspin forehand, back-spin backhand. All he had to do was make sure he gave her a good match.

At work, he told his friend Lloyd Forbes about all that had happened since he'd sought information about the Palmers, and reported on his chats with Joe Stanton.

"That's good, Colin. I was concerned you'd be lonely down there. And we won't be around until the renters leave. Quonnie people keep to themselves. It takes years for them to accept newcomers. But you're doing alright. Hey, you gotta bring her over for a drink. We want to meet her. Is she pretty?

Colin scrunched forward across the rim and lowered his voice.

"She's amazing! Incredibly bright as well as beautiful; vivacious, sweet-natured, warm and open... tender and giving,

NIANTIC JEWEL

the way authentic women are. I feel so alive when I'm near her. I can't get her out of my mind. Do you believe in love at first sight?"

The older man smiled and shook his head.

"Lust at first sight! Infatuation. Hold on, Colin! You've only known her a few hours. Don't get ahead of yourself here. Not to be a wet blanket, but don't read too much into the polished manners of the upper-middle class. She's been cloistered at Wellesley for the school year. It's only natural that she'd be playing the field in the summer. Or, maybe she's looking for strictly platonic male companionship – a chum. You'd be the perfect find. You're better than a homosexual: You're English!"

"I don't get it. What's the connection?"

"You're a handsome, straight guy. And she can have meaningful conversations with you. But best of all, she won't have to keep fending you off. You'll be a gentleman because you're English.... she can string you along because Englishmen are dumber than a doorpost. Dinner wasn't a date. Tennis isn't a date. She hasn't indicated even a glimmer of romantic interest, so far. These Wellesley women are heartbreakers, Colin. At Harvard, we used to say Romp at Radcliffe: Weep at Wellesley. It's the attraction of the unattainable."

Colin didn't like what he was hearing, but it grew worse.

"And what about her parents? They want the best for their daughter. In their affluent circumstances, that means the right kind of suitor – a doctor, a State Street lawyer, a high-tech honcho, an investment banker. Certainly not a journalist, a newspaperman. Don't get me wrong, but money marries money – especially in Boston. Just don't get your hopes up too high. I wouldn't want to see you hurt."

Colin pondered the reality check.

"What's wrong with journalists? It's a respectable living,"

"Are you kidding! We're the misbegotten, the scum of the earth. Journalism isn't a profession; it's not even a craft. We're voyeurs of life, purveyors of mass-produced banality. Only TV journalism's worse: Now that's the pits! It's not even journalism; it's infotainment – showbiz masquerading as significance."

He sat back in his chair and made an expansive gesture toward the newsroom.

"Just look at them all: the ink-stained wretches, the walking wounded. They couldn't function in the outside world. They're basket cases. This is daycare for lunatics. And the Gazette is the major leagues: one of the top 10 papers in the country. It's sad to think that it doesn't get any better than this.

"Half of them are here because it's the only thing they can do to eke out a living. The other half would pay to work here; they don't need the money, but they need a job for appearances' sake and the Puritan work ethic of their inbred Brahmin bloodlines. A job in the crass commercial world wouldn't cut it in their circles. The Gazette gives them prestige. This is a good place to hang out. If it's not that, they're here through the extended nepotism of the mass media. How many here are the offspring of the well-connected, the plugged in? It's incestuous! And we're all guilty, myself included.

Colin grimaced and waved him off.

"That's a wild exaggeration! There are plenty of talented people here. And nepotism and favoritism aren't confined to the Gazette. They're part of the human condition."

"Maybe so. But ask yourself what we do here? We titillate the baser instincts: 'Feed me fresh tragedies and disasters; who screwed up and got caught today?' After that's used up, we have to surround the ads with something, so we sensationalize the mundane and call it news. We do it for profit, and we don't care who gets hurt along the way.

"Journalism used to stand for something. Newspapers were public watchdogs. We exposed corruption and abuse of power by the government. But changing economics forced the families that had owned newspapers for generations and operated them as a public trust to sell out to media conglomerates that run them as profit centers.

"We're in the entertainment business now. Instead of publishing the Pentagon Papers and exposing pedophile priests, it's who makes the best cookies in town. No wonder people started getting their news from the Internet. It's just a matter of

NIANTIC JEWEL

time until the newspaper as we know it goes belly up – killed by corporate greed.

"If that sounds cynical, well that's what this business does to you. Get out, Colin, while you're still young and idealistic! Get your master's and your PhD and spend your life in the ivory towers of sheltered innocence!"

*   *   *

The discouraging words were ringing in his ears as Colin drove back to the farm that night.

His ardor faltered at the prospect of there being truth behind the hyperbole: Was she thinking of him only as a convenient tool to keep the Morton fellow off her back? No matter, he reasoned. We all act out of self-interest; without it, we couldn't survive. Even altruists expect a reward in Heaven. His goal was to get their self-interests to converge romantically. He told himself that any interest on her part was a step in the right direction. It gave him time to hang around and press his suit.

He sat on the veranda swing watching the last pink and purple hues of sunset recede from the thickening clouds. His emotions in turmoil, he immersed himself in accounts of the bloodiest battle of Metacom's War: the Great Swamp Fight of 1675, which took place 10 miles away in West Kingston.

The Narragansett under Canonchet (nephew of Canonicus who died in 1647) and the Niantic under Ninigret had remained neutral after the Pokanoket Wampanoag sachem Metacom (aka Philip) attacked Plymouth Colony in June 1675.

Metacom still trusted in the once-mutual understanding, long discarded by the Puritans, that natives and colonists were equal subjects of the king. His father Massasoit, who died in 1661 aged about 80, was the sachem who befriended the Pilgrims and saved them from starvation in 1621. The League of Peace in effect since then recognized the Wampanoag as a "friend and ally."

Both by treaty and royal decree, neither people had authority over the other. This remained the view of the British government and Rhode Island as well as of the Narragansett/Niantic, the only other tribal nation to still dare oppose Puritan hegemony.

Like the Wampanoag, they were committed to peaceful coexistence with the English since submitting to the crown in October 1636 and pledging "perpetual peace and friendship" to the Bay Colony. They reaffirmed their fidelity in 1644. Just two years later, sachems Canonicus and Pessicus had to fend off the Bay's claim of jurisdiction over them by reminding Gov. John Winthrop in a letter that they were "subjects... unto the same king."

Now, the Narragansett hoped to hold off the Puritan theocrats by diplomacy until the king could protect them as promised, but Charles II was preoccupied by turmoil in England and Europe. This left the Bay Colony free to assert a degree of autonomy that stretched to mediating "the king's pleasure" among his subjects in the absence of a royal decree.

On June 24, 1675, the very day war broke out at Swansea, Mass., the four leading sachems – Pessicus, Canonchet, Ninigret and Quaiapen – met with Bay Colony peace commissioners Capt. Edward Hutchinson, Seth Perry and William Powers at Worden's Pond 9 miles away. Roger Williams was also present to hear the sachems reconfirm their friendship toward the English. The pledge did no good.

Canonchet was drawn into the holocaust when he refused to turn over Pokanoket, Pocasset and Sakonnet Wampanoag women, children and elderly who had taken refuge with him. He was honor-bound to protect them through ties of consanguinity and the customary Native American obligation of hospitality.

The Pocasset squaw sachem Weetamoo was the widow of Metacom's elder brother Wamsutta (aka Alexander) who died in July 1662. The Indians believed he had been poisoned by the English a few years after succeeding his father. It now appears he may have died of appendicitis aggravated by the "physic" administered by Samuel Fuller, the Plymouth doctor.

Weetamoo reluctantly joined Metacom in the nascent rebellion when he retreated into her lands, then she split from him in

NIANTIC JEWEL

August and took her antiwar faction of about 100 people to seek shelter with "Ninicraft," also spelled "Ninicroft."

Historians assumed they came to Ninigret at Weekapaug, but it didn't ring true to Colin. Sources of the time sometimes alluded to both the sachem and his sister, Queen Quaiapen, as Ninicraft/Ninicroft, and she was then at her fort in North Kingstown. Five miles away at Wickford, Richard Smith Jr. wrote from his trading post to Connecticut Governor John Winthrop Jr. on Aug. 5 that Weetamoo and her people were in the area. On Sept. 12, he wrote again saying the Narragansett "sought favor" from the English for the Pocasset and Sakonnet to stay with them.

Smith was in close touch with Ninigret, but the letters, quoted in Daniel Berkeley Updike's 1937 biography, "Richard Smith: First English Settler of the Narragansett Country," never link Weetamoo to the Niantic sachem. Meanwhile, Ninigret was also in frequent contact with his neighbors Thomas Stanton and his sons, Thomas' son-in-law Rev. James Noyes and Tobias Saunders of Misquamicut, who would have reported Weetamoo's arrival even if Ninigret tried to keep it quiet for fear of enraging the English.

The long trek with women and children in the summer heat was another clue: Quaiapen was 17 miles closer than Ninigret. More likely, Weetamoo went to her sister sachem. With Quaiapen, she could count on female bonds for protection. With Ninigret, she'd be gambling against the Niantic's political interests, i.e. self-preservation. She was aware of his reputation for crafty diplomacy,

Maybe she had the prescience to know that in the fall Ninigret would present Connecticut authorities with the heads of some Wampanoag warriors. Both sachems were obligated to shelter refugees, but the Narragansett were better able to withstand English pressure to surrender them than the Niantic.

The clincher, Colin decided, was what happened to Weetamoo after the Swamp Fight: She fled with the Narragansett and fought alongside them until her death. Had she been with Ninigret, three scenarios were possible, each of which would have been documented: 1) she sits out the war at Weekapaug, 2) Ninigret turns her over to the English, 3) he refuses to give her up and the English slaughter the Niantic as well as the Narragansett.

The same path to Quaiapen may have been taken by another squaw sachem with whom she had kinship ties, Awashonks of the Sakonnet. She had succeeded her husband Toloney, who died in battle, and lived next to Weetamoo in modern Little Compton on the eastern shore of Narragansett Bay.

Awashonks shared Weetamoo's dilemma when war broke out: The young warriors wanted to fight with Metacom; she and the rest of the tribe, which included five sub-sachems, wanted peace. Unlike Weetamoo, she hadn't been forced to join Metacom in July 1675. Instead, she immediately sought refuge with the Narragansett, but after the Great Swamp Fight in December they were all fighting for their lives against the English.

Quaiapen initially fled to her brother Ninigret. The English found out, and he was summoned to Boston Sept. 15 to explain why he was sheltering her. He sent his son Catapazet in his place, claiming he was too old to travel. Upon renewal of the peace treaty, the Niantic agreed to deliver up Quaiapen. Not surprisingly, this never occurred.

All three squaw sachems may have been with Ninigret briefly after December, or Weetamoo and Awashonks may have gone west with Canonchet into Nipmuck country following the Great Swamp Fight. They returned a year later when the theater of war switched back to southern New England. In the final weeks, the Sakonnet surrendered, and ended the war fighting on the English side. By that time, Metacom had been abandoned by all but his few remaining Pokanoket.

When peace was restored, Awashonks was allowed to continue as squaw sachem although her son Mammanuah led a faction opposing her for control of the few small parcels of land not forfeited to Plymouth Colony.

She last appears in the historical record in 1683 when she, another son Peter, who was also her chief captain, and her daughter Betty were charged with infanticide in the death of Betty's newborn. They testified that the baby was stillborn and were acquitted. However, Betty, being unmarried, was punished

NIANTIC JEWEL

for fornication; Awashonks and Peter were chastised for ordering the whipping of the woman who reported the pregnancy.

William, a young son by her second husband Wewayewitt, went to grammar school until being disabled by palsy. Though her burial site is unknown, a boulder placed in Wilbur Wood, Little Compton, in the late 19th Century is inscribed: "In memory of Awashonks Queen of Sogkonate & friend of the white man."

*   *   *

Unhappily for the Narragansett, on July 15 some minor sachems along with Ninigret were coerced into a treaty pledging continued fidelity to the English and promising to deliver dead or alive any of Metacom's subjects in their midst. Hostages were demanded to assure compliance, including Canonchet's brother and his family, who were held at Hartford.

The scalps of at least 14 Wampanoag and Nipmuck warriors were duly presented, but Canonchet was called to Boston Oct. 18 to reaffirm the pact, again under the threat of war unless he complied. A deadline of Oct. 28 was set for the refugees to be turned over.

When the day came, Canonchet is famously said to have declared: "No, not a Wampanoag, nor the paring of a Wampanoag's nail." (He was not to know that Weetamoo would soon become his kinswoman when she divorced her second husband, the pro-English Petananuet, and married Canonchet's cousin and fellow sachem Quinnapin.)

Ostensibly as punishment, but with the ulterior motive of grabbing the tribe's lands by conquest, the United Colonies sent an army of 1,180 men, including 150 Mohegan allies, marching through a blizzard to the Narragansett stronghold in the Great Swamp on Sunday, Dec. 19, 1675.

The invasion was illegal since only Rhode Island and King Charles had authority in Narragansett Country. In granting the colony's 1663 charter, the king explicitly acknowledged that the Narragansett were under his protection and forbade neighboring colonies from invading Rhode Island to attack Indians within its borders. The three Puritan governments based their legitimacy on English law, but abided by it only when it served their interests.

The soldiers were led across the ice to the hidden sanctuary by "Indian Peter" Freeman, who had been captured a few days earlier by the Bay Colony's Capt. Samuel Moseley, a former privateer with a reputation for brutality. Only weeks earlier, he had a captive squaw, in his own words, "torn in pieces by dogs." He and his crew of Jamaican buccaneers and Boston riffraff, pardoned in exchange for enlistment, wanted blood and booty. They seized 18 Indians on their march from Boston and sold them into slavery.

Even innocent Indians were spoils of war. The army's commander-in-chief, Gov. Josiah Winslow of Plymouth, sent two boys similarly captured as gifts to friends in Boston. Though the son of a compassionate Pilgrim Father, Winslow was a slaveholder who unscrupulously acquired vast amounts of Indian land.

In his 1676 history of the war, Rev. Increase Mather of Boston, who regarded Indians as savages, maintained that Peter sought out Moseley and turned traitor "having received some disgust among his Country men." That he was indeed captured and cooperated, likely after torture, to save himself and his family is suggested by the fact that five months later he petitioned the Bay General Court for release of his wife, who had been taken as booty by Moseley despite a promise of freedom for his family in return for his services.

His wife was freed, but 10 years later he was making a similar petition regarding his daughter, a slave of Capt. Thomas Prentice; she too was freed. Such treatment of his wife and daughter seems unlikely reward for a voluntary collaborator.

A third possibility is that Peter was sent by Canonchet to lure the English to the most heavily defended part of the fort by telling them he knew the weakest point. But why lead the cold, hungry and dispirited soldiers to the fort at all when they could be harried to death stumbling around in a vast frozen swamp? Nor would such a stratagem require the sacrifice of Peter's wife and daughter.

The most believable scenario is that Peter's cooperation was secured by woolding, the preferred interrogation technique of the day in which a cord is tightened around the prisoner's head. Not in doubt is that the army would have perished in the frozen wilderness without him, yet he died vilified, and then was forgotten.

*   *   *

The several hundred wigwams crowded onto a fortified 4-acre hummock held about 1,000 women, children and old men. They were protected by probably no more than 100 warriors, given the confined space, although other estimates range from 200 to the tribe's entire fighting force of maybe 2,000 men. More plausible is that Canonchet and his main host were about 7 miles east at the still-unknown location of the tribe's great village in today's town of Narragansett, or with Quaiapen at Queen's Fort 11 miles away in North Kingstown.

Following heavy losses in two attacks, the English set fire to the village. When the smoke settled, the 100 warriors and 600 women and children lay dead; 300 were taken prisoner. English losses were about 100 dead and 150 wounded, of whom 40 died on the nighttime march through 3 feet of snow to Richard Smith's garrison at Wickford. Mohegan losses were about 50 dead and 80 wounded.

In his history of the war, Rev. William Hubbard wrote: "after much Blood and many Wounds dealt on both Sides, the English seeing their Advantage, began to fire the Wigwams, where was supposed to be many of the Enemies Women and Children destroyed, by the firing of at least five or six hundred of those smoaky Cells."

The massacre was described less reticently in "News from New-England," published anonymously in London a few months later: "ours had now a Carnage rather than a Fight, for every one had their fill of Blood."

By 1886, however, success was its own vindication. In his "Narragansett Fort Fight," the otherwise fair-minded historian Rev. George Madison Bodge would have no second-guessing: The carnage was "one of the most glorious victories ever achieved in our history, and considering conditions, as displaying heroism, both in stubborn patient and dashing intrepidity, never excelled in American warfare."

Even after the slaughter of their people, co-sachems Pessicus and Canonchet continued to seek peace while preparing for the inevitable. They made four fruitless overtures to the English in the next three weeks, time each sachem used to pursue his own ends. Pessicus was no friend of Metacom and correctly foresaw along with the tribal elders that war with the English would lead to disaster. Canonchet spoke for the young warriors in advocating a pan-Indian alliance to expel the English as the only means of survival.

The precious time was used by Pessicus to gather food stores and send hundreds of women, children and the elderly to safety among the tribes of northern New England, where he joined them until being killed by the Mohawk above the Piscataqua River in New Hampshire in 1677.

Meanwhile, Canonchet was marshaling his warriors to link up with Metacom and the allied tribes in Nipmuck country to carry the war to the English. From late January 1676 through early April, the Narragansett unleashed their full fury, attacking and burning towns and killing settlers, but often taking women and children hostage. By war's end, every house in mainland Rhode Island from Providence to Stonington had been put to the torch, except for one stone dwelling in Warwick.

The warrior army, including Nipmuck, Pocumtuck, Mahican, Eastern and Western Abenaki and many smaller tribes who joined the cause, destroyed a dozen Massachusetts towns and heavily damaged many more. There was a similar toll in New Hampshire and Maine. The final tally when fighting petered out in Maine in 1677 was 3,000 English dead from a population of 52,000, plus 10,000 head of livestock. A generation of settlement was wiped out, not to be approached again for almost a century.

Canonchet overshadowed the Nipmuck sachems Matoonas, Shoshonin ("Sagamore Sam"), Monoco and Muttaump as the insurrection's tactical leaders almost immediately upon taking up arms. By December 1675, Metacom and his several hundred

NIANTIC JEWEL

Wampanoag were in New York territory wintering in what was thought to be safe haven among the Mahican at Schaghticoke in the Hoosic Valley just north of Albany. He hoped to enlist Mahican, Mohawk and French manpower while buying French and Dutch munitions to lay waste to Boston and Hartford among other major towns in the spring.

The plan looked promising at year's end, by which time Puritan cold-heartedness had driven tribes like the Nipmuck, Narragansett, Pocumtuck and Agawam to the rebel cause. Metacom's own efforts won over the Mahican and 5-600 French-allied Indians identifiable by the straws they wore in their noses. By February, he had assembled close to 2,100 warriors. Meanwhile, the main Algonquian host of another 2,000 warriors and their families, including the Narragansett, were hunkered down in the Nipmuck strongholds at Menameset (New Braintree), Squakeag (Northfield), Quaboag (Brookfield) and Mt. Wachusett (Princeton).

*   *   *

Metacom knew he was safe from English attack in New York because Gov. Edmund Andros treated Native Americans as brothers. Fatefully, however. he intervened with his Mohawk allies against the rebel sachem as part of an ongoing diplomatic effort that forged the Covenant Chain. This crucial alliance between the English and the Five Nations of the Iroquois League – the Mohawk, Seneca, Oneida, Onondaga and Cayuga – secured North America for Britain. The chain of peace treaties remained in effect on the Canadian side of the border until 1982.

Andros was a staunch Anglican who hated the Puritans almost as much as he hated the French, who fought the British for Canada until ceding their colony on the St. Lawrence River in 1763. While he wished to take over the New England colonies for his patron, James, Duke of York, who held the Province of New York as his personal fiefdom, he couldn't stand by as Christians and countrymen were killed. He was knighted the next year for his diplomacy that turned the tide of war.

Sir Edmund finally got his wish in 1686 when James became king on his brother's death and ended Puritan autonomy by creating the Dominion of New England with Andros as governor general. Gifted though he was as an administrator, diplomat and militarist, he was so resoundingly unpopular as to be arrested and briefly imprisoned by the people of Boston in May 1689.

This coincided with the overthrow of James II in the Glorious Revolution that brought his Protestant daughter Mary and her husband, William of Orange, to the throne. The Dominion then collapsed and the colonies at first enjoyed then endured royal governors until the American Revolution.

The official view in London was that Boston's republican magistrates, not the loyal colonists, had brought the calamity upon themselves by stealing native land, neglecting their defenses and refusing military aid lest it compromise their independence. In the king's Privy Council, the prevailing opinion was that the Puritans had provoked the war by their bigotry, greed and self-righteousness and prolonged it by their autocratic conduct.

Royal patience was running out on the Massachusetts tyrants and warmongers, but not fast enough to halt the carnage. On Dec. 22, 1675, three days after the Great Swamp massacre, the king in council ordered the Bay Colony to send agents to answer a host of charges including customs fraud, theft from proprietary landlords and merchants, operating an illegal corporation, violating the royal prerogative, flouting statute law and making a mockery of the established church and political morality.

On Oct. 10, 1675, disturbing news reached Andros at Fort James in Manhattan: Metacom was cutting a swath of death and destruction through the upper Connecticut Valley as he headed for the New York border. The governor sent troops under Captain Brockholes to the Albany garrison with orders to arm the Iroquoian allies in the Covenant Chain in preparation for an invasion by the Algonquian, their traditional enemies.

Metacom was looking for help not trouble in New York, but by Feb. 12 he was being hunted by the Mohawk, the most dreaded of the warlike Iroquois nations. When Andros arrived in Albany March 4, taking advantage of an early thaw on the Hudson to ship

NIANTIC JEWEL

in more troops and munitions, 300 Mohawk had just returned with prisoners and scalps from a devastating attack on Metacom's camps.

Later, Puritan scribes put out a different version that ignores Andros' role and demonizes Metacom. In this classic piece of Puritan obfuscation eagerly reported by Rev. Increase Mather, a desperate Metacom attempts to set the Mohawk on the warpath against all whites by killing several warriors and making the English appear responsible. Then, improbably, a lone survivor exposes the deed and vengeance is exacted – all as if by divine providence.

By both accounts, Metacom lost hundreds of warriors. The battle and its consequences dealt the rebellion a fatal blow. For in that single encounter in New York, the war's outcome was decided – not by the Puritans but by Andros and the Mohawk.

Similarly, the war was not ended by the Puritans, but by Andros and the Abenaki. So denuded of English settlement had the wartorn northeastern lands claimed by both the duke of York and the Bay Colony become by 1677 that Andros feared the French would fill the vacuum if he didn't quickly reestablish an English presence.

First, he had to mollify the Native Americans who, as a result of mistreatment by Massachusetts traders and settlers, had expelled them from everywhere north of Wells, Maine. In August, he dispatched troops to build a fort at Pemaquid near Damariscotta and to open trade with the Abenaki tribes. Next he gave a green light to Boston to invite the ever-obliging Mohawk to rampage through the northern reaches, now occupied solely by Algonquian, including displaced holdouts from the southern New England insurgency.

Although the Mohawk sent several war parties east to take the heat off the remaining English settlements, the tactic achieved little, save for the death of Pessicus. It was left to Andros to negotiate peace. And so the signing of the Treaty of Casco April 12, 1678, officially ended Metacom's War with not a Puritan in sight.

89

Graham Griffith

*   *   *

Routed from the Hoosic Valley, Metacom fled back to the Connecticut River while his Pocumtuck and Abenaki allies went north to Canadian refuges. The dispersion crippled his ability to attack major towns. More ominously, his best hope for victory was dashed. Instead of winning over the Iroquois, who lived for war, he was now their mortal enemy.

Andros sent Lieutenant Gerrit Teunise out from Albany to find Metacom – not to deliver the coup de grace but to offer an olive branch. The defeat, the governor knew, made Royalist-Iroquoian power supreme beyond the settlements of southern New England. But there was a problem: Once unleashed, the Mohawk would slaughter not only their Indian prey but every Puritan man, woman and child who got in the way.

Andros' shrewd solution was to offer the remnants of the southern New England tribes a new home under his protection in the Hoosic Valley. In one fell swoop, he accomplished three ends: 1) Algonquian who settled there entered the Covenant Chain as allies of the New York English and the Iroquois; 2) settling the valley secured it for the Duke of York against the competing claims of Massachusetts and Connecticut; 3) settlement added much-needed population to the ducal domains.

Amazingly, Teunise located Metacom. He told him that in the spring the governor would plant a Tree of Peace in the valley and those who lived under it would be safe from Iroquois and Puritans alike. Hedging his bets until the asylum became a reality (which duly occurred in May), Metacom freed 100 English hostages to the emissary before continuing his flight from the Mohawk down the Connecticut Valley and back to the Menameset stronghold.

Despite Nipmuck and Narragansett successes in March and April, Metacom faced an increasingly hopeless struggle. The native alliance began to splinter with the Schaghticoke debacle and continued to fragment with the massacre at Turner's Falls May 19, 1676, in which hundreds of Nipmuck and River Indians died.

NIANTIC JEWEL

Late on May 18, Captain William Turner and 150 militiamen marching out from Hatfield found the Native Americans fishing at Peskeompscut (Turner's Falls in Montague), their position reported by two escaped captives. The huge encampment was attacked by surprise the following dawn.

Hundreds of native men, women and children died as the English simply stormed the sleeping village, firing into the wigwams. A massacre was underway until the arrival of warriors from a camp the English had overlooked forced Turner to break off the butchery and retreat. It was small consolation for the grievous Indian losses that he and 38 soldiers died trying to fight their way to safety at Deerfield.

Metacom's unified command disintegrated into factions. Some sachems, like their leader, wanted to fight to the end. River Indians like the Pocumtuck, Norwottock and Agawam would have negotiated terms, using the dozens of captives as bargaining chips. A third group favored buying time through subterfuge to fight another day.

Unknown to Metacom, the River Indians had opened peace talks even before the Battle of Turner's Falls; the Nipmuck followed in July. Such discourse and dissent as the autocratic Metacom tolerated was futile anyway. The Puritans were committed to eradicating Native American culture and to killing or enslaving as many natives as the Bible would allow.

Changing their failed tactics, Massachusetts and Plymouth began using the friendly Praying Indians they had incarcerated at the war's outset to track down the sick and starving rebels and their families. Mohegan and Pequot warriors were already a vital part of Connecticut's forces. Tellingly, only one settlement in the River Colony was destroyed in the war – the deserted town of Simsbury.

Each side burned the other's provisions when they found them. Soldiers and settlers, warriors and tribespeople alike went hungry. The English made do with meager but regular supplies, mostly from unscathed Connecticut and New York. The Indians were reduced to eating horses' hooves, bones, tree bark and the few English livestock remaining.

Their straits were shared by a 38-year-old minister's wife taken hostage Feb. 10, 1676, in a Narragansett raid on Lancaster, Mass. She was ransomed May 2 and wrote of her ordeal in "The Narrative of the Captivity and Restoration of Mrs. Mary Rowlandson." The 1682 classic describes her 3-month servitude to sachem Quinnapin and his wife Weetamoo as well as conversations with Metacom himself. Although harshly treated by Weetamoo and enduring immense physical and emotional suffering, including the death of her 6-year-old daughter Sarah in her arms, she experienced many acts of kindness and "not one of them ever offered me the least abuse of unchastity to me, in word or action."

*   *   *

The war never went right for Metacom. He was always out of sync with events. His numerous allies, including the powerful Nipmuck, Pocumtuck and Abenaki, had the English reeling at first, but winter came too soon, giving the colonists time to regroup and the natives time to starve and sicken. As Metacom often must have lamented, the war itself came too soon.

There is no doubt he wanted a showdown with the English – but a year later. He needed the time to create a unified native alliance from Canada to Chesapeake Bay and to stockpile munitions and supplies. But instead of taking on just the English, he had to fight on three fronts that also included friendly Indians and Nature herself in the form of winter exposure, hunger and disease.

If only the young warriors who started the war at Swansea June 20, 1675, had been patient.... If only the Narragansett sachems had seen that neutrality was impossible when the Puritans were bent on taking their land and would destroy them to get it.

Metacom was on the run from the beginning. Somehow, he spirited his people off Narragansett Bay's Pokanoket peninsula, where most of them lived, just as the English were about to pen them in. Crossing Mount Hope Bay in late June, he swept up Weetamoo and her Pocasset, but tarried too long. English soldiers

NIANTIC JEWEL

caught up with them July 19 in Pocasset Swamp, and ill-advisedly entered the vast cedar bog that was second home to the natives but alien terrain to their foes.

Seven or eight English were killed and others wounded before direct engagement was abandoned in favor of siege tactics. While a fort was being built, Metacom slipped the noose again about July 29 and crossed the Taunton River to safety. He paid a heavy price. More than 100 women and children had to be left behind. They surrendered and most were sold into slavery.

On Aug. 1, it was the turn of 50 Mohegan allies and 130 English to trap Metacom in a swamp at Nipsachuck (North Smithfield, R.I.) as he and Weetamoo headed north to Nipmuck country. A dawn battle on open land nearby cost the heavily outnumbered natives 23 warriors before they retreated into the swamp around 9 a.m. An hour later, Captain. Daniel Henchman arrived with reinforcements. He then took charge and, inexplicably, ordered the troops to rest.

By the next morning, the Wampanoag were gone. Henchman followed their tracks west until his food ran out, without ever getting close to Metacom, who thus spread the flame of war throughout New England.

In an equally impressive disappearing act, Weetamoo and her antiwar faction also slipped out of the swamp that night and headed south to Quaiapen in North Kingstown. Ironically, the Old Queen/Queen Magnus as she was also known, was to die in the same swamp 11 months later.

She and her people, plus the refugees they sheltered, spent the war until midsummer 1676 in safety at Queen's Fort. The rock bastion was never discovered by the English – nor betrayed to them – despite lying under their noses. It lay just a mile from Smith's trading post at Wickford, the army's headquarters during its brief but bloody sojourn in Narragansett Country. In late January 1676, Gen. Winslow marched northwest in pursuit of Canonchet and the post was soon abandoned. The Narragansett then burned it to the ground.

When Gov. Andros opened his New York refuge in May and it became apparent to Quaiapen that Metacom's War was lost, she

93

probably decided that asylum in the Hoosic Valley was better than death or slavery for her people in their homeland, and so she struck out northwest, trying at all costs to avoid contact with the enemy. She'd gone less than 30 miles before being discovered.

Weetamoo, now with only 26 of her original 300 warriors, may have left Quaiapen's fort at about the same time for the same reasons, but with a different destination in mind. She was probably returning to her Pocasset lands at Tiverton, hoping to gain favorable terms by surrendering to her neighbor and war hero Capt. Benjamin Church just as Awashonks had done. Weetamoo's band was surprised and captured in a swamp near Taunton Aug. 6, 1676. She drowned trying to cross the river to safety. Her naked body was found near the water in Matapoiset (Somerset, Mass.). The corpse was mutilated by the English and her decapitated head stuck on a pole and paraded through Taunton.

The July 2, 1676, massacre in which Quaiapen died was described July 4 by the United Colonies commander in "A Letter Written by Maj. John Talcott from Mr. Stanton's at Quonocontaug to Govr. William Leete and the Hond. Council of the Colony of Connecticut":

"These may acquaint you that we made Nipsaichooke on ye first of July and seized 4 of ye enemy, and on the 2d instant being ye Sabbath in ye morning about sun an hour high made ye enemies place of residence and assaulted them who p[re]sently in swamped them selves in a great spruse swamp, we girt the s[ai]d swamp and with English & Indian sould[ier]s, drest it, and with 3: hours slew and tooke prisoners 171: of which 45: prisoners being women and children that the [Mohegan] indians saved alive, and the others slayne… among which slaughter that ould piece of venume sunck (queen) Magnus was slayne."

Passing through Warwick en route to Quonochontaug July 3, Talcott then exterminated 80 of the sachem Potuck's warriors who had given themselves up in response to a June 19 Declaration of Mercy and were waiting the hear the terms of their surrender. In an earlier two-day period, Talcott's expedition killed 52

NIANTIC JEWEL

Narragansett men and 114 women and children while taking 72 captive.

Rev. Hubbard justified the butchery of women and children thus: "... being all young Serpents of the same Brood, the subduing or taking so many, ought to be acknowledged as another signal Victory, and Pledg of Divine Favour to the English."

As philosopher Thomas Hobbes had written 25 years earlier in his "Leviathan," "Thus, one man calleth... cruelty what another calleth justice."

*   *   *

But it was hunger and disease, not poetic justice, that forced Wampanoag and Narragansett warriors back east to their homelands in late March 1676. They desperately needed to catch and dry fish at the spring runs, retrieve caches of seed corn to take back to their families in the northern forests, and to plunder livestock where they could.

These imperatives inspired Canonchet's most famous victory, Peirce's Fight on March 26 at Central Falls, R.I., when Capt. Michael Peirce of Scituate, Mass., led 63 soldiers and 20 friendly Indians into a perfectly laid ambush. Only 10 friendly Indians survived.

A few days later, Canonchet appeared 4 miles away in Providence. Its 400-500 residents were long gone except for 30 holdouts who included 73-year-old Roger Williams. The former friends talked and Williams persuaded the sachem not to harm anyone. Instead he burned the 50-60 homes, including Williams', in what was then a small farming and fishing village.

Metacom's dwindling band of Wampanoag had a different homecoming. In contrast to mainland Rhode Islanders who evacuated to Newport or Portsmouth on Aquidneck Island, leaving Narragansett Country almost deserted save for English mounted patrols, Plymouth colonists kept their eyes peeled for Indians to kill or enslave. Metacom was constantly on the move, surviving one narrow escape after another. As the noose tightened, his wife and 12-year-old son were captured, later to be sold as slaves in Bermuda.

On Aug. 11, a native sought out Capt. Church and offered to lead him to the sachem's camp in a swamp at the foot of Mount Hope. Metacom had killed the man's brother, one of his counselors, for advocating peace. Church's English and Sakonnet troops encircled the swamp that night and began closing the circle at dawn Aug. 12. Metacom was among the first to reach the English line, where Caleb Cook of Plymouth and Alderman, a Pocasset Indian, had him in their sights.

Cook's gun misfired, leaving it to Alderman to shoot Metacom through the heart. Church had the rebel leader beheaded and quartered. The body parts were hung in a tree and the head sent to Plymouth, where it was displayed on a pole for many years. Alderman was given the disfigured hand Metacom burned in a firearms accident years before. He exhibited the trophy for tips in alehouses.

In a final irony, it was Metacom's own instincts that sealed his fate. Rightly or wrongly, he had the reputation of being first in retreat. Correspondingly, there is no evidence of him ever having been seen in battle. If true, being first in flight had worked well for him in the past. On this day, however, leading the retreat was a mistake. Just five Pokanoket perished. The rest escaped. The English lacked sufficient manpower for an effective cordon and the Pokanoket soon identified gaps they could slip through.

About 6,000 Native Americans died in the uprising, among them the sachems Canonchet in April 1676, Quaiapen, Pomham and Matoonas in July, Quinnapin (Canonchet's successor), Metacom and Weetamoo in August, Monoco in September and Pessicus a few months later. Captured combatants were tried and executed; ringleaders were beheaded and quartered. (They were traitors in English eyes, not prisoners of war.) A thousand noncombatant men, women and children were sold as slaves in the West Indies and Bermuda, forced into indefinite servitude in New England or given as booty to soldiers and native allies. Two thousand fled to New York, Maine and Canada.

NIANTIC JEWEL

In 1615, 100,000 Algonquian inhabited southern New England. Then came the "virgin soil" epidemics of European diseases to which Native Americans had no resistance – bubonic plague, smallpox, typhus, diphtheria, measles, yellow fever, chicken pox, influenza and mumps. Mortality rates in stricken areas reached 75-90 percent. By 1675, there were 12,000 Indians left; a year later, 4-6,000. National existence was over for southern New England's aboriginal people

*   *   *

After the insurrection, Narragansett Country became the subject of a lengthy dispute between the United Colonies and Rhode Island, whose pacifist Quaker government had been officially neutral, despite furnishing ships, supplies and care for the wounded. The lands lay within Rhode Island, according to its charter. Since 1644, sachems had sworn loyalty to the colony and to the English crown, which in turn acknowledged and vowed to protect the original rights of the Indians to the soil.

The Newport government assumed jurisdiction when peace returned, and recognized Ninigret and his heirs as the legal owners. But the other colonies' charters also seemed to include tribal lands. Now, they additionally claimed right of conquest under English law. They had no qualms about stepping on Rhode Island's toes since it was a renegade colony by virtue of its religious views and wartime neutrality.

In fact, as John Easton, a future governor, admitted in his 1675 tract "A Relation of the Indian War." Rhode Island had betrayed rather than protected the Narragansett. It considered the United Colonies' declaration of war on the tribe Nov. 2, 1675, to be illegal – a pretext to annex Narragansett Country/King's Province before the Crown made it part of Rhode Island – but remained silent.

Easton blamed the English for starting the war and acknowledged that as attorney general he had assured the Narragansett they had nothing to fear from the United Colonies. In fact, the invading army was under orders to kill or capture all

Indians it encountered in order to preserve the element of surprise for the all-out attack that followed.

A few Narragansett lucky enough to escape death, slavery or indentured servitude in the genocide and who had blood ties to the Niantic were allowed to live with them in Charlestown, as were some Wampanoag and Nipmuck refugees.

Ninigret, ever the master politician, had saved his 500 people from annihilation. He was keenly aware of the wrongs done to them, but was too intelligent to let these grievances destroy the Niantic. At every opportunity, he told the English he would never take up arms against them, and pointed out that Metacom's men had killed 11 Niantic just before the war began.

The Great Swamp Fight at West Kingston reinforced his conviction that the uprising was doomed from the start. The very next day he sent Niantic warriors to bury the dead, and promptly demanded payment of a charge of powder for each of the 24 English bodies they interred.

Yet still true to his people, he also found a way to help the surviving women and children whose wigwams had been burned, leaving them without shelter: The warriors from Weekapaug carried mats with which to build new wigwams – a godsend that must have saved dozens of lives.

The aid was to be kept secret lest it incur the wrath of the English, but Maj. Robert Treat, second-in-command of the United Colonies army, reported it to his superiors when his troops' returned to Connecticut a few days later. Hartford apparently turned a blind eye.

Colin imagined the massacre's aftermath and pondered how the frozen earth could have been broken open for the burials even if Ninigret's men brought iron shovels, which seemed unlikely. And the Indian mortuary practice of placing the body in a shallow pit covered with rocks wouldn't have been much easier. Alternatively, tomahawks could smash through the swamp ice, allowing the bodies to be placed in a watery grave – not what the English thought they were paying for, but a grave nonetheless.

Many of the dead were Connecticut troops killed in the first assault. Hartford officials were upset to learn that not only had

NIANTIC JEWEL

their men been left where they fell but that the corpses had been looted by their comrades from Massachusetts and Plymouth. An angry letter was sent to Boston demanding return of the stolen muskets and condemning the "surreptitious, uncivil, if not inhumane deportment towards the living & dead." Connecticut's distress may have eased when the full story became known.

So exhausted, cold and hungry were the "victors" after the battle that Commander-in-Chief Winslow, the man accused of poisoning sachem Alexander, was caught on the horns of a dilemma: Should he let them rest and eat what remained of the village's food stores, tend the wounded and bury the dead; or retreat posthaste to the Wickford supply base before Canonchet's warriors arrived to make easy pickings of them?

So the dead were stripped of their weapons and belongings, including coats that could save a shivering comrade's life on the 18-mile march – and abandoned. Had Winslow known that the overnight trek in the snowstorm would result in his Plymouth troops getting lost for hours and 40 more deaths, he might have heeded the advice of Capt. Benjamin Church to stay put. The dead lie in the Great Grave at what is now Smith's Castle in Wickford.

Church, originally a carpenter from Duxbury, Mass., settled Little Compton, R.I., then in Plymouth Colony, early in 1675, and became a war hero. His success came from using friendly Indians and adopting their tactics. Nearly 1,000 rebels were killed or captured by his men, including Metacom, and he himself captured Annawon, the Wampanoag chief captain. Despite being a Puritan and owner of two Indian slaves, he advocated peaceful coexistence and promised leniency to the 300 noncombatants who surrendered to him. It was a promise he must have known wouldn't be kept by his superiors; 511 Indians were sold into slavery at Plymouth alone.

*   *   *

When Ninigret saw the tide of war begin to turn, his fence-straddling turned into moderate support for the colonies. On Jan. 8, 1676, he sent a messenger to the English with a letter from

Joseph Stanton (Thomas' son) vouching for his allegiance. He offered to use his own wampum in one of two peace proposals he made for ending the war. They were relayed by Stanton, but fell on deaf ears. The English could never be sure Ninigret wouldn't outmaneuver them.

Six months later when Native Americans began to surrender en masse, when they were likely to be shot on sight or disposed of as slaves, whether combatants or not, Ninigret ensured his people's survival by negotiating a treaty formally delivering the Niantic to the English side.

After the deaths of Miantonomi and Canonicus in the 1640s, Ninigret became the elder statesman in Narragansett Country and chief negotiator with the English. He was repeatedly called before the United Colonies commissioners to answer charges of fomenting plots or falling behind in his tribute payments, but was always able to satisfy his interrogators. A favorite tactic when threatened with invasion was to submit to English terms, then once the heat was off to renounce them as having been obtained under duress.

On one such occasion, in 1650, Capt. Humphrey Atherton of Dorchester took him by the hair and thrust a pistol against his chest. On another, Maj. Simon Willard, sent from Boston with 270 infantry and 40 cavalry, told him to submit to Puritan authority or have "his head sett up upon an English pole." When Willard reported back to the commissioners, he was reprimanded for his leniency. Ninigret was actually held hostage in 1648. He owed 1,000 fathoms of wampum, but was freed after Roger Williams interceded for him.

On April 3, 1676, 20 Niantic warriors under Catapazet, Ninigret's son and chief captain, assisted in Canonchet's capture beside the Pawtucket River in Cumberland, R.I., by Connecticut and Pequot/Mohegan forces led by Captains James Avery of New London and George Denison and John Stanton of Stonington, another of Thomas' sons.

The first Englishman to question him was Robert Stanton, John's 22-year-old brother. "You much Child! No understand Matters of War; let your Brother or Chief come, him I will

NIANTIC JEWEL

Answer,' the sachem responded. Taken to the captains, he refused their offer to spare him and his men if he ordered all Narragansett rebels to surrender. The 43 warriors captured with him were then executed on the spot.

Canonchet was taken to Stonington, where the English agreed to let the Indian allies execute him. Told he would be put to death, he replied: "I like it well; I shall die before my heart is soft, or have said anything unworthy of myself." He asked that the sentence be carried out by Oneco, son of Uncas, the Mohegan sachem who had killed his father, Miantonomi, in 1643. (Afterward, Uncas reputedly followed the custom of eating flesh from a great warrior in the belief that his powers would pass to the victor.)

Canonchet's wishes weren't entirely respected. He was first shot by the Pequot sachem Robin Cassacinamon, then beheaded and quartered by Oneco and the quarters burned by the Niantic. The head was presented to the English at Hartford, where it was displayed on a post – the punishment prescribed for traitors.

By autumn, Connecticut expeditions had cleared the Narragansett Country of Indians, except for Ninigret's friendly Niantic along Block Island Sound. He lost much of his autonomy after the war, but kept the tribe and its lands intact into the 18th Century through a quirk of fate: Rhode Island, Massachusetts, Connecticut, the Atherton Company of land speculators and the Marquis of Hamilton through a grant from Plymouth Colony all claimed his territory, and none wanted to see a competitor occupy it. Rhode Island already held the rest of the equally disputed Narragansett Country since incorporating it as Kings Towne in 1674.

At stake was the most fertile land in New England – the plain of rich glacial deposits between the ocean and the Charlestown recessional moraine (a sinuous ridge stretching from Wakefield to Watch Hill). The 18th Century would see it gobbled up by large landowners, who established 2,000-12,000-acre plantations worked by African slave labor.

Since the postwar Niantic comprised three prior elements – anti-English, neutral and pro-English – Ninigret faced a tribal identity crisis. Gradually, they became known as Narragansett, and remain so. There was nothing in the texts to suggest that Ninigret made the decision to drop the Niantic name, but it bore his diplomatic hallmark: The Narragansett were the initially neutral element dragged into the war. And what better standard of Indian heritage was there to rally around than that of the once supremely powerful then tragically heroic tribe exterminated in a cruel and cowardly way defending the path of honor?

Or did the name change occur under a later sachem? Ninigret may have died of old age as the war ended, or lived until 1678. His birth date of 1600 is also approximate. He was succeeded by Weunquesh, a daughter by the first of his two wives, who was crowned at her fort on Chemunganock Hill in present-day Burlingame State Park in 1679. She died in 1686 and was followed by her half-brother Ninigret II (d. 1723).

Then came Charles Augustus Ninigret (d. 1735), his brother George (d. 1746), his son Thomas (d. 1769), his sister Esther, who refused to speak English (d. 1777), and her son George, the last hereditary sachem (d. 1779). He was killed by a falling tree, an event of ironic symbolism for the by-then denatured tribe. By 1766, only 315 Narragansett remained, according to Samuel Drake, who spent 14 years among them as a schoolmaster. An 1832 Census gave the same number, but listed only 7 purebloods.

The numbers were further reduced in 1775 when a Christianized group led by Mohegan Rev. Samuel Occum obtained a grant of land (allowing purebloods only) from the Oneida Iroquois nation. They sat out the Revolutionary War at the Mahican mission-fort at Stockbridge, Mass., before founding Brothertown, N.Y., in 1783. A second westward migration from 1833-40 saw the founding of Brothertown, Wisconsin.

*   *   *

It seemed to Colin that the more colonial history he read, the less he really knew. Surprisingly little could be taken as unquestionable fact. Historians made their own interpretations, often based on conflicting sources. Charged with creating a myth of national origin, the ethnocentrists and ancestor worshippers

NIANTIC JEWEL

among them had been far too credulous of evidence to support a heroic narrative and all too willing to suspend their disbelief, and with it the fundamental requirement of any science – a healthy skepticism. The past was massaged to please the present. National dishonor evaporated in the face of collective denial and the paramount necessity of a glorious patriotism.

Contemporary accounts differed widely or were infuriatingly vague, and the plethora of documentation provided by journals, diaries, letters and public records only added to the confusion. Even eyewitnesses, then as now, were unreliable, seeing what they wanted to see according to their biases and subject to the vagaries of memory.

Conversely, Native Americans had no written language. Their history was oral tradition with few artifacts surviving to corroborate it. Archeological finds sometimes turned prevailing wisdom on its head. Algonquian leaders were shadowy figures, our knowledge of them limited to white perceptions. The Indian's history was written by his enemy.

Since American English spelling wasn't standardized until Noah Webster's American Dictionary of the English Language was published in 1828, it was no wonder that difficult Indian names had many spellings, leading to similar names being confounded. Worse yet, sachems sometimes changed their names after life-changing experiences, at major rituals, or adopted a predecessor's name. In later life, Massasoit became Usamequin and finally Matchippa.

Literacy itself can make history difficult. Ninigret was also rendered Ninicraft, Ninicroft, Nenekunat, Nenekunnath, Nenekionats, Niniglud, Ninegrad, Ninegratt, Nenegrat and Nenegelett; at various times he was Janemo/Juanemo and Wonaconchat.

Canonchet/Quananchit/Quanonchet/Quananchett/Quanochu was also Nanuntenoo, Naananto, Nananautunu and the jaw-locking Nawnawnoantonnew. Mixanno/Mixam/Mexam was Mriksah and Meika or Meiksah. The name of Canonicus, who died in 1647 at about age 85, was adopted in the 1670s by his nephew Pessicus, Miantonomi's brother and co-sachem after his death in

1643 until 1676. Canonicus was really the Latin word for lawful or right, easier for the English than the more accurate spelling Woquacanoose, which Roger Williams rendered as Cawnownicus.

And few names had been spelt more ways than Narragansett. In his 1833 "Book of the Indians," Samuel G. Drake lists nine permutations not using an r (which the language does not contain) and alludes to those with an r as "still more numerous."

Coincidentally, Colin found himself looking at the words of Capt. John Mason, the Connecticut army commander mortally wounded at the Great Swamp Fight. Forty years earlier he had been a hero of the Pequot War and wrote a narrative of it containing the enigmatic statement: "History most properly is a Declaration of Things that are done by those that were present at the doing of them."

It seemed to capture the essential truth that the past is always subjective memory. Historians can't avoid being mythologizers. The now – the present – passes instantly into incomplete mental storage. First, the involuntary blinking of our eyes hides 5 percent of what is observable, rendering continuity virtual, not actual; our brains ignore the chronological blind spot for the sake of reason, without which nothing would make sense and we'd go mad. Second, only those experiences and perceptions useful for future action are imprinted for recall; extraneous junk would scramble the mind into a hodgepodge of dreams and nightmarish snippets of formless thought.

He was reminded again that history is written tendentiously by the victors. How different, he wondered, would be a chronicle of the same events observed by alien visitors?

He closed his books and turned off the veranda light, Sitting in the moonlight, he listened to Nature's nocturne and tried to pick out the trills, chirps, staccato whines and katy-DIDs of crickets, cicadas and katydids in the trees and grass from the bleats, quacks and snores of frogs and toads in the pond. A halo framed the full moon. The earlier cirrus clouds had become cirrostratus, indicating that the tropical storm had changed direction and was nearer to the coast.

CHAPTER 7

LOVE MATCH

He either fears his fate too much,
Or his deserts are small,
That puts it not unto the touch,
To win or lose it all.
JAMES GRAHAM,
MARQUIS OF MONTROSE

At 7 a.m. Sunday as Colin opened the pasture gate to let the waiting cows into the barn, the rising sun hid behind a glaze of translucent altostratus clouds. A steady Southeast wind ruffled the treetops and rippled the misty pond. He cursed to himself, knowing that rain was on its way and the tennis rendezvous in jeopardy.

By early afternoon, the wind had dropped and the overcast sky had bright spots among the dark nimbostratus clouds, But he knew this was only a brief window of fair weather before the winds picked up and the downpour began.

He decided against calling her, and drove up to the Palmers' at 1:55 precisely. She emerged from the portico as he pulled up beside it. Her short tennis dress with a scooped neck revealed 3 inches of enticing cleavage, which he tried not to notice as she handed him her gear and with a cheery smile got in beside him.

"I'm glad you didn't call it off. I don't know how much tennis we'll get in before it rains, but this is ideal: nice and cool, no glare, no wind. Let's go for it!"

Graham Griffith

She leaned forward to retie her sneakers, giving him a clear view into her bodice. He quickly returned his eyes to the road.

"I don't know how well I can play when you look so gorgeous. How am I going to keep my eyes on the ball?"

She blushed and laughed it off.

"I'm sure you'll find a way. And I could say the same about you!... There's a storm coming, you know. The Weather Channel said it changed direction and caught everyone by surprise. There are mariners' warnings from Cape May to Cape Cod and travelers' advisories after 5 p.m. They expect 2-4 inches of rain and high winds. Maybe thunder and lightning. It'll get here during an astronomical high tide, so there could be coastal flooding. The surf should be amazing! I love a big storm, don't you?"

"This will be my first, apart from Nor'easters in Maine. Thunderclaps and lightning are awesome. It feels like the end of the world... I'd better keep the cows inside tonight."

"Gosh! I forgot about your cows. I remember when I was little, Mr. Stanton used to let us sit on the wall and pat their noses. They seemed to like it."

"They do. They love to be touched. Come back with me after tennis, if you'd like. It's milking time at 4, but I have to leave for work around 5. I'm not looking forward to the drive."

They pulled up to the empty courts before she could respond. She took their gear while he put the top up, and they did their warm-ups and some volleying. Then they were ready to start.

She served first and aced him three times with deep, kicking balls that flew by him. He retreated to the baseline and won the next point with a forehand return just inside the crosscourt line. The next serve whipped down the centerline, forcing a weak left-handed shot into her corner. She countered with a powerful two-handed forehand down the line. which he could only lob back. She let it bounce, before smashing it into the open court.

As they passed at the net to change ends, he pointed to her racquet.

"So you're a leftie. I'll have to make adjustments."

"Yep. I got it from Mother. But you can't complain; You play with both hands."

NIANTIC JEWEL

His first few serves did everything he wanted, but she returned them with ease. When he added more power, he lost placement and double-faulted. Her groundstrokes were flawless and she had impeccable form. After one of the few long rallies, she showed her fast footwork and fitness by chasing down balls he'd rocketed into opposite corners, then coming to the net and finishing him off with a drop volley to take the game.

The rest of the set continued in much the same vein with her pace and placement pinning him behind the baseline, His left-handed serves sometimes wrong-footed her and he had success with drop shots when he ran out of gas in long rallies and had to go for winners to end the point. But, she was holding her serve automatically, while he couldn't get a first serve in and his indifferent second serve was often crushed. She hit the ball so hard, he had no time to change hands and too often was caught off balance. Most of all, she never gave up on a point and had the legs to outlast him. Before he knew it, he'd lost the set 6-2.

They took a break to sip water on the bench. He caught his breath and sized up his deteriorating situation: Nothing was working. There was only one thing for it if he was to give her a decent match.

"Would you mind if I use a sliced serve? I know some people don't like it... not tennis; dirty play. Only, right now, I'm not giving you much competition. You're just too good."

She shrugged her shoulders.

"I've seen slice before. Not very often, but I can handle it. No problem! Nothing within the rules is dirty."

She stood up and gave him a broad wink before heading toward the baseline.

"I doubt it'll work, though."

Things didn't start well. It took him awhile to get the angle, loft and distance he needed on the sliced first serve and she stood close in anticipating it. But the deep conventional second serve that followed had her out of position. Then the slice began to work. He was serving aces on balls that landed 2 feet beyond the net and spun back into it. She came in even closer and took one serve on the volley. He laughed and protested mildly.

"I don't think you can do that. You have to let a serve bounce. Rule 9b."

She gave a shriek and swiped at the net with her racquet.

"Rats! I don't know why I did that! Your point."

He was serving for the set at 5-4 when another problem came up: Improbably, the ball spun back over the net and died. She threw up her arms in disbelief and claimed the point.

"I've never seen anything like that! But it's my point. The ball's in your court and you failed to return it. Rule 20."

It seemed ungentlemanly to mention that she hadn't returned it to begin with, thus losing the point. So, ahead 30-0, he let it go and won the next two points.

They took another break, during which she kidded him.

"That was more fun. Where did you learn to play like that? You have terrible form, you know. Too much wrist."

"I know! I've tried unlearning it but can't. It's the same with golf. I play wrong-handed. Lessons don't help. I can't learn from others. I have to find my own way; otherwise it's no fun."

"But you have fun, right? That's all that matters... It's fascinating how you rely on intuition so much. It's a gift you have. You're a never-ending surprise. It's exciting! You're definitely not normal!"

He felt a flush of embarrassment and returned the backhanded compliment.

"You're the most exciting woman I've ever met. I'm staggered by your brains and stunned by your beauty. You're sensational!"

Playfully, she bounced the face of her racquet off his knee, and stood up.

"Take care, Sir Galahad. The wise man said woman begins by resisting man's advances and ends by blocking his retreat.... C'mon, before the rain starts. You're mincemeat! I can change tactics, too, you know."

Her gaze switched to the sky behind him, continuing upward as she craned her neck to take it all in.

"Wow! Look at those clouds. The sky's full of tennis balls. Someone up there's having a joke with us."

Colin paused in silent wonder.

NIANTIC JEWEL

"They're mammatus. They may be tennis balls to women, but to the chaps who name clouds they're breasts. Mamma is breast in Latin. They're quite rare. I've only seen them once before. Aren't they magnificent? Well, maybe not to someone who has her own… They're caused by cold air descending from a cloud shelf. Things are very unstable up there."

As if on cue, thunder rumbled in the distance. A few large raindrops fell, the sky darkened and the wind picked up. At the baseline, she held up a palm to check the rain, and called to him:

"We'd better make this a mini tiebreaker: first to 7 with a 2-point lead?"

"Jolly good."

She held her serve in a long point that had him digging low balls off his feet. Clearly, she was going to exploit his tired knees. His first serve revealed another problem: All the slicing had made his elbow sore. The ball arced high and landed deep, giving her ample time to dispatch a forehand into the corner behind him. He switched back to a flat serve. Surprised by the change, she returned short. He replied deep into the ad court and came to the net, where he answered her passing shot with a perfect drop volley. 1-2.

A lightning bolt sizzled behind her as she aced him down the middle on the next point. Then a high-kicking serve into his chest forced him to bail out. She took his pop-up on the volley and dispatched it out of reach. Retrieving the balls, he noticed she'd backed up, expecting another speed serve. He tried to mix it up with topspin to her backhand, but her footwork was too good. She returned at his feet. His knees twinged as he dug it out, and she was waiting at the net when the ball arrived. Guessing that she'd whip a cross-court forehand, he raced to his right and made a desperation lunge. Implausibly, the ball collided with his racquet and popped over the net for a winner. 2-4.

*   *   *

As they changed ends amid increasing raindrops and gusts of wind, an SUV pulled into the parking area. Two mixed-doubles pairs in T-shirts and cutoffs came through the gate behind Juliana. They greeted her and proceeded to the bench beside the empty court, where one of them distributed racquets, balls and cans of beer from a carryall. Then, each with a racquet and a beer in hand, they started to hit the ball around.

Three points from defeat, Colin mulled his options for what could be his last serve. The interruption had checked her momentum. If he won this point, anything could happen. He shook out his elbow and went with the slice. Seeing the ball's high arc, she scrambled to get her racquet under the spinning bounce, which zipped off the strings to skip high over his head. He ran it down at the baseline and at full stretch managed to flip back a lob, leaving him off court to watch her make a graceful smash. 2-5.

He batted the balls to her then took his position to receive the coup de grace. It was enough to be on the same court with such a goddess, he mused, and to ogle her under the guise of competition. Abruptly, she caught her toss in midair when the male nearest Colin waved his beer can and called to her:

"We're playing wet T-shirt tennis, Juliana. Come and have some fun for a change – like we used to. Remember? Let it all hang out!"

She ignored him and hurriedly served a soft ball that Colin returned deep to her backhand. She countered with a cannonball into the corner. He could only block it back, and remained on the defensive, running up and down the baseline, until lack of breath forced him to drop-shot her. She sprinted for the ball only to get wood on it, sending it into the net. Her next serve whistled by his head before clanging the fence. The follow-up was delivered with equal force right down the line. He made a left-handed stab and caught the ball in the center of his racquet, hurtling it back with transferred velocity into the far corner.

Serving at 4-5, he drew her wide with a ball that darted off the sideline, leaving an impossible angle for the return. But his relief at evening the score was short-lived when his next serve bit hard on landing and, for a second time, skipped back over to die in his court. His heart sank as he realized he couldn't change a rule interpretation he'd already accepted. Now she would serve for the match. He retrieved the ball and bounced it to her. She frowned sympathetically.

"Bad luck! But never say die!"

She bounced the ball a few times, as if in hesitation, before serving another creampuff. His return anticipated using speed off the serve, and when there was none, it landed at her feet. She hammered it at his body and he was lucky to volley it back. They exchanged two more close volleys until he mishit one over her head. She back-pedaled and lobbed. He ran around it and replied with a crosscourt forehand. She hit a forehand down the far line. He ran it down and stabbed it back into the open court. But his fate was sealed. With perfect placement, she ripped a shot down the opposite line. He scrambled for it and lunged, but too late, leaving him sprawled out on the court. She ran to the net.

"I'm sorry. Are you hurt?"

His knees and elbow ached as he picked himself up.

"Just my pride. Good shot! No mas! I surrender."

The player who had called out to Juliana approached him with the ball, which had lodged in the fence. Colin went to take it, but the young man pushed it into his chest, forcing him back a step.

"I've been watching you play. That's not Quonnie tennis. You don't belong here. Your car doesn't have a Cove sticker."

Colin put the ball in his pocket.

"Thanks… The guest card's in clear view on the dashboard. And if your court conduct is Quonnie tennis, I'd rather not belong."

The split second of the cocking arm telegraphed the punch that followed. Colin wheeled away from it on his heels and came back around to see his assailant slip on the slick court and fall face-first. He got up with blood running from his nose and started toward Colin again. The other players began to come over, and Juliana called out from the net:

"Stop it, Tom."

Colin backed away.

"I'm not going to fight you."

But his tormentor kept advancing.

"We'll see about that, jerk."

Colin dropped his racquet and stood his ground, watching his antagonist's body movements like a matador taking the measure of a charging bull. In one fluid motion, he sidestepped the lurching, barrelhouse punch, grabbed the arm under and over with both hands, and, turning the locked elbow into a fulcrum, executed an Irish whip. He released the arm as the airborne adversary somersaulted and came to rest spread-eagled on his back.

After a few anxious seconds, the aggressor sat up, supporting himself on one hand while rubbing his tailbone with the other. The impact spattered nose blood over his yellow shirt and pale-blue cutoffs, where it spread out in scarlet patches on the damp clothing.

As the others gathered around, Colin gave him a hand up.

"Go back to your game. Your friends are waiting. But first, let's shake hands. No hard feelings, and we'll forget it."

There was a pause until a female partner nudged the dazed young man.

"Go on! Shake, you idiot."

They shook, and both groups went to their benches as the rain fell heavier from the dark sky. Colin sighed in despair.

"I'm really sorry. I didn't mean for that to happen. Who is he?"

"Tom Morton. Blotto, as usual. No need to be sorry. You did me a huge favor. Now maybe he won't bother me anymore."

She looked up at the leaden sky.

"Every dark cloud has a silver lining."

"I should have made the cheeky rascal apologize for that crude remark he made to you."

"No. You were splendid. I think he's had enough for one day."

She patted his shoulder as they left the courts.

"Was that kung fu or karate? Where did you learn to do that?"

"My uncle used to take me to wrestling matches at Liverpool Stadium. It's basic WWF stuff – applying leverage in the right place at the right time."

*   *   *

NIANTIC JEWEL

He opened the car door for her.

"Should I take you home?"

A plaintiff look came into her eyes.

"After all that, I think I could use a nice cup of tea."

"Me too... You're a good sport. You didn't let him ruffle your grace and good humor."

"Only because I know what he can be like."

Colin gave a brief chuckle as a thought came to him.

"Of course! He can't help it. He's a reincarnation of his namesake."

"What d'you mean?"

"Thomas Morton scandalized the Pilgrim Fathers, causing them no end of grief between 1625 and '42. He was an Elizabethan libertine hounded by pious killjoys. The community of reprobates he led at Mt. Wollaston, overlooking Boston Harbor and next door to Plymouth Colony, conducted drunken orgies around an 80-foot maypole – a pagan phallic symbol.

"They called their settlement Merrymount, delighting in the double entendres it afforded: Merry mount, Mary mount, Mare mount. Initially, the settlers were 30 young men. They enticed Indian women to their debaucheries by plying them with liquor.

"As I recall it, Gov. William Bradford wrote in 'Of Plymouth Plantation': 'They... set up a May-pole, drinking and dancing about it many days together, inviting the Indian women, for their consorts, dancing and frisking together (like so many fairies, or furies rather) and worse practices. As if they had anew revived & celebrated the feasts of ye Roman Goddess Flora, or ye beastly practices of ye mad Bacchanalians'."

Juliana giggled girlishly.

"Your gift for recall makes you a natural storyteller. Tell me more. Did he come to a sticky end, the way this Thomas is headed?"

"Not really, although he spent plenty of time in Puritan jails. He was about 71 when he died. He'd been a lawyer in England, the son of minor gentry, making him well situated to take part in the bawdy revels of the Elizabethan Age, which ended in 1603 when he was 27.

"When Thomas, his partner Capt. Wollaston and their 30 indentured laborers started their fur trading post and farming/fishing venture in 1625, the nearest English settlements were Plymouth 25 miles south and New Salem about the same distance north across Massachusetts Bay. Boston didn't exist until 1630.

"The partners fell out when Wollaston sold some of his men into slavery in the Virginia tobacco plantations, to where he fled in 1626. This gave Thomas the chance to put into practice his ultraliberal social theories. He viewed the Indian way of life as 'civilized and humanitarian' and promoted the carousing as a means for his men to find brides and create a fully integrated Christian society drawing on the best of both cultures.

"To the Pilgrim Fathers, he'd committed the despicable sin of having 'gone native' and sunk to the level of the depraved heathens, as they thought of the aboriginal peoples. Actually, Merrymount was hurting their purses more than their moral sensibilities. The trading post prospered since the Indians preferred to sell their furs there rather than at Plymouth. It was also attracting secular immigrants who threatened to subvert the Puritan dream.

"So in June 1629 Plymouth sent in the militia under the iniquitous Myles Standish to break up Merrymount. They chopped down the maypole and arrested Thomas. He was marched to Plymouth, placed in the stocks and pelted with garbage before being tried, convicted of selling guns to the Indians and marooned on the barren Isles of Shoals off the New Hampshire coast. Knowing who he was, the mainland Indians supplied him with food until he could catch a ship for England.

"Either he had a martyr complex or was a masochist because he returned the following year only to be arrested, tried and shipped back to England, where he became a celebrity in 1637 with his best-selling book 'New English Canaan.' In it he denounced the Puritans' genocidal policies and wrote admiringly of Native Americans.

"Amazingly, he came back for more abuse in 1642, this time spending months imprisoned in Boston until his health began to

NIANTIC JEWEL

fail. He was granted clemency and spent the last four years of his life in Maine."

Juliana cast him a pensive glance.

"I don't know about reincarnation, but Young Tom seems to share Old Tom's personal demons. He's really very smart. It's a pity he's dogged by self-destructive tendencies."

Colin shook his head.

"He has to be daft to throw away a friendship with you."

*   *   *

The cows were huddled at the pasture gate when the green Jaguar pulled into the farmyard and as close to the kitchen door as Colin could get. One of them bellowed as the pair ran indoors out of the torrential rain. Colin put the kettle on and got out the Royal Doulton teapot and two cups and saucers, trying not to trip over the purring cat, which was walking figure-eights between his legs.

"Would you be 'mother' while I let the cows in. They get grumpy when they're sopping wet. There's Typhoo tea in the caddy... and fresh towels in the bathroom if you want to dry off."

"Sure. This is a neat old house. Take your time. I'll enjoy looking around."

When he got back, she was in the inglenook by the window, toweling her hair with one hand and sipping tea with the other, cradling her cellphone against her shoulder.

"Hi, it's Jewel. I'm taking tea with Colin at the farm!... Yes, we had to cut it short. And Tom showed up with his group and tried to make trouble, but Colin was superb.... Tell you later... I'll ask him. Be home in an hour. Love you, too. 'Bye."

She put the phone on the table and motioned him to sit beside her.

"Mother was asking if you like lobster and corn – for tomorrow night."

"A whole lobster? I've never had one before."

"It'll be your baptism then. You've got a treat coming! You can put them in the steamer, if you're up for it! They won't be Mr. Stanton's, but they'll still be fresh off the boat – not even caught yet. This is the best place for lobster, anywhere! And Mother's the best seafood cook! You'd better come with an appetite."

"You're making me hungry already, but you'll have to show me how to eat it. I have no idea what to do."

"It's easy. You just use your fingers, and forget about table manners! The same thing with the corn. Mother has a special recipe. You've never had corn like this! She roasts the ears in their leaves on the barbecue. We all help get it ready."

There was a childlike quality about her enthusiasm that touched him. She finished drying her hair, and asked for a brush. They watched the rain dance on the pond and atomize into a layer of mist. In the distance, lightning streaked through the black sky, followed seconds later by thunderclaps. The confined space made brushing difficult with him beside her. He caught her hand and shifted position.

"May I?"

She gave a self-conscious laugh and released the brush.

"If you'd like to."

He brushed in long, gentle strokes, sometimes taking a strand in his free hand and drawing it out, then running it between his fingers, not wanting to let go.

"Your hair looks burnished when it's damp. The colors change in the light: Here it's red; here it's auburn; and here it's strawberry blonde. It's so beautiful."

He bent in front of her to reach the other side. Their eyes met and she smiled demurely.

"You are my dashing Sir Galahad!"

It was the trace of a quiver on her slightly parted lips that held him motionless for a second before an ineffable attraction drew him in ever closer. Their lips met softly at first, then more firmly in response to the incredible sensations coursing through him. He realized ecstatically that she was returning his kiss with a passion. The tip of her tongue flickered between his lips, compelling him to suck it further inside where he tasted her nectar before she withdrew. He followed her and she drew him in, their tongues pressed together. When the muscles tired, they nibbled on each other's lips again until, sated, she broke it off and nestled her head

NIANTIC JEWEL

against him. He held her close. Slowly, he regained control of his emotions, and began stroking her hair.

"I've wanted to do that since I first saw you."

She eased back to look up at him.

"That was perfect timing. Was it all you'd hoped it would be?"

"It was out of this world! I'll never be the same again!"

"Me, too. You're a dynamite kisser – and cuddly, too!"

They sat in silence for a while, hugging and watching the storm. He kissed her forehead and she squeezed his hand. He was trying to absorb the magnitude of all that had happened when bellowing from the barn signaled that it was 4 o'clock and the cows were growing impatient.

As they shared an umbrella on the way over to the barn, he asked her about the name she'd used on the phone.

"Jewel? It's something my family saddled me with. You're never to call me that! You have to promise. I get embarrassed in public. Daddy started it when I was little, because he's such a big softie. Then Mother and Joel took it up. I don't mind, as long as it's just in the family. But to everyone else, I'm Juliana!"

"I promise. Does that mean we're going to be friends?"

She stopped in the middle of the farmyard, where, curtained by cascading rainwater under the umbrella, she put her arms around his neck, pulled his head down and planted a long, ardent kiss on his lips.

"More than friends! I don't kiss friends like that! Now, show me how to milk a cow."

*   *   *

Beside the barn, Colin opened the door to the chicken coop to prove that Eric really existed. He looked harmless enough now, sitting quietly in the straw litter, surrounded by softly clucking hens, but watching every move with beady eyes. Juliana quipped that the injured foot was a lame story. Ducking her head, she stepped into the coop, whereupon Eric, true to form, sprang to his feet, and with wings flapping and tail feathers spread let out an ear-piercing shriek that startled them both. She backed out adroitly and he shut the door.

"You see what I mean? All those concubines and he's still bad-tempered. He's a testimonial for monogamy."

"Well, isn't he just protecting his progeny – in the eggs you take? Look what we've done to animals through domestication. No wonder he's angry. Animals have rights, too. It's ethically objectionable, the way we enslave and exploit, let alone kill and eat, other living creatures – domesticated or not. Or is that anthropomorphizing?

From under the umbrella, he caught sight of the cat peering at them through the kitchen window.

"Look, there's Molly watching us as if we're fools to be out in the rain. She certainly seems to be curious about us, but I don't know what she's thinking, any more than I know what Eric's thinking. Or whether they think at all in the way that we have thoughts. Whether their pain is the same as ours.

"We ascribe human characteristics to pets because we form emotional attachments to them. So we don't eat them. I could eat Eric, though. In his case I feel negative attachment. But when the animal is a cut of meat or a fillet of fish, I don't give it a second thought. Out of sight; out of mind...."

Juliana huddled close to him for the few steps to the barn, and finished the thought he'd left unspoken.

"... even though you're aware, intellectually at least, of being an accessory after the fact to an animal's suffering. If we knew enough about central nervous systems, we could draw a line for purposes of meat-eating between creatures that feel pain on being put to death and those that don't.

"I'd say all vertebrates do. So no more mammals, birds, fish, reptiles or amphibians for dinner. Nor lobsters, to be on the safe side. That still leaves an incredible amount of biomass: I can't imagine an insect hurting, nor mollusks or worms; certainly not fungi, algae, bacteria or plants.

"When Mother teaches ethics, she likes to ask her students: Do we need to kill or exploit any living thing to feed ourselves? Apparently not. We can synthesize the organic compounds we need to survive: amino acids to sustain the body and carbohydrates to fuel it.

"Before that became possible in the 19th Century, the Jainists of India came quite close. Their ancient religion considers all life forms equal, so they can't even kill plants. That excludes root vegetables from their diet. But they do `exploit' plants by eating other nonessential parts. Still, they're the only vegetable rights advocates I know of."

Colin put his arm around her waist to draw her closer.

"I like your mum's impish sense of humor… Fate threw Homo sapiens a curveball by turning us into omnivores with moral sensibilities. The further removed we are from the killing, the quieter are the pangs of conscience. Given the ultimatum `Eat animal products or die,' we'd always place ourselves above the animal. It's an instinctual imperative.

"Vegans can't eat meat or animal products with a clear conscience because they're no longer necessary for survival. They can choose not to do a `wrong,' as they see it. But only relatively recently have most people in the industrialized nations had access to a balanced vegetable diet.

"A person's moral compass is a subjective mental state, and our treatment of animals puts us in a quandary because the ethics have attained a clearer focus. For now, I think we can eat meat without necessarily feeling guilty. It's a matter for an individual's own belief system. In 50 years, the social acceptability of killing wild animals could be very different. Attitudes toward trophy hunting and slaughtering them solely for their fur have changed radically in a short space of time."

*   *   *

She opened the barn door while he angled the umbrella over them as they entered.

He introduced her to Angel, who mistook the attention for feeding time. Bleating in anticipation, the calf rose up on her hind legs, forelegs braced against the baled wall of the pen, looking for the pail of milk. He let her suckle his fingers while Juliana stroked the snow-white blaze of the forehead and cooed baby talk.

She helped him carry over the three milking-machine units, then a pail of soapy water, which he sudsed up with a washcloth. He washed the udders of the first cows to be milked, plugged the air hose into the overhead pipeline and attached the tubular suction cups, while she watched.

"I don't think I'd like having those rubber things pulling on me like that!"

He took one of the pulsating cups and placed her hand over it.

"The suction's quite gentle, for an 800-pound cow. I think they'd rather a machine milked them than a calf. Angel would suck my arm off if I let her!

He brought over the stripping pail and stool, and tucking Juliana up against the hindquarter of the herd's most docile animal, placed her hands on the nearest teats.

"Just pull down and squeeze the teats against your palm one at a time, so you establish a rhythm."

Two jets of milk rat-a-tat-tatted into the pail. She squealed in delight and went at it with abandon.

"This is so neat!"

"You're doing great! When the milk stops coming, move on to the other teats. Give the first two time to refill, then come back to them. I'll be changing the machines."

When he went back, she was rubbing her hands.

"There's no more milk coming, and my hands ache. Am I finished?"

He knelt down and guided her hand.

"Getting the rest involves something different. Place your thumb and forefinger at the top of the teat and slide them down – as if you're squeezing toothpaste from a tube. Then more milk will come, and you can go back to squeezing with your palm. When your hands get tired again, switch back. That way, the different muscles can work and rest."

She soon got the hang of it and gave him a knowing glance.

NIANTIC JEWEL

"It's no wonder your tennis game's all wrist... they're overdeveloped from milking. I'm going to work on that whether you like it or not!"

The hint of possessiveness only served to endear her to him. It made him feel connected. He didn't know if it was maternal instinct, a product of bonding or a control trait. But if she wanted him as much as he wanted her, she could have all of him, no matter where it led.

Afterward, she looked through his bookshelves while he changed for work.

It was still pouring when he pulled up beside the Palmers' portico. He offered the umbrella, but she declined.

"You'll need it... I'm worried about you driving in this. Do you really have to?"

"I don't want to... I don't want to leave you, but it's Sunday and there's only a skeleton crew. I'll take my time getting there. It's a small Monday paper, so it won't matter if I'm late."

She leaned across and he met her halfway in another torrid kiss that steamed the windows. Then she opened the door and he handed her the tennis bag. He reached for her free hand and held it.

"I won't be able to think about anything else but you until I see you again."

"I'll miss you too, but it'll be tomorrow before we know it. And I'll be dreaming about you. Please be careful. I've just found you: I don't want to lose you."

CHAPTER 8

UNHOLY TRINITY

To be philosophy's slave is to be free.
SENECA

The cluster of dancing red, yellow and blue lights refracted through the downpour into a pyrotechnic display on the windshield as Colin turned into the jug handle from Route 1 to Sunset Beach Road on his way home at 3 a.m. The wrecker with its grim cargo passed by him before he reached the accident scene at the bend. As a yellow-slickered policeman waved him through the emergency vehicles, he could see the snapped utility pole and the downed wires.

Torrents of water ran down both sides of the road and flooded it entirely beside the pond. The few streetlights were out, leaving only the headlights to pick out the swarming, wind-whipped leaves before they splatted against the car. So disorienting was the total darkness and the howling fury that he would have missed his turn into Niantic Drive were it not for the Cove Association sign. The gale churned the thickets on either side as he drove through, creating a tunnel of eerie calm amid the litter of stripped branches and twigs.

Halfway up the farm track, he saw the yard light above the kitchen door and gave a sigh of relief: The propane generator had kicked in when the power went out. He wouldn't have to hand-milk in the morning and the tank would stay refrigerated. Safe in bed, he felt exhilaration over the astounding turn of events with Juliana. It seemed too good to be true. There was an underlying

NIANTIC JEWEL

sense of impending doom that her feelings would change overnight. He had a bad dream in which she met him at her door and backed away in revulsion when he tried to kiss her.

He awoke at 7 to sunlight streaming through the window. The memory of the dream surfaced briefly until overcome by a picture of her in his mind, accompanied by a feeling of joy. The storm was over: The power was back on. Summer had returned.

There was cleanup work after the regular chores: debris to be raked from the farmyard, some shingles to be nailed back on the barn. He was too excited to take his Monday morning nap after Sunday's late shift. Instead, he went to the Charlestown liquor store and picked out a bottle of Stonington Vineyards' Chardonnay to take to the Palmers'.

On the way back, he stopped at Hoxsie's Nursery, where he cut a posy of pink bleeding hearts for Juliana and blue forget-me-nots for her mother. Beds of the taller cutting flowers lay flattened from the storm; there was damage to the corn and tomatoes. Ed Hoxsie was unconcerned: A day or two of sunshine would set them straight again. He was more saddened by the accident at the bend, which had killed a young man from Sunset Beach.

No sooner had Colin stepped into the kitchen than the phone rang. It was Juliana.

"I had to call you before you come over tonight...."

He was gripped by dread, as if teetering on the edge of a cliff, about to fall.

"... because I've been worried about you. You got back alright then?"

It was hard for him to breathe, and the words came slowly.

"The commute was an adventure, but I thought of you, and everything was fine. How about you? How long was the power out?

"I don't know. I was asleep, dreaming about you."

His heart took a leap.

"I was afraid you were calling to cancel... that you'd thought better of it; that you'd seen things differently in the cold light of morning."

123

"I don't know what happened. I can hardly believe it. It's not like me to be so… spontaneous. I feel so at ease when I'm with you. No, I'm not calling to cancel. Don't even think such a thing. I can't wait to see you! Mother and I want you to come early, 6:30, so we can talk inside – just the three of us. Remember what I said about something you'd be interested in?"

"Yes, I remember every word you've ever said to me. I'm crazy about you."

"It's mutual, so just don't you go having a change of heart. I warn you, I'm not a woman to be trifled with… and I'm not kidding. See you soon. Oh, don't dress up. I'm blowing you a kiss. 'Bye."

He felt like dancing for joy, but decided a more useful release would be picking up deadwood blown onto the pastures. It was there by the pond that a movement registered in the corner of his eye, followed by a splash. He looked up in time to see an osprey sink its talons into a bluefish 50 feet offshore. It was a violent struggle with furious beating of wings as the bird strained to pluck its squirming prey from the water. For a moment it seemed as if the foot-long fish would drag its captor under with it. They hovered at the surface while the raptor's deadly claws had time to do their work: With surgical precision they had stabbed into the spinal cord and in a few seconds paralyzed the victim.

Laboriously, the osprey gained height inch by inch on its 5-foot wingspan until a critical point was reached and it flew back to its nest atop the white oak in the sheep pasture, the fish's silver underside glinting as it passed overhead. Colin wished he had seen the headlong swoop at 80 mph from more than 100 feet, but knew that only the culmination of such silent marvels were sometimes witnessed by man: the bottom of the dive when the feet come down to strike into the water and the wings begin beating.

At 5:30, after his work was done, he showered, splashed on some Bay Rum and changed into a pale-blue polo shirt with white Bermuda shorts and blue high socks.

*   *   *

NIANTIC JEWEL

She was waiting at the portico when he drove up. It wasn't until she had picked her way barefoot over the gravel to the parking area that he felt the full effect of what she was wearing. Up close, she radiated feminine allure in her pale-blue tank top with spaghetti straps and tight white shorts. He gathered up his offerings, got out and handed her the posy.

"I've brought you these bleeding hearts. They're miniatures of mine struck by Cupid's arrow."

"That's so sweet! What a romantic you are."

She inhaled their fragrance before reaching up on tiptoes to kiss him on the mouth. Before he could respond she dropped back to her heels and touched his lips with two fingers.

"Later! We should go in now."

She took his hand and led him through the hallway into the kitchen behind, where a barefoot Alise Palmer was fixing martinis. They shook hands and he gave her the posy and the wine. She thanked him and surveyed the matching outfits.

"You two look like peas in a pod. What a coincidence that you dressed alike... Let me get you a drink, Colin."

"Thank you. A glass of water, please."

"Ben's on the patio. Why don't you join him. We'll be out with the drinks."

The big man was nattily dressed in a cherry shirt stretched taut over the potbelly, and yellow pants. He gave Colin another crushing handshake as he pulled up a chair, but this time Colin met it with equal force.

"How's the newspaper business, my boy?"

Colin wondered if it was a pro forma inquiry or whether he really wanted to know.

"Not so good. Terrible actually. It's slowly dying. The paper's been drowning in red ink for years. Advertisers spend their money on the Internet. Circulation's down from more than a million copies a week to about a quarter of that. Craigslist killed Classified advertising, and online advertising at Gazette.com can't replace the lost revenue. Never will. Jobs are being eliminated all the time. The foreign bureaus in Jerusalem, Berlin and Bogota were closed years ago.

Graham Griffith

"The way people get their information has changed forever. Why pay for a dead tree version of the news when you can get it free online during downtime at work? It saves time at home to spend with the family.

"It's a bit like dinosaurs waiting for an evolutionary change to reinvent themselves as birds. Newspapers can only pray for a technological miracle to save them. Or a new business model by which they'd become nonprofits or cooperatives. In the meantime, they could go extinct. Don't buy any stock, unless you don't mind losing money in the public interest. Democracy would be the worse without them though."

Ben Palmer nodded.

"That's for sure. But what about your career? I thought you were getting a master's."

"Yes, in history. That's where I want my career to be. Journalism isn't the life for me – not for anyone in their right mind! The toll on body and soul isn't worth the meager reward, unless you're oblivious to what it does to you."

"So will you go back to England when your visa expires? You must get homesick."

The two women came with the glasses and sat beside them. He looked at Juliana and felt the thrill of her presence.

"Well, I don't have to go back. I have a Green Card, and in four years can become a citizen. I'm hoping something will keep me here, but first I have to earn my credentials."

Juliana chuckled at his ambiguity.

"First you have to earn your dinner. You can help us with the corn. And Daddy, you should light the grill."

*   *   *

She pulled Colin to his feet and he followed the women back to the kitchen, Alise Palmer sat him at the breakfast island, handed him an ear of corn and showed him what to do.

"We're doing roasted corn on the cob. Peel back the leaves like this, without breaking them, and remove the silk. I'm going to slather the ears with butter and sprinkle them with Cavender's

NIANTIC JEWEL

Greek seasoning. Then you fold the leaves back in place and tie them with string. They go on the grill for 15 minutes; turn them once, and they're done!"

Juliana was chopping lettuce for a salad when her father called from the patio:

"Can someone get me another martini, please?"

While she saw to it, her mother came over to Colin, grinning puckishly.

"I'm really glad you and Juliana have hit it off. She's been talking about you incessantly since Friday night. I think she's stolen you from me!"

He felt a flush of embarrassment, and hoped it didn't show.

"She's wonderful! Amazingly bright and astonishingly beautiful, just like her mother. She takes my breath away. You must be very proud of her."

Her fingers fidgeted momentarily.

"Thank you, we are. And she's a charmer, just like you! But flattery aside, you two have much in common. Juliana tells me you have a singular gift that leads to feelings of isolation. Well you're not alone. We have an affinity that goes beyond being mother and daughter. There's an unspoken communication between us. Call it female intuition carried to a higher level, or something like the telepathy between identical twins. Sometimes, it allows us to know what the other's thinking or physically feeling.

"When Juliana was 7, she fractured her arm skateboarding in the driveway one Saturday afternoon. I was on my computer and felt excruciating pain in my arm. Simultaneously, I heard Juliana screaming. It was the same between my mother and me, and between her and Juliana.

"My mother was staying with us here when she died four years ago. She was 87 and frail with a heart condition. We used to make up a bed for her in the study off the dining room because she needed a walker or a cane to get around and couldn't manage the stairs.

"She died in her sleep. During the night, I woke up to find her standing at the foot of the bed in her nightie. She said to me, 'Take good care of Juliana, dear. You're both very special.' With that, she turned around and left. At the time, it never occurred to me how she'd climbed the stairs, and I must have gone back to sleep. When she didn't come out of her room for breakfast, I went in and found her."

Juliana returned and took a seat next to Colin as she listened.

"I wish now that I'd woken Ben so I'd know if it was a dream or an apparition of her spirit departing. But the really astonishing thing is that when I mentioned it to Juliana that morning, she'd had a parallel dream/visitation with the same words spoken, but about me, didn't you, dear."

Juliana nodded and Colin felt a tingle down his spine.

"That's uncanny. How do you explain it?"

"Only by metaphysics and parapsychology – what Ben calls supernatural mumbo jumbo. That's why we're in here. Anything unscientific, immeasurable, unorthodox makes him uncomfortable – the fear of the unknown. So we spare his feelings. Philosophically, I can deal with it from a rational, scientific perspective. That's what ontology, etiology and epistemology are all about: theories of being, reality and ultimate substance; causes and origins; the nature, sources and limits of knowledge...."

"It's an intuitive understanding in the female line going back generations. My mother was well aware of it. She had sympathetic labor pains when I gave birth to Joel and Juliana, for example. Her mother told her that the women of our family inherited it through a Native American ancestor. There was a foremother in the early 19th-Century who was supposedly part Narragansett. She even had an Indian name: Daughter of the Moon. Sometimes the bearers were proud of their Indian heritage and powers; sometimes not. That's why it's undocumented oral history...."

Juliana touched her mother's arm and continued without a pause:

"... How we came to Quonnie is interesting. After Daddy's company became successful, he started looking for a summer cottage on the Cape. But one day at Roche Bros. supermarket you were reaching for sunscreen at the same time as another woman, and you got to talking about how you were going to the Cape to look at a property. It turned out that her parents live here year-round and she knew this house was on the market...."

Alise Palmer took up the story as if on cue:

"... Ben wasn't interested. Bostonians go to the Cape. We're not happy unless we're sitting in traffic. But I insisted on taking a look, and something told me this was the place. When Ben saw the beach and discovered the driving time is an hour less than the Cape, he agreed to make a bid – and we got it! Later, when my mother saw it, she fell in love with it, too. It was then that she told me about Daughter of the Moon. We both felt at home here."

A thought struck Colin.

"I've been studying Narragansett history. Theoretically, you could validate part of the oral history by DNA testing with a registered member of the nation. There are 2,400, including 300 in Charlestown. Most are in New York, Wisconsin and elsewhere as a result of migrations long ago. The offices, community center and health clinic are on Route 2, within the 1,800 acres of land around Schoolhouse Pond and Indian Cedar Swamp that was returned to the tribe in 1978.

"Rhode Island had illegally detribalized the Narragansett in the 1880s and scooped up their 922-acre reservation for $5,000, even though many didn't want to sell. Only a 2-acre plot containing the church and burial ground was spared. The 324 men, women and children were each paid $15.43. The state then divided the land into lots, most of which it auctioned at $1.37 an acre; the best land went for $50 an acre and swampland 25c.

"This was exactly what the US government was doing with reservations across the country under the 1887 General Allotment Act, so Washington let it happen. Its sponsor, Massachusetts Senator Henry L. Dawes, turned his own state's disastrous 1869 Indian assimilation law into a national policy aimed at further dispossessing Native Americans of their land. The act abrogated a slew of treaties with Indian nations to open roughly a million square miles to white settlement. It and the almost as infamous Burke Act of 1908 weren't repealed until 1934.

"In Rhode Island's case though, the land grab violated the 1790 Indian Trade and Intercourse Act, which forbade anyone but the

United States from dealing directly with tribes. When federal policy changed with the 1934 Indian Reorganization Act, the Narragansett were retribalized as a nonprofit corporation. Federal recognition of the sovereign nation came in 1983.

"The tribe had to reclaim its identity after 250 years of public policy that left Native Americans socially degraded, culturally disintegrated, politically excluded and economically exploited. The 1833 Census listed 100 Narragansett in Charlestown. Only seven had exclusively indigenous genes, and they were all elderly women. After taking their land, white Americans just wanted Indians to disappear. If they weren't 'full-bloods' they weren't really Indian, the thinking went – but they survived. When the New England Indian Council was formed in 1923, its motto was 'I still live.'

"After all, Indianness isn't about racial purity or skin color. If a single drop of 'black' blood could make me officially African American under the 'one-drop rule' of the Jim Crow laws most states had between 1910 and 1925, then a drop of 'red' blood can make me Native American. It's racialist nonsense, of course, to assign heritage according to a racial hierarchy based on skin color, so that I can't be Indian if I have black or white skin.

"Federal and state laws are still rife with blood quantum restrictions, even though the Supreme Court ruled the 'one-drop' rule unconstitutional in 1967. Interestingly, Native Americans were spared its worst effects because of the Pocahontas Exception, made primarily for the benefit of prominent Virginia families claiming descent from the Powhatan heroine. They were spared being classified nonwhite if they had no more than one-sixteenth Indian blood...."

Juliana tapped his shoulder to interrupt.

"Perversely, a drop of supposedly superior 'white' blood won't make you anything! There's a term for that white supremacist rubbish, you know. The anthropologist Marvin Harris called it hypodescent. He said it happens when racial heritage governs membership in groups with a superordinate-subordinate relationship and when someone with a lineal ancestor in a

NIANTIC JEWEL

subordinate group is classified as a member of it... Sorry, I had to get that off my chest...."

Colin found himself admiring her exquisite profile as the literal image of her tantalizing figure of speech popped into his mind's-eye.

"Anytime. I'm all for getting things off your chest... I was going to say that none of us is pure anything if you go back far enough. American antimiscegenation laws to secure white racial purity were a few thousand years too late: The Europeans were already contaminated. But they didn't know about genes then, or Massachusetts wouldn't have banned mixed race marriage in 1705 and Indian-white marriage specifically in 1786. The laws weren't repealed until 1843.

"I have 'drops of blood' or, more accurately, bits of DNA from all my ancestors. I can draw my racial or ethnic identity from any of them I choose. Let's hope that DNA analysis will relegate blood quantum to the scrap heap where it belongs before it victimizes more people... To be a Narragansett tribal member I'd have to show a direct line of descent to someone on the state's detribalization roll in 1881; therefore I'd have Narragansett genes, and may identify myself through them if I wish.

"Unlike the people, the language itself is extinct, as classified by linguists. Its Y-dialect was one of more than 20 Algonquian languages. It ceased being spoken around 1810. Quite a bit survives in oral tradition and in the historical record, thanks mainly to Roger Williams. Some tribal members and academics can speak that part of it."

Alise Palmer began to muse as she set places at the island:

"I don't think I want to find out that badly! I like the idea of having a few bits of Indian DNA along with the English, Scottish, Irish, Dutch, German and who knows what else. I'd rather be a product of the melting pot than of a particular ethnicity. The mindset makes it easier to be objective, easier to embrace a less nationalistic, more humanistic worldview. I'm me! It doesn't matter who my forebears were. I like the sentiment of the legend. It provides a cause for our inherited female effect, even if only in broad metaphysical terms. I wouldn't want to lose that!"

Juliana shook her head.

"Mother, you're hopeless! Everything doesn't have to be cause and effect. It's inhuman! It's all well and good for the material universe in which things have to obey the laws of physics, but not for living creatures with psychological states that allow spontaneity.

"Cause and effect works predictably only in external space/time, not when the so-called effect is filtered through internal time, through a kaleidoscope of heterogeneous impulses with qualitative differences, until the ever-changing singularities coalesce into the concrete resolution of our choice. Then you can't pinpoint a cause or predict an effect. Time and space interact only in the external world. There is no space dimension internally, and the two kinds of time can't be confused!"

She clapped her hand to her mouth.

"I'm so sorry Colin! We don't always talk like this. It must sound like so much psychobabble to you."

Before he could respond, her mother threw up her hands.

"OK, OK! I didn't mean it literally. It's just a romantic notion. I don't want to get to the bottom of why we have super-intuition or why Colin has super-recognition. Everyone's unique; some more so than others. The idea was to make Colin feel comfortable with himself. Let's leave it at that for now. Ben's on vacation and we need to make lighter conversation, but you can always talk to us, Colin, dear... Now, you two take the corn out to the grill while I cook the lobsters."

$$*\qquad*\qquad*$$

Colin perused the evil-looking crustacean on his plate and the knife, fork, crackers and pick with which he was meant to subdue the blood-red beast. He poked it with the fork, seeking a point of entry on the tough shell. Then he turned it over and stabbed with the pick at the glistening white underbelly. The whole thing seemed impenetrable. He looked around to see what the others were doing, but they were watching him in amusement. At last, Juliana spoke:

NIANTIC JEWEL

"Well, you started off right by turning it over. Now watch me. I like to get all the meat out at once so I can discard the rest into the waste bowl and make room on my plate. Snap off the tail from the body, like this. Then break off the flippers and push the tail meat out from that end with the fork. Now, twist off the claws, open them with the crackers and remove the meat. Use your pick to get the meat from these four pockets where the claws attach. You can break off the legs and suck the juice if you want, but I don't. Cut the meat into chunks and dip it in the melted butter as you eat it. Now, you do it."

Colin followed her lead and extracted the tail meat.

"What's this black line down the middle, and the green and red stuff in the body?"

"Oh, I forgot! Take out the black line. It's the alimentary canal, and you don't want that! The green is the tomalley, the liver; the red is roe, the female's eggs – lobster caviar if you add salt. Mine's a male, so there is none. Try them. You can't be a New Englander until you do. They're an acquired taste, but full of nutrition."

He put some roe on his fork, salted it and took the plunge. It stuck to his teeth and he felt like spitting it out, but managed to swallow it.

"That's good! A bit like fishy peanut butter. I think I'll leave the tomalley for another time, though."

Alise Palmer pointed her fork at him.

"Then you're half a New Englander – you're an Englander."

Ben Palmer groaned.

"You see what we have to put up with, Colin. I pity her poor students. I've never eaten roe or tomalley in my life. They're disgusting! But I could eat lobster meat all day."

Colin caught Alise Palmer's eye.

"It's delicious! The corn, too. How do you cook a lobster?"

"Well, you fill your lobster kettle three-quarters full of water and bring it to a boil. Then I add 8 tablespoons of salt – two for each quart. Better yet, if we're having lobster and I'm going to the beach, I take a gallon milk jug with me and fill it with real saltwater. I put the lobsters in one at a time and bring the water back to a boil each time, just to be sure they die as instantaneously

133

as possible. Put the lid on and simmer for 20 minutes; take them out and let them drain. That's all there is to it!"

Juliana put her hand over his and squeezed it.

"Now that you're finished, I can tell you that lobsters are scavengers of all the guck on the ocean floor. They also eat sea stars, crabs and worms. That's why they're so good for you! And some live to be 100."

He resisted the urge to plant his lips over her mischievous smile, and before he could respond more appropriately, her father jokingly thumped the table with his fist.

"Chin up, Colin! You know, women are never so much attached to us as when they make us suffer. They're cruel and cunning."

Alise Palmer leaned over and kissed her husband on the cheek.

"And you deserve every second of it because you're a Neanderthal where women are concerned. Colin, on the other hand, is enlightened, cultivated and refined. He knows women, as the progenitors, are innately superior to men. We'll spare him when we end our vile subjugation, but not you. You'll be castrated with a clam rake!"

Her husband winced.

"Say it's not true, Colin. You haven't been infected with their feminist propaganda, have you? They're too dangerous to gain equality. My wife's fond of quoting Socrates on the subject: 'Woman once made equal to man becomes his superior.' Well, you ladies can quote me on this: After man came woman, and she's been after him ever since."

Juliana poked Colin with her elbow.

"No, Daddy. Adam was a huge mistake. That's why God made Eve so different... Go ahead Colin, tell him about the Earth Goddess."

He felt trapped between a rock and a hard place.

"Shouldn't we be leaving the war of the sexes behind us? The ideal state is an equilibrium: an equality of the sexes that respects our differences, honors our special roles and recognizes our mutual interdependency. It seems to me the path to that is through love. I love women because they're not men like me. They

NIANTIC JEWEL

make me whole. They actualize me into a genuine person. My happiness lies with women – so to speak – not other men.

"As I see it, the union of a man and a woman creates a whole greater than the sum if its parts. While men and women want and need each other, our bodies are subject to the laws of nature. We can achieve sexual intercourse temporarily and remain proximate in a domestic partnership, but it's through spiritual intercourse, through love, that we truly become one and transcend our self-limiting corporeal state with all its primal instincts.

"Love enables us to subsume our self-interest in a greater good: the welfare of our partner and resulting children who add more love to the reservoir. Only through love can we liberate ourselves. Freedom needs a love object, because there is no freedom without the limitation of being committed to a mate.

"Paradoxically, the sacrifice of our independent identity furthers our self-interest and, in the larger scheme of things, the propagation of the species. Applied to the human animal, survival of the fittest means survival of the most loving because our capacity for love has been the basis for the astonishing progress of Homo sapiens. It took the mind to a higher level.

"When I identify with my own sex to the detriment of the other, when I take comfort in the sympathetic gender bonding of close same-sex friendships, I'm avoiding the total commitment of myself through love to an opposite-sex other that will transform me. When I do that I remain static, unfulfilled…."

He glanced at Juliana and her mother, and gave a wry smile.

"How's that for psychobabble?…That's my theory anyway. I only hope I can find someone to share that depth of love with, but maybe it's too idealistic."

Alise Palmer raised her eyebrows.

"Not to women, although they'd be surprised at an American male who described love in those terms. European men are less afraid of their emotions. They're more passionate. That's good when they're being considerate and caring; not so good when the passion expresses itself as machismo and male chauvinism. But, at least, a woman knows where she stands. Here, men suppress their emotions so much that we don't know what they're feeling.

135

"You should trust your intuition. You're young, and should shoot for the stars… But don't think idealism and romantic love are only for the young. The trouble is that men – present company excepted – betray their ideals and their lovers. Too often, they're perfidious: untrustworthy and unfaithful. It's no wonder that many women prefer the company of women.

"Men are one-dimensional. They have this obsession with an idea of sex, which they pursue but are unable to realize because they're focused on self-gratification rather than mutual pleasure. So they skip from woman to woman, doomed to disappointment…."

Juliana rallied to the cause:

"… Women are better at sex – after we've shed our male-imposed inhibitions – because it's only one level of our emotional lives. Men can't decide whether they want a virtuous Madonna or a volcanic mistress, and they don't understand that women are both. The prize is right before their eyes, if they could only see. Instead they project their conflicted longings onto women and see their own image in women's clothing."

Ben Palmer glanced at each of the two women.

"How did we get here from there? I love you both for who you are, not as extensions of me. And I deplore infidelity. Most men I know are monogamous. You two are generalizing beyond belief. It's an underhanded feminist tactic. I'm a product of the Zeitgeist I was raised in. Blame that, why don't you. My mother shaped my attitudes toward women more than my father. So if men aren't all that women would like, blame the mothers of America! You're climbing up the wrong pole – with all its Freudian implications…. Colin is going to think we do nothing but argue."

His wife started clearing the dishes.

"I think you started it, Ben, and I did say present company excepted. You're both wonderful: You're the exceptions that prove the rule. I'll get your black Russian, and you and Colin can talk while we clean up."

Colin got to his feet to help.

"I can scrub the lobster kettle, if you'll let me. It needs big hands, and, besides, you did all the cooking."

NIANTIC JEWEL

Juliana gathered plates and followed her mother over to the dishwasher.

"You get the rest of the night off, Mother. You and Daddy sit and have your black Russians. Colin and I can handle this."

They worked side by side while, in the background, her parents talked about the summer and the storm, their voices rising and their laughter increasing as the liquor took effect. She put the last pot away, then turning to them announced:

"I'm going to show Colin the outside while there's still some light. Can I get you anything while I'm over here?"

Her father lifted his glass.

"Another of these if you don't mind, Jewel. And don't stay out too long."

*   *   *

The deepening twilight had already brought darkness to the island of pin cherries and tall rhododendrons that screened the house. As they crossed the driveway hand in hand, Juliana let out a sigh.

"I wish Daddy didn't drink so much. Sometimes it worries me. It's only at weekends and on vacation, but when he starts he doesn't stop. I suppose it's the pressure of running a business…. Oh, mind the steps here."

Colin was surprised to find they were descending into a dell with plantings of hosta and begonia bordering a small lawn. In the center, a gray wooden bench circled the branching trunks of the largest tree. She led him to the far side and sat down, pointing to the birdfeeders hanging from the canopy.

"This is our sanctuary. The cardinals officiate over it! The birds are roosting now, but in the daytime it's full of chickadees and sparrows, blue jays, goldfinches… Now's the time for bats, if we're still. You're not afraid of bats are you?"

"Not if you stay close."

He put his arm around her waist and, turning her toward him, kissed her full lips softly at first and then with rising passion. She wrapped her arms around him, returning his kiss with equal fervor and hugging him closer. He stroked her hair while covering her face with kisses. When he reached her ear, he swirled his tongue around the orifice and murmured:

"It was so hard not being able to hold you until now. I never want to let go of you."

She sought his lips again and pushed her tongue between them. They feasted on each other, sucking tongues in another long embrace until, breathless, she slid down into his lap and stretched out on the bench.

"You're a wonderful kisser. It feels so good being in your arms."

He placed a hand on her stomach and leaned down to kiss her again. Slowly, his hand moved up to her breast and cupped it. When her body remained relaxed, he began kneading the fullness while their lips stayed locked together. Then he brushed his lips over hers.

"You're so beautiful. I love your body."

He moved his kisses to her neck and shoulder, but when he took a spaghetti strap in his teeth, she put a hand over it.

"No, don't. I don't think I'm ready yet. We need to know each other better."

A wave of remorse swept over him. He removed his hand and placed it over hers on her shoulder.

"I'm sorry. You're right. I promise I'll never do anything that makes you uncomfortable. Will you forgive me?"

She kissed his hand.

"Of course. It's just that I don't believe in the physical without the spiritual, and that takes time, for me. Sex without commitment is like eating raw meat: It satisfies the body without nourishing the soul. When the two come together, there's carnal nirvana; the narcotic of unified bliss. I want to be in love body and soul, or not at all.

"Daddy says French kissing is a green light, so I'm sorry if that happened. But I like tongues, if it's alright with you. I like your body, too. You have a great body. If we started making love, I'd never want to stop... But the brain's the most erogenous zone of all, don't you think?"

NIANTIC JEWEL

He kissed her again, probing freely with his tongue until she held it with a vacuum and gently sucked on it before allowing him to catch his breath and speak.

"You exude sensuality. I don't know whether I'm more attracted to your mind or your body. They're both sublimely erotic. Each feeds into the other... You embody dualistic interactionism, in psychospeak!"

She pressed his inner thigh with her hand and exclaimed only half in jest:

"Stop! You've no idea how arousing that is to a psychology major... But, now that you mention interaction, how experienced are you? You're a hunk, and young men have casual sex, right?"

Once again, her outspokenness touched him, and he kissed her forehead.

"I told you: I don't make friends easily. There were only two relationships that outlasted the second or third date. They were long-term, but somehow never went beyond petting. Casual sex never appealed to me... How about you? You must have to fight men off."

She snuggled against him and patted his hand.

"Maybe if I wasn't at a women's college. I don't know. The ones I'd have to fight off, I wouldn't go out with in the first place... but same as you really with dating, except for Tom Morton, and that was always with clothes on... So we're both virgins with some experience. That's cool!"

He decided now was the time to bite the bullet.

"While we're on the subject, I have a confession to make: Just before we met on the beach, I was climbing the rocks and saw you sunbathing with your top off. I couldn't help it. I didn't see anything. There you were, just for a few seconds. I felt badly, and climbed back down immediately. I've been wanting to tell you. I hope you're not angry with me."

She gasped and put her hand to her chest.

"Good grief! That means you'd seen more of me than any man has, before we'd even met!... I know kids can't climb up there. I've never been able to, so I thought it was safe... I do remember getting a feeling, now that you mention it. You're sweet to tell me though. I hate having guilty secrets, too. You're forgiven."

He told her about the inscription on the rock, and now she voiced concern.

"We used to go down there together, but I didn't know he'd done that. I wouldn't have let him. I don't want it there. Is there a way to get it off?"

"Don't worry about it. The lichen's almost grown back over it. It'll be gone by the end of summer. Let it fade away."

"I suppose you're right, but you're the only one I want to be connected with. You know that."

They kissed and held each other close until she sat up suddenly, just before her mother called out from the portico:

"Time to come in, Jewel. You don't want mosquito bites."

She pulled him to his feet and called back in a muted voice:

"Too late, Mother. I've already been bitten, by a different bug."

She pecked his cheek, and they walked back with their arms around each other's waists, her head nestled against his chest.

NIANTIC JEWEL

CHAPTER 9

RIPE FOR ROMANCE

Let men tremble to win the hand of woman,
unless they win along with it
the utmost passion of her heart.
NATHANIEL HAWTHORNE

In the days that followed, Colin felt a happiness he'd never known, or thought possible. They were inseparable. She phoned in the mornings to arrange tennis matches or afternoons at the beach. They took trips in the Jaguar to Newport and its Gilded Age mansions, Smith's Castle and the picturesque harbor at Wickford, the amusement arcades at Misquamicut, the boutiques at Watch Hill, the casino and Mashantucket Pequot museum at Foxwoods, the Tomaquag Indian Memorial Museum and Queen Quaiapen's Fort at Exeter, the Museum of Primitive Culture at Peacedale and to Burlingame State Park, where they walked in the woods.

She showed him the historic sites nearby: Fort Ninigret, Coronation Rock, the Narragansett Indian Church, the Royal Indian Burying Ground and the Great Swamp Fight monument with its haunting if inaccurate inscription: "Attacked within their Fort on this Island the Narragansett Indians made their last stand in King Philip's War and were crushed by the United Forces of the Massachusetts, Connecticut and Plymouth Colonies in the 'Great Swamp Fight,' Sunday, 19 December, 1675."

(Inaccurate because the fort's exact location within the Great Swamp is a mystery, but fieldwork subsequent to the monument's erection in 1906 by the Rhode Island Society of Colonial Wars has ruled out this spot. Less excusable, it seemed to Colin, was the phrase "last stand," given that the war's chronology was always well known and the Great Swamp Massacre, as the tribe rightly calls it, marked the beginning, not the end, of the Narraganset's reluctant involvement in the war.

(Here we go again, he thought: history written by the winners. Who would ever know from visiting the site that hundreds of women and children were slaughtered here? Maybe war's greatest evil, he decided, is its power to cleanse the victor of its obscenity.

(It seemed to be an ironic facet of the denial that otherwise scrupulous historians as well as careless guidebook scribes usually misidentified even the general location of the infamy. The site is near the hamlet of West Kingston, 2 miles from the village of Kingston, both in the town of South Kingstown, adjacent to North Kingstown – a source of confusion resulting in such nonexistent permutations as West Kingstown, Kingstown and South Kingston.)

Either he ate dinner at her house or they cooked at the farm and spent evenings entwined in the wicker loveseat or the swing chair on the veranda, listening to his iPod's SoundDock and watching sunsets on the pond. They talked of their lives and families, of history and psychology, until it seemed he'd always known her. He told her of his alcoholism; she confided she'd been anorexic at 15. Friday nights, they explored restaurants; on Saturdays, he hurried back from Boston, milked the cows, and by 10 they were dancing at a nightspot. They were a couple.

Her parents took to him, apparently glad that she was happy and getting out. They didn't question him about the relationship and he didn't ask how she characterized it to them, although he knew they were a close family. Apart from holding hands, they toned down their intimacy in front of them.

She was less inhibited one night at the Palmers' when her friend Juanita stopped by. They were with her parents on the patio when a car came up the driveway. Juliana spotted it and jumped to her feet.

"It's Juanita! C'mon Colin. You're going to meet my best buddy. She's adorable."

NIANTIC JEWEL

She took his hand and led him through the living room to the front door.

"Juanita's parents have a house here. They come up from New York at weekends, but they're from Guatemala. Her dad's a diplomat at the UN and her mum teaches Spanish. Mother saw them on the beach one day and introduced herself. That was six years ago, and we've been best friends ever since. We're the same age. She helps me with my Spanish and I help her with her English, although I need it more than her. You can barely detect an accent. She's a political science major at Columbia. I've told her all about you."

At the portico, Colin recognized the scarlet Audi coupe as the car he'd braked to avoid on his first visit. Seeing it again three weeks later provided a reality check: There was a disconnection in his mind, as if the other time was in a different life. So much had happened in such a short time that he struggled to establish continuity. He didn't take in the shapely, raven-haired Latina approaching them until Juliana ran forward and hugged her, amid kisses and squeals of delight. They caught up on each other's news, speaking Spanish at a speed that denied Colin all but a few words. Finally, Juliana stepped back, planted a burning kiss on his lips and drew him toward the young woman in the smocked turquoise dress.

"Juanita, quisiera que usted satisficiera a mi cariño, Colin. [I'd like you to meet my sweetheart.]"

"¡Amperio hora, su cariño! [Ah, your sweetheart!]... Mucho gusto, Colin. I'm very happy to meet you."

"El placer es el mío, senorita... ¡Usted es muy hermosa! [The pleasure is mine... You are very beautiful!]"

She turned to Juliana in embarrassment.

"¡Usted no me dijo que él hable español! ¡Espero que él no escuchara! [You didn't tell me he speaks Spanish! I hope he wasn't listening!]"

Juliana shrugged and pecked his cheek.

"¿Quién sabía? Él me está sorprendiendo siempre. [Who knew? He's always surprising me.]"

He patted her shoulder.

"Don't worry. You two are far too fast for me. I hardly caught a word."

Juliana started into the house while he held the door.

"I was only telling Juanita what a cutie you are, in Latina vernacular. And if you understand that, you're in trouble."

*   *   *

The days rolled into one another like a never-ending dream with only the onset of an August heat wave marking a point in time. Inland, the 98-degree heat filled emergency rooms, but sea breezes kept Quonnie Cove 10 degrees cooler. Even so, the stifling afternoons were made bearable only by frequent dips in the 70-degree ocean.

They were at the beach with her mother one such afternoon. Alise Palmer was reading in her chair beneath an umbrella. Colin was rubbing sunscreen into Juliana's bronzed back as she lay on a towel in the shade of a second umbrella. He hoped her mother hadn't noticed that the task was taking far longer than it should, and had turned into a sensual massage. Even if she did, he wasn't sure he could stop, emboldened as he was by the soft purring that rewarded his kneading of the warm pliant flesh.

Juanita's melodious greeting abruptly ended the forbidden pleasure. She had arrived that morning and had come to find Juliana. Colin spread her towel while she kissed the women and settled in beside Juliana. She'd heard on the weather forecast that a hurricane was forming in the mid-Atlantic, headed for the Caribbean. Then she pointed out to sea.

"Look, Block Island has submerged again. Maybe the Blockheads know the hurricane's coming this way."

Colin noted the fair-weather haze obscuring the island.

"It's been like that for days, ever since the heat wave settled in... Is that what Block Islanders are called – Blockheads?"

Juliana turned toward her mother.

"Tell Colin about the Blockheads, Mother."

Alise Palmer looked up from her book and smiled nostalgically.

NIANTIC JEWEL

"Oh, alright. When the children were little and liked scary stories, I told them there was a legend about why we can't see the island on days like this: Block Island is really an alien outpost. Thousands of years ago, even before the Native Americans came, extra-terrestrials colonized it as a listening post on Earth. Their intelligence and technologies are far beyond anything we can imagine. They don't have material bodies – just minds.

"But on Earth, when they first came, they needed a container to prevent the atmosphere from crushing them. So they used protoplasm, the essential living matter of all animal and plant cells, to make boxes their minds could live in. They didn't need arms and legs or bodies. They would have looked like blocks – hence Blockheads. Then, when humans came to the island, the aliens took over their bodies. Now, the Blockheads look like everyone else...."

Juliana took up the story:

"... The reason the island disappears is this: They draw their energy from hot magma inside the earth. They convert the thermomagnetic power into sustenance as well as electricity to run everything. Deep down, there's a volcanic vent they've tapped into, but they can't bring the raw energy to the surface because that would blow the island apart. Instead, they take the island to the vent, where the water pressure allows a safe transfer. Because they're so smart, they were able to reengineer Block Island to submerge whenever they need a recharge...."

Juanita broke in:

"... The haze is like a smokescreen, while they do it. The island isn't there!"

Colin peered into the distance while pondering the scenario.

"I think I see the ferry from Point Judith heading over. What happens when it arrives, or doesn't?"

Juliana gave him a playful slap on the wrist.

"Shame on you! You underestimate Mother's myth-making ability. As soon as you enter the haze, the Blockheads take control of your mind. They implant virtual perceptual experiences so that everything appears normal. It's the same for the real people who live there. The Blockheads can override our satellite- and Earth-based sensing technology to make the island appear to be there when it isn't...."

Her mother nodded in agreement.

"... It's a bit like the brain-in-a-vat conundrum in Philosophy 103, or the `Matrix'-type movies it inspires. It may be subjectively irrational, but that doesn't disqualify it from being a sound argument. It's logically and physically possible, given that we don't know all there is to know. There's no way to disprove the legend, believe me.

"Your Aussie philosopher Karl Popper knew that science often errs and that pseudo-science may happen to stumble on the truth. Scientific proof can lead to false knowledge because proof requires a standard in order to be confirmed, and a standard requires a proof that can show the standard to be true. We're contaminated by the human condition. Popper would have thought the legend to be no better or worse than a belief in God...."

Juliana continued the thought:

"... That's because neither exposes itself to falsifiability, or testability. They allow no empirical knowledge to be drawn from them; they can't conflict with possible or conceivable observations. You can't disprove a negative – something that doesn't exist to begin with.

"Popper was expanding on what your John Stuart Mill said a century earlier: that for a proposition to be true, it must overcome all possible objections. The legend does that because it questions human knowledge itself by invoking a superior Blockhead intelligence `greater than which cannot be imagined,' to use St. Anselm's ontological argument for the existence of God. The legend is true a priori – based on reason independent of experience. If I can think it and believe it to be true, it is."

Colin appealed to her mother:

"How does that work? I can imagine those herring gulls over there attacking us, but I don't believe it will happen?"

Alise Palmer stretched her lean legs and tugged at the bottom of her lilac swimsuit.

"It's like this: If an intelligence `greater than which cannot be imagined' exists in your thoughts, then it can be imagined to exist

NIANTIC JEWEL

in reality, which is greater. So if it exists in thought alone, then an intelligence greater than which cannot be imagined actually can be imagined. But that's impossible. There exists, therefore, something than which a greater cannot be imagined, both in thought and reality."

He tried to penetrate the haze that now enveloped his mind.

"Well, say I'm over there today and the Blockheads control my brain, I could prove it by jumping off the 150-foot cliffs at Mohegan Bluffs. If I survive, I know it's the virtual me. If I die, it could have been the real me or the virtual me, since they have the power to kill the virtual me regardless. My knowledge of surviving certain death would prove the legend true, wouldn't it?"

Juliana reached for his arm and pulled herself up against him.

"Good try, but no cigar! You can't be sure the Blockheads are the only explanation. God might have saved you. Anyway, the Blockheads can erase memories. Just accept Anselm's answer to the skeptics: 'I don't seek to understand so that I may believe. I believe so that I may understand'."

He stroked her hair away from her face, savoring the profile of her rounded nose and bee-stung lips.

"I believe! Tell me the summer will last forever so I can believe it will."

She clasped his hand over her heart and kissed it.

"It will, for us anyway. I believe that... Now for some not-so-good news. Mother and I have to go up to Wellesley tomorrow morning for a videoconference call about the book. We'll be back late Thursday. I wish we didn't have to, but you'll be alright, won't you?"

Her mother grimaced in distaste.

"Sorry. I had a call this morning. I don't want to go either, but it's unavoidable. And we need to pick up mail. Can you live without her for a day?"

Juliana kissed his forehead.

"I'll cook you something special tonight. What's your favorite English grub?"

"Have you ever tried liver and onions? I bet I could get liver at the Charlestown Mini Super."

She made a face, before burrowing her nose into his chest.

"It sounds vile, but OK. I'll try anything once – except I've no idea how to cook it?"

"All it takes is a skillet. You sauté the sliced onions in butter, take them out and put the calves' liver slices in for 5 minutes, turning them until they're brown, not red. You'll love it!"

Juanita pursed her lips and laughed.

"She'll either love it, or hate it! In Guatemala, we call it higado y cebollas. It's peasant food. ¡Buena suerte, miel! [Good luck, honey!]... Now, who's coming with me for a swim? Vamos!"

*   *   *

It was dusk when they finished eating by candlelight. She had a few bites of liver before begging off and filling up on salad. The congealed appearance, squishy texture and gamey flavor had her reaching for her napkin more than once. He regretted his poor choice but was glad he had dinner mints to clear the aftertaste. Later, they snuggled in the loveseat, watching the last pink veils disappear from the sky.

As night fell, they walked hand in hand across the sheep meadow to count the somnolent animals under the white oak. An osprey returned to the nest high in the canopy as they approached.

Her voice hung sweet and soft in the humid air.

"Let's cut through the dunes and walk Little Beach. It's magical in the moonlight."

He helped her over the stone wall beside Sunset Beach Road and they crossed to a sandy path where the only sound was the muffled drumbeat of the surf. Deep in the grassy hummocks, the waxing moon illuminated a brick pillar rising incongruously from the sand. She stopped beside it.

"It's the chimney of a cottage destroyed in the '38 hurricane. The sand's swallowed up everything else. There were cottages all along here then, but now it's protected seashore. Daddy's a hurricane buff, so I've heard all about it. He says 200 summer homes and four hotels were lost on Quonnie Neck and almost as many at Charlestown Beach. Then in 1954, Hurricane Carol demolished a few more and damaged others before Connie and Diane finished them off in '55."

He stepped over clumps of beach grass to touch the ghostly relic.

"I wonder if anyone drowned here? They wouldn't have had much warning back then."

"I don't know if they were among the 39 who died in Charlestown. Daddy says 700 were killed and 1,800 injured in GH38. That's what they call it: the Great Hurricane of 1938. They didn't have names then, but it wouldn't have mattered. No one knew a hurricane was coming. It had winds of 120 mph and drove the ocean 17 feet above high tide. There was $400 million damage to Long Island and New England; 63,000 homeless. Imagine what it would be like today."

They walked on in silence, she leading the way along the narrow trail, until the ocean lay shimmering in front of them. A dim spectral light bathed the strip of deserted beach between the rocky headlands of Quonnie Cove and Sunset Beach, dissolving into darkness near the dunes and around the boulders at water's edge. She took his hand and led him along the black corridor beside the sandbanks. Opposite a break in the rocks where the glistening water lapped against the shore, she pulled him down and wrapped an arm around his shoulder.

"This is the only place you can swim on Little Beach. It's ideal for skinny-dipping. Juanita and I sometimes come here at night."

She turned to hear his reaction, but the perfect angle of her lips so close to his led him to kiss her instead. They dropped back against the dune, clasped together, devouring each other in passionate hunger. When their tongues finally disengaged, she brushed her lips back and forth across his while murmuring softly:

"This is for tomorrow. But let's make the most of tonight."

Graham Griffith

With that, she got up, took a few steps toward the ocean and shed her clothes. The deep shadows hid all but her indistinct outline as she half-turned to him:

"I'm going in. Are you coming?"

He glanced sheepishly up and down the beach, then felt foolish for not trusting her.

"Wait for me. I've never done this before."

She giggled exuberantly and started sprinting across the moonlit sand, calling back:

"No way! You have to catch me. You're Neptune and I'm Salacia – being salacious"

From the water's edge, he could see her swimming farther out than he thought safe. He waded in chest deep and began floating, aware only of the ocean gurgling in his ears and the moon and stars above. When he raised his head and swirled his limbs for stability, the agitated water glowed with phosphorescent plankton.

He had his feet down with his eyes at water level, watching the silver moonbeams dance on the surface, when she burst up from the water 10 feet in front of him. She swam over laughing and gasping. Before he knew it, she jackknifed her legs around his waist and hooked her arms behind his neck.

Reflexively, he grabbed onto her bottom to keep his balance, which pushed her breasts into his face. He moved his head from side to side between the luxuriant mounds, alternately kissing each one until he had worked his way to the firmer flesh of her wide areola and the protruding nub at the center. Taking it in his mouth, he began to suckle, drawing in more and more of the heavy breast. Her nipple softened from the warmth of his swirling tongue, then engorged and stiffened as her giggles became sighs. The intimate contact broke with a pop when, as suddenly as she'd jumped onto him, she launched herself off and swam to shore.

She was bent forward, shaking her hair dry when he caught up with her in the darkness of the dunes. He was a few yards away when she straightened up to watch him. Even in the gloom, the moonlight played on her swaying, upturned breasts and exquisite form. She noticed the effect on him and curtsied.

"Sheathe your mighty sword, Sir Galahad. I'm a defenseless maiden. Have mercy, I beg of you."

He dropped to his knees and kissed her hand.

"I come to honor your virtue, my lady, not to ravish it. Let me be your champion and place my sword at your service. 'When beauty fires the blood, how love exalts the mind.'

"My, you are gallant."

She knelt down with him and sought his lips with hers. They fell into each other's arms, collapsing onto the sand in a frenzy of kissing and caressing. When their eyes finally met, he felt a warmth that radiated deep into his soul. The words welled up spontaneously, unchecked by inhibition:

"I love you... madly, passionately, desperately. I love you with all my being. You make me whole."

She touched his cheek with her hand.

"It's all happened so fast. I've never felt like this before. It's wonderful... as if we were meant to be together. I love you, too."

They kissed again, tenderly now, and lay together in joyful silence, absorbing the full meaning of their affirmations. When the warm breeze gave way to the chill of night, they dressed and walked back to the farm.

CHAPTER 10

BROKEN HEARTS

To love and win is the best thing;
To love and lose the next best.
WILLIAM MAKEPEACE THACKERAY

The next night, they talked on the phone. He told her he'd opened his books, but couldn't study for thinking of her. Yard work and housecleaning were all he could apply himself to, because in those rote tasks she had free rein over his mind. She told him about her day. On the drive up, she'd confided to her mother that they had a serious relationship.

"Mother said she and Daddy have grown fond of you. She knows you're special; not like all my old boyfriends who flunked her male sensitivity test. She was telling me about her summer romances, and how that was all they were. I suppose that's what it looks like to her, but I know it's different with us. We don't have to part after Labor Day. We'll take up in Boston where we leave off in Quonnie.

"I can't wait to show you the Wellesley campus. It's so beautiful in the fall. We'll take walks around Lake Waban and spoon on the benches beside the water. I'll take you browsing at the Wellesley Booksmith; we'll have ice cream at White Mountain Creamery... You can tell I'm mad about you. I'll have your whole life planned out if you're not careful! I miss you. I love you more each day. I'll call tomorrow afternoon when we're leaving. We should be back by 6."

It was all he could do to speak without his voice breaking.

NIANTIC JEWEL

"Without you here with me, it feels as if I've been cut in half. It hurts so much. I yearn for you. It seems impossible that I could have found someone as wonderful as you; that you care for me as much as I care for you. In the back of my mind, something keeps telling me it's just a dream, and soon I'll wake up, desolated. I won't believe last night really happened until I feel you in my arms and taste your warm lips again. Hurry back, my love. Your face is engraved in my heart."

*   *   *

The phone rang while he was finishing off Juliana's leftover liver for breakfast. Although she hadn't liked it, the connection to her made it comfort food to him. A sweet rush of adrenaline accompanied the fanciful thought that she was calling because she'd somehow sensed he was thinking of her.

Moira O'Neill's brusque, self-assured voice put an end to his whimsy. She and her partner Tara wanted to come down. Boston was unbearably hot. The story she was working on was at a standstill. People were out of town and unreachable. It was dog days in the news biz, so they could skip out at noon. They were dying to get in the ocean and play Scrabble on the beach. He told her they'd picked the perfect day, and gave directions. He'd have grinders and soda waiting.

The moment he hung up, Juliana was back on his mind. He wanted to have something to give her when she returned. On his way home from the deli at Michael's Shell on Route 1, he stopped at Galapagos boutique, hoping for an inspiration. When he saw an eternity band set with small sapphires and diamonds, it reminded him of the color and sparkle of her eyes. He knew he had to get it for her, even if it did break his monthly budget.

The gift box on the kitchen table was the first thing Moira noticed when she and Tara arrived. He regretted leaving it out, but before he could grab it, she picked it up and gasped sarcastically.

"Oh Colin, is this for me? You shouldn't have!"

153

"No Moira. It's for someone special. Put it down. You'll have to settle for a grinder."

She pouted, and he went to the refrigerator, glad to change the subject.

"Michael's grinders are worth driving down for. We can split the three I got between us and try some of each. There's a Ninigret: honey ham, Swiss cheese and honey mustard; Quonnie Delight: chicken salad, lettuce and tomato; and Michael's Italian: spinach, artichoke hearts, black olives, roasted red peppers and mozzarella."

Tara took the box and put it out of Moira's reach.

"It looks like jewelry – for his honey. Who is she, Colin?"

He told them with an odd mixture of reluctance and exultation while they ate their grinders, which at least reduced the ribbing to a minimum.

They changed into their swimsuits and drove to the beach, where they laid out their towels near the shore but well away from the clamor of children building sandcastles and splashing in the surf. They cooled off in the water, then settled in to a game of Scrabble, lying on their stomachs around the magnetic board.

He asked Moira about her latest expose. She shook her head in chagrin.

"You've got to laugh to keep from crying. I expose DPW employees who go in late, drive around the city doing nothing, then leave early, and they're more likely to be promoted than fired. And what about the FBI letting 'Bulldog' get away again after I found him for them? Either they naively told the wrong people in the Garda they were coming or 'Bulldog' still has friends in the Boston FBI from when he was an informer and made patsies of them. We're living in a madhouse. Everything sucks."

Colin saw the sandglass running out on his turn. With a sigh, he put down three of his six vowels to score a feeble four points with "iota."

"That's how much luck I'm having – a very small amount. The day started out great with your call and finding the gift, but now I'm jinxed. I'm getting terrible letters... Tell me about your

NIANTIC JEWEL

sleuthing in Ireland. Maybe that'll distract you, and give Tara and me a chance to catch up."

Her face brightened and a sparkle came to her eyes.

"That was fun! It was so great going back to Inveran and seeing the cousins again. We say cousin, but they're really distant relatives. I'd met Caitlin and Siobhan three years ago when I went over there to find myself before I came to the Gazette. Inveran was the ancestral village. It's in the remote west on Galway Bay, but only about 50 miles from Shannon Airport, which made it attractive to 'Bulldog' as allowing a quick getaway if needed.

"I was staying at O'Flaherty's Pub, because there aren't any hotels. One day, I was in the post office-cum-store and got talking to the spinster sisters who run it, Caitlin and Siobhan. We found out we were kind of related. They wanted to know all about the genealogy I'd compiled, and insisted I stay with them. We hit it off immediately. I had a marvelous time. The countryside is wild and beautiful. It's like stepping back in time. Most of the people speak Gaelic.

"Since then, we've kept in touch. I send them Gazettes with my byline. One had a story about 'Bulldog' with a photo. Lo and behold if I don't get a call from Caitlin last month saying two couples were renting Baltyboys Grange on the outskirts of the village, and one of the men looked like 'Bulldog'. Plus, every month, a thick brown envelope postmarked Boston came addressed to 'Mr. Stephen Dedalus' at the Grange.

"Well, the sisters are no dummies. They're quite well read, in fact, and know their Irish authors, like James Joyce. Stephen Dedalus is the hero of his 'A Portrait of the Artist as a Young Man' and also appears in 'Ulysses'. Now they had a man who looked like 'Bulldog' using a suspicious name and getting packages, possibly containing cash, from Boston.

"I suspected right away that the sender was his brother Brendan, the disgraced public official who used his clout to protect 'Bulldog'. He's fond of flaunting his erudition – he liked to quote from the Classics during his political career. It was probably his idea to hook up 'Bulldog' with the FBI – the ultimate protection!

Graham Griffith

"The Gazette went for it immediately. The sisters weren't so keen at first. They thought the phone call would be the end of it: They'd give me the tip, I'd pass it on, the Garda would show up and arrest 'Bulldog' and I'd have a story. I had to tell them we needed photos, and could I stay with them for a few days using the cover I had from my last visit.

"They didn't want to get that involved: Firstly, there are no secrets in a little fishing village; secondly, Siobhan's the postmistress and shouldn't be talking about who's getting packages from where; and thirdly, it could be dangerous for them. Even now, it could get them killed if 'Bulldog's' IRA friends find out, so you can't mention this to anyone. Anyway, it wasn't until I'd gone into some detail about the 13 murders 'Bulldog's' wanted for that they came around. The part about the four female victims persuaded them...."

Colin rose to a crouch to stretch his shoulders, just in time to see Alise Palmer step off the boardwalk with her beach chair and bag. He waved, but she was turned away, heading for an open spot farther up the beach, His heart leapt as he realized Juliana was back early. Then it sank when he remembered he'd left his cellphone in the car and would have missed her call. He cursed to himself and lay back down, drawing a puzzled look from Moira.

"Sorry. I had to stretch... So that's why your story implied that the tip came from someone at the South Boston Postal Annex."

"Right... to protect the sisters at this end. At the other end, the villagers don't know I'm with the Gazette: To them, I'm an American relative of their beloved sisters, and they don't talk to prying strangers, anyway... So I get over there, put on my Irish brogue and blend in again. Caitlin and Siobhan live above the post office, which is across the street from the pub.

"On Saturday nights, 'Bulldog' and his girlfriend, Louise O'Day, and the other couple ate at the pub. 'Bulldog' and Louise never talked to anyone, but the second couple passed themselves off as their gardener/chauffeur and cook/housekeeper. Actually they were bodyguards hired from the IRA.

"From the living quarters above the post office, it was easy to snap them coming and going. Then I went inside the pub and

NIANTIC JEWEL

walked by their table while talking on my cellphone, but I was really taking pictures. They had no idea.

"Next, I staked out the Grange entrance by hiking across the fields to some woods in front of it. The house is set back near the cliffs and surrounded by high walls with iron gates, so I couldn't see anything. But I found a tree I could climb up, and got some nice telephoto shots over the wall.

"By this time, I had enough on them, but I wanted to try one more thing – and got lucky. I charmed a fisherman into taking me out with him in his dory on the pretext of photographing puffins nesting in the cliffs below the Grange. When we got there, I could see a table and chairs set up near the edge of the cliffs. No sign of life though. We had to wait an hour for someone to come. I got some great puffin pictures!

"The next thing I know, there's gunfire. The birds fly screaming from the cliffs, and I'm thinking we're both dead meat, right? My life ends here – another of `Bulldog's' victims. I duck down behind the gunwales, afraid to move an inch. Then Rory, the fisherman, starts laughing at me and says, `They're shooting clay pigeons up there.' I look up, and there's `Bulldog', rifle in hand, right on the edge of the cliff. I zoom in with the camera just as he starts fiddling with his belt buckle. I couldn't believe my luck! That's his telltale mannerism, you know. He's so vain, he has to look just right at all times, even to his buckle being absolutely straight... The rest is history."

They played out the Scrabble game, but Colin couldn't concentrate for thinking of Juliana. He thought of going over to introduce the women to Alise Palmer, but wondered how it would look without a long explanation. It was getting close to 4 o'clock and milking time. Moira and Tara took a last dip while Colin packed up.

*   *   *

He was folding his towel when he saw Juliana on the boardwalk. He waved excitedly. She started toward him, then stopped. Holding up a book, she pointed in the direction of her mother, blew him a kiss and beckoned him to join her.

He turned to see Moira and Tara come running out of the water, giggling inanely. As they approached, Tara veered off to one side and, while his attention was on Moira coming at him, she circled around and crouched down behind him. When Moira bumped into him soaking wet, he fell backwards over Tara and grabbed out reflexively, catching a finger in Moira's black bikini top, which came away in his hand. She fell on top of him, her bare breasts against his chest, the three of them sprawled on the sand, the women convulsed with laughter.

Moira was climbing off him, her breasts in his face, when he glanced up the beach, hoping the spectacle had gone unnoticed. To his horror, Juliana was stopped in her tracks 30 feet away. As their eyes met, she gasped in shock, turned on her heels and ran away groaning.

The women were too busy laughing to notice, until Colin frantically scrambled out from between them. They followed his gaze as he watched Juliana disappear up the beach and heard his anguished moan:

"Oh nooo. This can't be happening. Juliana saw it all. She'll never come near me again. It's all over. You lunatics have ruined me."

Tara finished re-tieing Moira's top and gave him a sympathetic hug.

"C'mon Colin. We're really sorry, but it was an accident after all. Just innocent fun. We'll go over and explain it wasn't your fault, won't we Moira?"

Her partner peered over Colin's shoulder and frowned.

"Oh shoot! I think it's too late for that. Look! There's a redhead and an older woman leaving the beach... Maybe it's just as well. There could have been a scene if we'd gone over. Better let her cool down. I know I'd be upset if I were straight and saw my guy sandwiched between two mostly naked women, one of them topless even. She'll be alright when she knows we're married... You've got to admit, it was funny."

NIANTIC JEWEL

The humor escaped Colin. He was racked by the pain of betrayal he imagined Juliana to be feeling.

"Thanks a lot, Moira. I don't want either of you talking to her. Don't you think you've done enough damage already? It's worse than you know. It appears to her that I hooked up with two bimbos while she was away. Then she comes back unexpectedly and catches me in flagrante delicto with both of you on her beach in plain view of her own mother. I've got to go to her now while the perception can be corrected, while the memory's fresh and can be infused with the truth before it imbeds. There's no time to lose."

Moira gave him a playful push.

"You're the only schmuck who could call me a bimbo and get away with it. Cut the psychobabble and get a grip. You make it sound like a psychiatric crisis instead of a simple misunderstanding. Showing up now will just make matters worse. She won't see you, believe me as a woman. She'll just get even more angry… But you know her better. If you want to give it a try, let's go! We'll stay in the car unless you need us."

*   *   *

Just as he'd feared, there was message from Juliana on his cellphone in the car. Tears welled in his eyes as he listened.

"Hi Sweetie! I don't know where you can be. I tried the farm and left a message. I worry when I can't reach you! It's 2 o'clock and we're ready to head back. Mother wanted to shop for a swimsuit at Talbot's, but I told her I was miserable. Then she felt guilty. We'll be there just after 3. I'll drop off my stuff and come over. Can't wait to kiss you! I love you."

Tara saw the tear on his cheek and passed him a tissue.

"Lighten up, honey. It'll bring you closer together after you make up."

Moira turned on the radio.

"Listen! Hurricane Hannah's veered away from the Caribbean, headed for Bermuda. One of the projected tracks would bring her to New England. That's good news, Colin. Your problem's solved if we all get killed!"

They spent the rest of the short trip over to the Palmers' in silence.

Alise Palmer came to the door barefoot and carrying a book. Her impatient look gave the impression she'd been interrupted, but she smiled wanly when she saw him.

"I was half-expecting you, Colin. Juliana told me what happened. I'm afraid she's not taking it well at all. She's in her room and wants to be left alone. There's nothing you can do. I'll tell her you came by."

He wrung his hands forlornly.

"What Juliana saw at the beach must have looked absolutely awful…."

Her mother put up her hand to stop him.

"I don't want to know, Colin. It's between the two of you, though I have to say it surprised me."

He turned to leave, then reestablished eye contact.

"Please, I owe you an apology, too. The horseplay was foolish, but what resulted was an accident. The ladies involved are friends from the Gazette: They're a married couple. I didn't know they were coming until this morning. Please tell Juliana that. I can imagine what she's feeling, and it's tearing me apart."

Alise Palmer's expression brightened. A gasp of laughter escaped before she reached for his hand and patted it sympathetically.

"You poor boy! Forgive me, but that's priceless. I believe you. It's so bizarre, you couldn't possibly be making it up. Now I feel awful for jumping to conclusions. Of all people, I should know appearances can't be trusted. I'll tell Juliana when I call her for dinner, unless she comes down before then. Now's probably not the right time. She's in shock. Her emotions are in turmoil and need to settle down."

"Whatever you think best. Thank you for listening. Tell her I'm so sorry… and that I love her."

"I will. And don't worry."

NIANTIC JEWEL

He returned to the car feeling that maybe the black cloud was lifting, but painfully frustrated that it could be hours before Juliana knew the truth. In the meantime, she might make an irreversible decision. All he could do was hang on, and hope for the best.

After he'd related the conversation, Moira tried to lift his spirits.

"While you were gone, we were talking about what we should do. We'll go home now if you want to be alone. Or, we were thinking we could stay until her fury subsides, and then the two of us would take a shot at trying to see her on our way out. But now that her mother knows about us and is on your side, she's sure to let us talk to her, in a while.

"So how about we put it out of our minds for the next hour. We won't mention it. Never happened! You show us how to milk a cow, like you promised. Then we'll head out. We'll stop by her house and play a get-out-of-jail-free card for you. We'll call you when we're back on the road – with good news, I bet. How does that sound?"

"I suppose you're right. Thanks for wanting to help out. I'm just worried that her mind's already made up. But if anyone can change it, you two with your blarney can. OK, I'm sold. Not another word about it."

There was a setback when Colin retrieved the message Juliana had left at the farm. He contrasted the joy in her voice with what he thought she must be feeling now, and saved the call in case it was the last he'd get from her. The somber mood lifted when he heard the cows lowing impatiently at the pasture gate. He was 20 minutes late, and they knew it.

Milking time was fun for Moira and Tara. They squirted each other with milk, and after meeting Angel asked how there could be a calf without a bull to father it. He explained as delicately as the subject permitted:

"When a cow's lactation period ends and milk production drops off, she goes into estrus, or 'heat', signaling that she's ready to have another calf and begin a new lactation. It's not economical to keep a bull for that purpose, now that we have Artificial Insemination technology. It allows semen to be collected from champion bulls with the best genetic traits and transferred into the lowliest cows, resulting in superior offspring. It just takes a vet to perform the procedure by hand. AI in cattle paved the way for human AI. Does that answer your question?"

Tara stroked Angel's back and mused:

"That's good for the gay cows, but not for the straight... Can cows be gay?"

"Bisexual is probably closer. Bovine sexuality is raw mating instinct. The first indication that a cow's in heat is when you see another trying to mount her. The pheromones released by the first cow act on the testosterone in the second. Luckily for us, cows are better mothers than lovers. Humans wouldn't be where we are without their milk, butter, cheese, beef and hides, even the motive power of oxen that the Third World still depends on."

Moira looked at the Jerseys waiting patiently in their stalls to return to the pasture for the night.

"They're beautiful, and so gentle."

"Affectionate too. Each has her own personality... There are beauty contests for cows, you know – at state fairs and agricultural shows. I used to judge dairy cattle as a teenager in the English version of 4H."

"Only because you were too nerdy to judge the dairy queen contest, I bet."

"No Moira. Dairy queens might appeal to you, but not me. And they wouldn't let adolescent boys be judges, would they. That's for the married men! Anyway, it's easy to size up a beauty queen. The finer points of a champion dairy cow are more complex. They can't hide anything. No makeup, no padding. You can even open their mouths to check inside."

"Whatever, cowboy. It's all meat on the hoof to the male animal, isn't it. Pursue, subdue, possess. For women, it's the pursuit of happiness; for men, it's the happiness of pursuit... Talking about meat, what will happen to Angel?"

"She's blessed! She'll join her mother in the herd, replacing an old cow who doesn't turn a profit anymore. But the next calves will be sold at 16 weeks and slaughtered as veal. There's no room

NIANTIC JEWEL

for more cows here and there aren't many dairy herds left in Rhode Island."

Tara sighed forlornly.

"That's so sad. I'll never eat veal again."

*   *   *

Half an hour after they left, Colin was sitting by the phone, imagining the worst, while he waited for Moira's call. Bleak scenarios crossed his mind: Juliana was still too upset for her mother to talk to her; Moira and Tara had made themselves objectionable; her father or Juanita had intervened against him; she'd decided he wasn't worth the grief.

His eyes welled up again when he toyed with the blue box holding the eternity band. Not knowing was worse than the finality of catastrophe. He pictured her vulnerable, open smile, and he ached. He remembered their embraces, her words of love, and wondered how he could live without her. Feelings of loneliness and impending doom swept over him. A long-dormant craving returned: He needed a drink.

The futility of his desire struck him as so ludicrous that he laughed out loud. He kept no alcohol and couldn't leave the phone to get any. Then he realized there was something worse than losing Juliana: losing her and sliding back into the pit of alcoholism. The allergy he cited socially as to why he didn't drink was only half of the clinical description – "an allergy plus an obsession" – of the incurable, progressive and fatal disease he had battled since his parents died.

On his way over to the refrigerator, he shook his head in wonder at the insidiousness of the affliction that, no matter how long since the last drink, was ready to strike whenever he dropped his guard in a crisis. Fat chance, he thought as he put ice cubes in a tall glass and filled it with equal parts apple juice and water. The tricks he'd learned to stop cravings in their tracks kicked in reflexively nowadays. There would be no "wet thinking."

The diluted apple juice had the umber color of a highball with the faint aroma and taste of whiskey, but the sweetness made the similarity incongruous and counteracted any desire for the sourness of alcohol, in the same way that no one chases chocolate milk with beer. He remembered that food also dulls the pangs of the body, and found unexpected comfort in a banana.

Mentally, he turned the craving on its head. Rather than try to block it, he embraced it with the "full script" technique of imagining the pleasure of that first drink, followed by its consequences: another and another, inevitably, until full sedation and unconsciousness; day after day until, in a few weeks, the toxic buildup sapped his body and warped his mind; then the bottom of the pit, the primeval void of darkness, the mirror of utter loneliness in which he faced his own death mask. At rock bottom, the giddy ride was over, the fall from grace complete. Life was unbearable.

He welcomed the memories of desolation that resurfaced. Twice, the Grim Reaper had beckoned him at the fork of two roads to Hell: the first, a shortcut by his own hand; the second, the longer, living death of alcoholic madness. It wasn't that he had chosen life on those occasions. His polluted mind was too feeble to make rational decisions.

He couldn't even decide if suicide required courage or stupidity. Wasn't bravery just folly with good luck; folly simply bravery with bad luck? He had lived in a perpetual stupor, which qualified him as stupid. But courage means not fearing death, which he didn't; it offered release from torment. If suicide is the ultimate transference of pain, shattering the lives of those who love us, no one would suffer on his account; he was alone and unloved. It was all a confusing blur.

What saved him was something beyond his control. It was only later, while learning everything he could about his alcoholism, that he found a name for it – the life force.

Swallowing the last of the banana, he realized that dealing with the craving was taking his mind off its cause. His empty gaze rested on the pond beyond the kitchen window and the inglenook in front, where the cat warmed herself in the late afternoon sun. He went over and picked her up, tucking her into the crook of his elbow while he stroked her head.

NIANTIC JEWEL

"Molly, we're going to have an AA meeting. Just you and me. Alcoholics need to talk. Hearing ourselves lends commitment to `dry thinking'."

He took Molly's purring as encouragement and returned to his chair with the cat in his lap.

"Hi, my name's Colin and I'm an alcoholic. It's been 18 months since my last drink. I started drinking heavily at 18 after my mother died in a car crash. My father was inconsolable. He ended his life a year later in what the coroner called `an accident while cleaning his gun'.

"I was in college, and showing up drunk for class. I was miserable. A professor urged me to get help, so I went back to the psychiatrist who'd treated me for depression the year before. She told me about Alcoholics Anonymous and suggested going to some meetings. I didn't think I was an alcoholic; I just liked to drink and had a good reason to.

"At the same time, I knew I had to quit. The life stories I heard at AA gave me comfort in knowing I wasn't alone with a drinking problem. But AA's religious overtones weren't for me, and I soon stopped going. It had scared me into not drinking, though. And fear of the consequences kept me dry.

"Back then, I didn't know that neither fear nor willpower can overcome an obsession. The paradox of alcoholism – that you love your killer – has to be fought with a paradox – that you can't trust yourself. I didn't know that lapses were inevitable until I accepted a Higher Power.

"After three years of sobriety, I thought I could return to social drinking. In 30 days I was back at the bottom of the pit, my livelihood in peril. An understanding employer knew that journalism leads to alcoholism among those genetically disposed and to alcohol abuse in many others unable to take the stress. The company was willing to keep me if I got help, but, as for my career, I was a marked man, a weak link. I was an alcoholic.

"This time, the treatment was a little different. A psychiatrist saw me through the immediate crisis – I had a suicide plan – and prescribed an SSRI for a few weeks. He put a greater emphasis on AA, since I now acknowledged my alcoholism. Instead of the large open meetings I'd been to before, where few get the chance to speak, I happened upon a Twelve Step group, where everyone speaks briefly.

"I'm a shy person, so baring my soul to 150 strangers was a terrifying prospect: I was content to listen. A 12-step group suited me better. Studying a step each week with mainly the same 20 people meant that we got to know one another. After a few weeks, speaking wasn't a problem. And I felt better afterward because I was unburdening.

"History has always interested me, and AA's is amazing. I read AA books: the Big Book, 'Twelve Steps and Twelve Traditions,' and 'Living Sober.' It became clear that I'd previously rejected AA without knowing much about it. Belief in a Supreme Being is offered as a basic matrix, but AA isn't a religious movement. God is a metaphor for spirituality, a way to connect with our soul. Without spirituality there can be no recovery. Belief in God isn't required; belief in a Higher Power is. For me, that's the life force.

"I knew I was onto something in AA with the very first step: 'We admit we're powerless over alcohol – that our lives are unmanageable.' That was me.

"The next two steps are the big hurdles for nonbelievers: 'We believe that a Power greater than us can restore us to sanity' and 'We've decided to place our wills and our lives in the care of God as we understand him.'

"Luckily, my psychiatrist had turned me over to an alcohol counselor. Her approach was cognitive behavioral therapy or mindful awareness: rearranging my maladaptive processes of thinking and perceiving through self-reflection. That led me to meditation. As a farmboy, it was only natural for me to seek in Nature the spirituality I'd lost in the Wicked World. Walking in the woods, meditating, restored my spirit.

"I went back to the Romantic poets I'd read: Goethe, Wordsworth, Coleridge, Byron, Keats, Shelley. But biographies are my favorite, and one on Thomas Carlyle, who championed the antimaterialism of Schiller and Goethe, led me to his own admirer, Emerson, and the other New England transcendentalists: Thoreau, Alcott, Fuller and Ripley.

NIANTIC JEWEL

"It seemed that transcendental meditation was exactly what I'd been doing: seeking the nature of reality through the process of thought rather than through the objects of sense experience. Its antiauthoritarianism in holding that intuition is the supreme source of knowledge appealed to me, as did its celebration of the mystical unity of Nature.

"That sparked an interest in ontology, the nature of being and reality: first Darwin's naturalism, Hume's skepticism and Mill's libertarianism (only because they're British), then the German giants – Kant's ethical individualism, Fichte's and Hegel's humanist idealism, Marx's socialism and Nietzsche's life-affirming (but antidemocratic) moralism. To understand my basic psychology, I read Freud and Jung."

Molly yawned and stretched while swatting her tail against his arm.

"You're right, Molly. I'm boring you, and have gone way over my allotted time. Would you like to say something?... OK, I'll get back to 'God as we understand him.' I couldn't figure out why I was still alive and not drinking. It was if an unknown hand had intervened: a Higher Power. But what was it? It didn't make any sense for there to be a God who would save me but not others. I hadn't even asked to go on living. All I'd wanted to do was die; to get it over with.

"Well, the soul-searching meditation and exposure to the great metaphysical thinkers gave me the idea of a life force flowing through Nature, using every living thing as its vehicle to the next generation; a Kantian noumenon unable to be known through perception; a power independent of the physical laws of the universe in its death-defying ability to reproduce into the future.

"This scared the heck out of me. It means that the life force doesn't care about the quality of my life; that's for me to deal with. (Not that it could care, being inhuman and amoral.) Neither will it easily let go of the life it's lent me; it clings on tenaciously like a candle flame until the last glimmer is spent. It won't ever give up on me, or let me give up on it, without a superhuman struggle.

"That's what makes suicide such a bad bet for a rational, balanced mind. The life force is working against us. It doesn't mind if we're crippled in a failed attempt, as long as we're still alive, even barely. Ironically, things can get worse at the bottom of the pit. Nor does it mind if we live out our lives in madness. Our suffering is irrelevant. And what if we change our minds after the die is cast? Then, irony of ironies, we await death as ludicrous losers, wishing we'd chosen life. Much better, then, to embrace this awesome power and use it to promote our happiness.

"Now Molly, you ask why I'd believe in a such a far-fetched notion. Well, members can't interrupt speakers at AA meetings, but you're allowed. This is where it gets interesting. If you look up 'life force' in the dictionary, it refers you to the entry for élan vital, French for vital force; in Bergsonian philosophy, 'the original vital impulse which is the substance of consciousness and nature.'

"Henri Bergson (1859-1941) was a French philosopher, a dualist who believed that the world contains two opposing tendencies: the life force and the resistance of matter against it; we know matter through the intellect, but perceive the life force and the reality of time through intuition. He said there are two kinds of time: One is external space-time, which is measurable; the other is internal duration in terms of life experience (or psychological time), which isn't.

"His doctrine of vitalism proposes that life in living organisms is caused and sustained by a vital force distinct from all chemical and physical forces, and that life is, in part, self-determining and self-evolving. He doesn't credit Hinduism for his inspiration, but it seems to extend the concept of an abstract life force the Hindus call Brahman.

"I'd stumbled independently upon the strands of a belief system that Bergson had rigorously woven together in his 1907 book 'Creative Evolution'. The idea of a life force goes a step further than Darwin's 'natural selection' and the Neo-Darwinists' incorporation of modern genetics into his theory. All three leave room for a Supreme Being to have set things in motion, but none is contingent on Him or Her existing.

"Now I had a tangible Higher Power to correspond to AA's God as we understand him, plus the self-knowledge to embark on Step 4: to make a searching and fearless moral inventory of myself. This

NIANTIC JEWEL

crucible of conscience was a searing exercise in humility. It sparked a spiritual awakening that made the remaining eight steps come naturally.

"Sometimes I think AA's founders, Bill Wilson and Dr. Bob Jones, had the Seven Deadly Sins – pride, covetousness, lust, anger, gluttony, envy and sloth – in mind when they devised Step 4. I wouldn't call ordinary lust a sin, because we wouldn't be here without sexual desire. And sloth is a value judgment. Covetousness and envy are practically synonymous; it's only in their excess – as jealousy – that they're destructive. Gluttony is better called greed. That leaves us with pride, anger, greed and jealousy, to which I'd add untruthfulness: Five Deadly Sins.

"In modern terms, we'd call them character defects. That's what Step 4 and its constant revisiting through Step 10 are all about: righting the moral compass we've distorted by the lying necessary to protect our drinking. Once I'd made a fresh start and rediscovered my innate spirituality, the crushing burden of guilt and self-loathing was lifted. I was free again to experience the joy of life.

"That's what AA did for me. I'll always be grateful, even though I don't attend meetings anymore. It's there if I need it. If that sounds selfish, it's only because I don't expect others to share my notion of a Higher Power. Vitalism works for me, but when I've tried to explain it at meetings it didn't help people grappling with God as we understand him. Those unable to believe can always use AA as their Higher Power. It's just as effective. They depend on AA attendance to stay dry, but any belief system involves dependency, and the fellowship of AA is therapeutic. Plus, they're able to give back by helping others. I don't fulfill that part of Step 12, although I'd do whatever I could for anyone who wanted help to stop drinking. At some point, I'd mention AA and take them to a meeting, if they wanted."

Molly meowed and roused herself. He felt her claws extend as she stood up on his bare thigh, then pressing down with her hind legs she sprang to the floor and wandered away. He winced and rubbed his leg.

Graham Griffith

"You're not staying for the end of the meeting, Molly? We have to close with the Serenity Prayer. It was written by Reinhold Niebuhr, the American religious and social thinker, and adopted by AA:

> God grant us the serenity to accept
> the things we cannot change,
> The courage to change the things we can
> And the wisdom to know the difference.

*   *   *

The craving was gone, replaced by the sinking feeling that preceded it. He glanced at the tambour clock on the mantelpiece. It was 6:02, but the Westminster chimes hadn't struck the hour. They needed winding. He busied himself with it and allowed the second hand to hypnotize him as it jerked through its course, watching helplessly as time passed. After a couple of minutes, he stretched his arms and walked over to the window. On the pond, a dozen boats sat motionless on their moorings off the Quonnie Cove dock. Farther out, a water skier sent up sheets of white spray. Near the breachway, a small cabin cruiser returned from a day's fishing in the Sound. Overhead, the osprey circled, and high cirrus clouds on the southern horizon reminded him that Hurricane Hannah was somewhere out there. He was about to turn on the weather radio when the phone rang. The lump in his throat caused him to answer with a croak.

"Colin? Are you alright?"

"Hi Moira. I had to clear my throat. Thanks for calling. How did it go?'

"Sorry it took so long. We got lost in those blasted lanes after we left the Palmers'. It was sheer luck that we ended up on Route 1. Why don't they…."

"Stop Moira. You're killing me."

"Sorry Colin… You're all set."

"How do you mean?"

NIANTIC JEWEL

"We fixed it all up, idiot! She's a knockout, Colin, and really nice, although I hate to say that about a WASP princess. Tara just said she's perfect for a WASP prince like you."

"And...."

"Oh, you want to know what happened. Well, her mother came to the door. We thought she was the housekeeper or something. They don't look anything alike. She certainly doesn't dress like a Wellesley swell. Anyway, she knew who we were before we'd said a word. She said she reads my stuff. How do you like that? She'd told Juliana the whole unlikely story and said to go see her. She was sitting under a tree in that sunken garden in front of the house. Her eyes were all red and teary. She looked heartbroken, and so vulnerable we just wanted to go hug her.

"It was amazing how quickly she brightened up after we introduced ourselves and she saw us holding hands. By the time we'd finished explaining and telling her how devastated you are, she was feeling a little guilty. I guess our version meshed with yours enough to remove any doubt in her mind. She said, 'Oh God! Poor Colin. I have to go see him.' Then she thanked us for coming and offered us both a drink – hard stuff mind you! You know how hard it is for Gazeteers to turn down free booze, but we did – for you Colin. We thought it was so sweet of her to offer hospitality, given her condition. I don't think I would have had the good manners to, but there you are.

"I guess she just wanted to talk to someone because she asked how long we'd been friends. That gave us a chance to extol your virtues, meager as they are. We must have done a good job though. Her eyes welled up and she had to get out the Kleenex. Then we did have a group hug.

"As we were leaving, Tara had the presence of mind to test the waters. She told her you both had to come over for a Scrabble night when you get back to town. And Juliana said she'd like that. So there you are. You'll be able to give her that ring after all. I'd better go before she shows up at your doorstep. You owe us a bottle of Jameson. Ciao."

She was gone before he could say anything. He smiled wanly as he hung up the phone, thinking she knew he'd be too choked up to talk. A conditioned reflex to the emotional roller-coaster ride he was on made him fill the tea kettle before going outside to sit on the stoop. From there, he could look down the farm track to the road.

Two boys on bikes emerged from the Quonnie dock entrance, trying not to collide as they steered with one hand while holding their buckets in the other. They'd been crabbing, he thought, and were headed home for dinner. As they approached the bend by the farm gate, one dropped behind and the yellow Mini Cooper came into view. It stopped to let them pass, then turned up the track.

He watched, frozen, wondering whether to stand up and wave or retreat into the house. The honking of the horn drew him to his feet, and he stood awkwardly immobile with his arms at his side until making eye contact. She was smiling as she pulled up beside him. He smiled back and waited for the engine to die before opening the door.

"Hi Juliana... I'm so sorry for all...."

Before he could get any further, she hopped out of the car, threw her arms around his neck and kissed him hard on the lips. He pressed her to him, wanting to devour her. She sucked greedily at his tongue, then released him and covered his face with kisses.

"I feel so stupid after meeting Moira and Tara. I let my emotions run away with me. Forgive me for doubting you. I know I shouldn't be so possessive. But I love you so much...."

The pleading look in her moist eyes was more than he could bear. He cradled her face in his hands and returned the shower of kisses.

"I love you with all my heart. You're everything to me. I wanted to die when I thought I'd lost you. Now, I'm the happiest bloke alive."

They both tried to sniffle back the tears that ran down their cheeks and mixed together on their lips as they kissed again. Their sighs turned to muffled giggles at the taste of the salty lubricant, until she broke off and began kissing his face dry. Then she took his hand and brushed it with her lips while looking him impishly in the eye.

NIANTIC JEWEL

"I think we just shared bodily fluids. Was it good for you?"

"It was wonderful – but I can imagine better."

She smiled demurely.

"All in good time, Sir Galahad. I want it, too – when we're both sure it's for the right reasons. I love your mind first and foremost. It turns me on, and I won't be satisfied until I've explored every crevice. I'm hungry for you. Sex should be the dessert in a relationship, don't you think?... Talking of appetites, that reminds me: I picked up some takeout at the Hitching Post. It's on the front seat. You haven't eaten have you?"

"No, I'm starving. What did you get?"

"Fish and chips and a clam plate. It was my backup plan. I was afraid you might have decided to throw in the towel again, like you tried to the first time we went out. So if I couldn't get to your heart through your head, I was going to go through your stomach. You told me how the English love their fish and chips!"

"You're amazing. There's nothing I'd like more – and I've got the kettle on for a cup of tea."

*   *   *

She warmed up the takeout in the microwave while he poured the tea. He noticed the gift box on the table and put it in his pocket for later. They talked about her trip, renewing the closeness of two nights before, as if the unpleasantness had never happened.

"We heard some bad news on the radio coming down. Hannah's 500 miles off the Virginia Capes, making a beeline for us. If she doesn't spin off to the east overnight, they'll have to issue evacuation warnings from Sandy Hook to Cape Cod."

"What happens then?"

"Everybody gets out, dummy."

He frowned and felt a rush of anxiety.

"It's only voluntary, right? The animals have to be cared for. Well, the sheep and fowl will be OK, but the cows need milking or they'll get mastitis. It's a painful inflammation of the udder that can make them very sick. They'll have to be inside, so they'll need to be fed, and calmed down if they get scared, or they'll injure themselves."

Now she looked alarmed, too.

"If the warning changes to an order, it's mandatory. The police come around and tell you to leave. I don't think they forcibly remove you if you won't go, but you have to sign a disclaimer and pay the cost of being rescued, if it comes to that. They close the roads and shut off the power. You'd have to be insane to stay. I won't let you."

She smiled and patted his hand.

"No sense in worrying tonight. Hannah's three days away. Maybe she'll be far out to sea by morning."

"You're right. Joe Stanton's due to call tomorrow. He'll know what to do."

They cleared the table and went on the veranda to watch the last of the sunset. She stretched out on the loveseat with her head in his lap, where he could stroke her hair. He leaned over and brushed his lips against hers, until she turned it into a French kiss of swirling tongues. With his free hand, he pushed the near strap of her blue bra-top dress over her shoulder and reached under the smocked bodice to cup her breast, which he gently kneaded. The large nipple hardened at his touch and she began to moan softly, her chest rising and falling, pushing more of the yielding flesh into his palm. She broke off the kiss and looked up at him.

"Don't stop, but I have to move my head. There's something in your pocket that feels like a rock."

He laughed and reluctantly removed his hand to pull out the box, which he placed in the top of her cleavage. She peered down at it.

"Why are you laughing? What is it?"

"I missed you so much that I wanted to get you something. So this morning I went to Galapagos and found this."

She unwrapped it on her chest, then opened the lid and sighed.

"It is a rock – little rocks! Are they sapphires and diamonds? It's beautiful."

"It's an eternity band – a token of my love for you. I hope it fits. I had to guess the size."

NIANTIC JEWEL

She put it on and raised her hand to display it.

"It fits fine. You took into account my chubby fingers. It's gorgeous. Wait till I show Mother! I'm speechless with joy... Thank-you."

She circled his neck with her arms and pulled herself up to kiss him.

"I'll love you for all eternity."

CHAPTER 11

HURRICANE HANNAH

God moves in a mysterious way
His wonders to perform;
He plants his footsteps in the sea,
And rides upon the storm.
WILLIAM COWPER

A southerly breeze was slowly pushing the mist off the pond when Colin let the cows back into the pasture at 8 a.m. Wispy cirrus clouds told him that Hannah was taking her time moving up the Atlantic Seaboard. He took a deep breath of the cool morning air. It would be another glorious day, another idyllic afternoon at the beach with Juliana, another romantic night out with her.

Over breakfast, he watched The Weather Channel, Hannah had indeed turned northeast, but traveling at only 15 mph, and as long as she hung around there was the chance she could spin back west. With winds of 90 mph, she was a Category 1 hurricane – for the time being. The warm moisture she was picking up from the ocean, where surface temperatures were over 70 degrees, meant she could strengthen quickly into a Category 2 with winds up to 110 mph. Then this gigantic spinning top would become entirely unpredictable, raising fears that Hannah could suddenly make a fast break west toward Long Island and southern New England. As a precaution, the National Weather Service advised people to evacuate those coastal areas.

NIANTIC JEWEL

He felt uneasy, and called the Palmers' to see what they were thinking. Ben Palmer answered the phone.

"Good morning Colin. I hear you had quite a day yesterday. I wish I'd been at the beach to see it. How are you feeling?"

"I'm the luckiest chap alive. It was like being on Death Row and getting a reprieve... I was calling to see what you thought of the evacuation advisory. Will you be leaving?"

"Alise is going late this afternoon. She has a premonition of impending doom. I told her Hannah's 600 miles out to sea, but she won't listen. It's an emotional thing. Juliana and I want to wait awhile, but I'm keeping The Weather Channel on. The surf should be spectacular tomorrow. There's nothing like witnessing Nature's power to make you appreciate life – as long as you're at a safe distance. I bet Alise a dinner at Shelter Harbor that nothing's going to happen. She can spring for it since we're going to have to fend for ourselves without her... Juliana's over at Juanita's, but I'll tell her you called. Any message?"

"Just that I'll see her at the beach."

He felt a growing anxiety as he went about his chores. He had a healthy respect for Alise Palmer's prescience. Yet maybe she was just being prudent, probably along with many others. If her intuition were infallible, surely her husband would be taking her qualms more seriously.

While he waited for Joe Stanton's call, he checked the lobster boat's mooring lines and scouted around for loose objects that a gale could hurl through windows – buckets, rakes, trash barrels. When the call came, he was relieved that the old man was on top of the situation and shared Ben Palmer's Yankee equanimity.

As a boy of 6, he had narrowly survived the '38 hurricane, but the trauma affected him for years. GH38 had struck without warning around 4:30 p.m., Wednesday, Sept. 21. Sheltered in the farmhouse from the fury of the wind and rain, Joe, his parents and two younger siblings watched the pond rise up the slope of the pasture. When the surging water entered the house, they retreated to the second floor, where they huddled terrified as the windows were blown in. His most vivid recollection was the pressure inside his head and the ear-splitting, inescapable roar, which gave him nightmares for years.

The family emerged unscathed, and for the solid old house in its carefully chosen location it was just another hurricane. The farm was devastated – livestock killed, the barn and sheds wrecked, all vegetation destroyed by salt, trees uprooted, the heartbreaking mess – but his parents' sweat and toil brought it back.

Colin tried to interrupt the reminiscence, anxious to know what he should do, but there was no stopping the flood of memories:

"... The nightmares stopped after I got used to the close calls when nothing happened. Then came Carol in '54. By that time, they had better forecasting, so there was an evacuation. Thank God, because that was the worst since '38. A lot of oceanfront cottages, even small wooden hotels, were swept away. We didn't leave though, and never have.

"In those days, there was a big storm once a decade. Now it's twice – and the population's skyrocketed: city folk and their summer homes with an ocean view. It's only a matter of time until the next big one. With all the bells and whistles they've got to track hurricanes nowadays – satellites, planes and what have you – they can get everybody out, but there won't be much left on the oceanfront to come back to.

"Trouble is, the bureaucrats have to cover their backsides, don't they? So they'll issue evacuation orders just to be on the safe side. The last time was Hurricane Bob in '91. Apart from a bit of flooding on Surfside Avenue, it didn't amount to a hill of beans here. That was when they closed the roads and I had to get a pass to cross the police line....

"I've got a hunch that's what they'll do with this one, whether it comes any closer or not. They've never had a drill to see if they can get people out. If I were you, I'd stop by the police station and get your pass early. Don't wait until they make it official, or you'll be standing in line. They can call me if there's a problem. I've known the chief all his life. His name's Brad Kenyon."

A rush of anxiety swept over Colin. The old man was leaving him no room to back out. He felt the familiar tug of the flight response, then overcame it by seeking reassurance.

NIANTIC JEWEL

"You're sure nothing bad can happen then – if the worst comes to the worst?"

"Hell no! If you weren't a farmer, I'd tell you to go. But you know the animals need someone there. Even at worst, there shouldn't be much of a mess. The last storm took down the deadwood and tested the generator. The house is 18 feet above the pond. It would take a Category 5 for a storm surge to reach it. You've battened down everything...."

"The only other things I'd do, if Hannah does decide to turn nasty, is hitch up the tractor and trailer, and haul the lobster pots to the shed. Then, on a high tide, tow the Old Queen off her slip and halfway to the big boulder in the pasture – the one the cows use as a rubbing rock. Run a bow line to it and a stern line to a dock piling. Allow some play in the loops so she can ride up with the water. That'll keep her out of trouble in a Southeast wind. Forget the anchor: It could do more harm than good... The window shutters actually close, not like the fake ones nowadays. But don't bother with them unless there's a gale... You'll be a lot safer where you are than on the roads with damned fools rushing to get out."

*   *   *

Colin recounted the conversation to Alise Palmer at the beach a few hours later. They sat together, sharing an umbrella, while Juliana and Juanita sunbathed in front of them. The water was full of children riding their rings and boards off the big lazy rollers that thumped ashore with cascades of foaming white water. Alise Palmer yawned and stretched her slender arms as Colin finished his story.

"It's easy for old Joe to give advice from New Hampshire. I understand about the animals and that you have nowhere else to go. But I can't see putting yourself in harm's way for them. Come with me to Wellesley and spend the night. Then Juliana would come too. Just until the coast is clear – no pun intended... Look at how the surf's picked up since yesterday. Ben needs his head examined if you ask me. I'm really worried, Colin."

"Is it a sense of foreboding?"

She gave a scornful laugh.

"Heavens no! Don't listen to Ben's nonsense. I don't have precognition. I'm not clairvoyant! There's an evacuation advisory. I'm not the only one with common sense. Juanita's parents are leaving in the morning, and they just got here yesterday. Ben can stay and watch the surf if he wants. He'll leave if the forecast changes. Hopefully, he won't be caught up in a mass exodus… He's a hurricane buff, but not foolhardy. Forgive me, but you, on the other hand, don't know what you could be getting into."

"You have a good point. I'm trusting that Joe knows what he's talking about when he says the house is safe. I don't think I can back out now though. He's likely to drive down, and if anything happened to him I'd never forgive myself… Oh well, maybe it'll all blow over."

Juliana lifted her head and grimaced.

"Did I hear that right? You're making puns as bad as Mother's now. It's contagious you know."

*　　　*　　　*

Ben Palmer was sipping a martini on the patio and listening to his weather radio when Colin arrived at 7:30 to take Juliana to dinner at the Wilcox Tavern.

"High surf tomorrow. Hannah's stalled 300 miles north of Bermuda; winds of 98 mph. This one's an enigma: so far north without a definite track. She could do anything, or nothing. Thank God for technology. She's far enough out that we'll get ample warning if she moves this way – assuming she doesn't come at us at 60 mph like GH38: 700 miles from Cape Hatteras to New Hampshire in 12 hours.

"That one was 500 miles wide at landfall with an eye diameter of 43 miles and dumped 6 inches of rain. Block Island had sustained winds of 82 mph; 121 at the Blue Hill Observatory outside Boston, with gusts of 186. There were 50-foot waves. Katrina in '05 pushed a 28-foot mound of water onto the Gulf Coast; Camille's storm surge in '69 was 22 feet."

NIANTIC JEWEL

Colin checked the sky, which had begun to cloud over from the Southeast.

"Hannah's sending her cirrostratus heralds to warn us she may drop by. We won't know if she plans on coming until the dark altostratus show up. She'll still be hundreds of miles away then, and could change her mind. Not until really dark stratocumulus or nimbostratus appear will we know she's only hours away. That's when the rain starts and the wind picks up."

Ben Palmer chuckled.

"That's not bad for a farmer's forecast, but I'd rather have real-time data I can depend on – and early."

Juliana stroked her father's hand.

"He means satellites and sensors – and telecom equipment his company can provide, for a price."

"You'd better believe it. There was no warning in '38. It wasn't until months later that they pieced together what happened. Information technology would have saved hundreds of lives. And that's only part of the electronic equipment we have now. Better tools mean better science. There's still a lot of guesswork to meteorology, but we're getting there.

"The days of crews risking their lives in hurricane hunter planes are numbered. Now there are robotic aircraft that fly at 1200 feet to monitor winds and the flow of heat and moisture. Weather satellites show cloud tops. Infrared sensors chart the warm eye. Radar and microwave sensors map rain. Dropsondes on parachutes feed temperature, pressure. humidity and wind data into computer models...."

*   *   *

There were whitecaps and mist on the pond when Colin's internal alarm clock woke him at 6:15 a.m. Saturday. Below the open window, eerie specters began emerging from the ground fog as the cows glided silently to the pasture gate. He had a busy morning ahead of him before leaving for Boston at 11, and wanted to get an early start. Rolling over in bed, he watched the sun rise with a coppery halo and heard the surf pounding beyond the dunes. The sweet scent of virgin's bower drifting through the open window cleared his head. His senses registered the stillness and humidity of the warm air. It would be another marvelous day.

By midmorning, he had worked up a sweat loading 18 lobster traps onto the trailer and stacking them in the shed. The Old Queen looked bizarre sitting in the pasture, where he'd been instructed to haul her with the antique Allis Chalmers tractor. Long ago, in the '50s, her dowdy pale pink had been a sleek cherry red, but she could still handle the light tasks of semiretirement and was as much fun to drive as the Jag. Still, making preparations for a storm seemed like a waste of time.

The sun had burned off the morning haze revealing a brilliant blue sky with swelling cumulus clouds as he drove to the police station on Route 1A to see about getting a pass. It was an improvement over the cover of cirrostratus from the previous evening despite signaling that unstable air remained in the upper atmosphere.

Brad Kenyon was standing next to a large-scale wall map of the town when Colin was shown into his office. The balding, mildly overweight police chief looked up from the clipboard he was holding and came over to shake hands as Colin introduced himself over the crackle of the police radio. A friendly smile came with the penetrating eye contact of a shrewd judge of character.

"So you're the green Jaguar at the farm. How's it going? We all miss Joe – last of the Quonnie old-timers. What do you hear from him?"

Colin filled him in and explained his reason for coming. The chief listened with pursed lips and nodded. Peeling a 4-by-6 orange card from a block on his desk, he stamped and signed it, then slid it into a plastic sleeve.

"Here you go. Let's hope you don't need it, but we're ready for anything. If there's a mandatory evacuation, everyone'll be notified by the Reverse 911 system. We'll be going to every house on the shore; some folks'll need help getting out. After that, the roads will be closed and power and water shut off. There'll be a cruiser at the end of Sunset Beach Road. If that floods, you'll be cut off, and cellphones don't work in hurricanes. No offense, but

NIANTIC JEWEL

I'm glad it's you sticking your neck out rather than old Joe: one less worry... Good luck, and give Joe my best."

Dark thoughts enveloped Colin on the way to work. Hearing the police chief talk about disaster plans had unnerved him. What had he gotten himself into? He felt trapped, not in control anymore; he wanted to get away from it all.

At the Rhode Island Veterans Cemetery on Route 2, a state police cruiser waited at the exit. Colin took his foot off the gas and watched in despair while the needle crept down to the 45 mph speed limit. Let it be a routine patrol, not a radar trap, he prayed to himself. In the rearview mirror, he saw the cruiser turn south. He sighed with relief that he hadn't shown brake lights to attract attention. Reflexively, he programmed a Mozart CD, knowing it's impossible to feel despondent with Mozart playing.

Soon after 6, he was editing a silly season story about a rare blue lobster caught off Cape Ann when slotman Lloyd Forbes slapped his hand on the copy desk and pointed to the bank of TV monitors overhead.

"Look at that! Hannah's moving out at last – drifting East at 10 mph. My vacation's saved, and you'll be off the hook, Colin. Come Monday, we'll be on the beach with our honeys. I'll finally get to meet Juliana."

Try as he might, Colin failed to come up with a fresh headline for the summer chestnut he'd been saddled with. At least it hadn't run since last year, he rationalized. Maybe the blue lobster was a rite of summer; no August would be complete without "Lobster has the blues."

*   *   *

Heartened by the weather news, he was in good spirits when he arrived at the Palmers at 9:45. Juliana came out as he drove up and got in the car the moment it stopped. She gave him an eager, probing kiss.

"I missed you so much."

Before he could answer, she leaned back against the door and threw her arms apart to show off her sheer lime dress.

"It's new. What do you think?"

His eyes traveled up from the handkerchief hem to the surplice neckline.

"You look devastating. It's very becoming – mostly because of what's inside."

She looked down at her cleavage.

"It's not too much is it? Daddy bought it for me this afternoon. We went to Watch Hill while it wasn't so crowded. Of course, I had to visit J.C.'s. He would have preferred something more... demure. But I told him everything at J.C.'s is in good taste. Well it's true!"

Colin put an arm around her shoulder and playfully lowered his head.

"May I have a taste?"

Impetuously, she pressed his face into her bosom. He inhaled her fragrance, then kissed the warm luxuriant flesh, working his way up her neck to the tumescent lips and a long embrace. She sighed contentedly and sank back in her seat.

"That was very tasteful... You should have seen the surf this morning. It was big. The ocean was foaming. You could feel the shock waves when the rollers snapped on the beach. The pounding hurt my ears after awhile. A bunch of teenage guys were surfing. Daddy was like a little boy. He was so happy. He always wants to buy us things when he's happy. Then when I was making him dinner, we heard about Hannah. That made his day."

*   *   *

After his farm work Sunday morning, Colin went over to the Palmers' for brunch. Juliana and her father were at the breakfast bar, he with a New York Times and she with a Gazette, when he let himself in.

He marveled at how vibrant she looked in the sparkling morning light. Everything about her seemed to shimmer: her fiery hair, the bright yellow tank top, the dazzling white shorts. She offered a cheek, which he nuzzled longingly until her father

NIANTIC JEWEL

frowned and, putting down his Bloody Mary, rapped on the stool beside him.

"Pour yourself some coffee Colin. Then I want you here, next to me... You're right on time as usual. Just as well, or there'd be nothing left. Juliana's blueberry pancakes go fast. I picked up the berries at Hoxsie's while I was getting the papers at Michael's. You can't get any fresher than that, but what she does with them is culinary magic...."

He paused to rub his stomach.

"I'm blessed – or cursed – with two gourmet chefs. As you can tell... I must warn you though: She's high maintenance, and I should know. Thugs want your money or your life, but women demand both. You saw what she shook me down for yesterday. And you're partly responsible. I don't think she got it to wear for me."

Juliana looked over from the stove.

"I'm going to tell Mother you called us thugs. And you can't blame us for your business lunches. Everything we cook for you is low-calorie – because we love you."

Colin cleared his throat as she handed him a plate of pancakes.

"Thank-you.... er, in all fairness Ms. Palmer, your dad didn't say women are thugs; he alluded to them as being worse than thugs."

She swatted him with a potholder just as his cellphone vibrated in his pocket. He recoiled in surprise, then felt foolish when she started giggling:

"I'm sorry. You looked just like the Cowardly Lion the way you jumped. Serves you right, Mr. Smarty-pants."

He reached for his phone to check the caller ID.

"It's work. I'd better take it."

When he'd finished, Ben Palmer grimaced.

"That didn't sound good. What's up?"

"They're having early deadlines. Hannah's gone berserk. She could be here by midnight. The Gazette's in winter storm mode: an earlier press run with fewer editions so the delivery trucks have more time to get through the wind and rain, flooded roads.

Everything's two hours ahead. I'll have to leave at 3, and milk the cows early. They won't like having their routine changed."

Ben Palmer shook his head in frustration.

"Goddamit! Turn on The Weather Channel will you Jewel? Better yet, I'd rather hear this from my honey on Channel 7… and get me another Bloody Mary."

She reached for the remote on the counter behind her and brought to life the 65-inch Sharp Aquos on the rear wall. Meteorologist Bonnie Breyer was pointing to swirling bands of red, yellow and green:

"You can see in these Doppler radar images from the past 24 hours how the phenomenon we call eyewall replacement caused Hannah to change direction. A second wall forms around the eye; the inner wall collapses and the storm weakens; the outer wall contracts and replaces it, strengthening the storm again. We saw this with Rita in 2005, but not the directional change.

"In Hannah's case, the weakening halted her northerly progress when she came up against the Bermuda High, leaving her to drift East along its boundary. The strengthening changed all that. It's given her the impetus to drive for the low-pressure trough moving north along the East Coast.

"Don't ask me how she knows it's there or why she's drawn to it. The laws of magnetism say opposites attract and equivalents repel, but not in this case it would seem. The answer probably lies in the upper atmosphere. Conditions there determine a storm's path, and we have little data about the upper atmosphere far at sea. Predictions are difficult because when areas of high and low pressure move, their influence on a storm's track changes too."

"As of now, Hannah is a Category 3 hurricane with winds of 117 mph. She's moving West-northwest, picking up speed as she goes. Landfall is predicted overnight between the Jersey Shore and Cape Cod. If you're in those coastal areas, you should leave as soon as possible. Mandatory evacuation orders are in effect. This is a very dangerous storm. The eye, where the most destructive winds are located, is 30 miles in diameter,

"A lot can happen in a short time, so stay tuned for updates. Hannah's still 500 miles out to sea – 18 hours away at her current

NIANTIC JEWEL

speed of 29 mph. That's exceptionally high. Hurricanes usually travel at 10-13 mph. So let's hope she slows down and comes ashore in daylight. But if her directional velocity continues to increase, that would be good news and bad: good because faster-moving storms produce less rain; bad because there's less time to evacuate...."

Ben Palmer waved his hand dismissively at the screen.

"She's forgetting GH38 at 60 mph and an eye 50 miles wide... You can turn it off now Jewel. She's ruined my breakfast. I should have known something was up when those gulls and gannets came flying over. The seabirds are getting out of the way. Damnit! Alise was right all along. That's what irks me most, plus Colin will be here to see it and I won't."

Juliana gave him a piercing look.

"How can you say that, Daddy? It's a Category 3 and could get worse. The situation's changed. Colin didn't sign on for this."

She reached over and took his hand.

"It's not quitting to abandon an idea that's become insane. After you get out of work, you'll spend the night with us in Wellesley. Promise me."

Caught off guard, he took a sip of coffee to buy time.

"I'm confused... How can this happen? And what's this Bermuda High that was supposed to prevent it?"

Ben Palmer nodded knowingly.

"It's a cool, high-pressure area that forms over the Atlantic in hurricane season. Warm, low-pressure cyclones move westward along its southern edge until they meet warm air coming off the continental landmass. That turns the storms to the Northeast before they hit land. This year, the Bermuda High is farther West than normal, forcing storms to travel West longer and make landfall before turning Northeast. That's what gave us last month's storm. What's different here is the eyewall replacement....

"But Jewel's right. I was joking. A hurricane is a screaming demon. Even a Category 1 releases more energy every hour than an atom bomb. Stay with us. You don't want to be here the way things look. After I tape the picture windows, we're gone."

Colin thanked him for the offer and turned to Juliana.

"I'm having second thoughts. I don't think Joe had this in mind. If the cows panic and injure themselves, it's going to happen whether I'm here or not. But I won't get out of work until 12. I can't keep you all up way past midnight. They'll have cots set up at the Gazette, or I can stay with Moira or Lloyd on Savin Hill. Unless there's a drastic change for the better, though, I'll stay in Boston. Anyway, we'll be talking. How's that?"

She laughed and shook her head.

"Better, but not good enough. I don't trust you! The roads in Boston will still be fine at midnight. It'll take you 20 minute to drive to Wellesley, and I'll be the only one up. If you're not right there with me, I won't be able to sleep. You're coming!"

As if to seal the matter, she leaned over to peck his cheek, lingering just long enough as her lips brushed by his ear to murmur "You won't regret it."

*   *   *

Tension was high when Colin walked into the Gazette newsroom at 4 p.m. Instead of the bare-bones crew for a lazy Sunday afternoon in August, bodies moved in all directions, whipping up a buzz of excitement and anticipation. What should have been a quiet refuge from the din of Expressway traffic was a babble of overlapping conversations. Reporters awaiting their storm assignments gathered under the TV monitors near the copy desk, forcing him to make a detour to reach his chair.

Within minutes he caught the fever of being part of a Big Story; the rush of adrenaline that news junkies live for; the thrill of feeling Significance pass through them as they processed the facts of a major event into information for the masses. In doing so, a quantum of its energy adhered to them, bestowing a brief glow of validation and self-importance.

A collective gasp from the rubber-neckers followed by a brief, stunned silence brought him down from the high. Hannah had accelerated to 40 mph and would make landfall around midnight.

NIANTIC JEWEL

He reached for his cellphone to call Juliana. There was apprehension in her voice.

"We took the Route 2 evacuation route just as the police said to when they came by the house. But we hadn't gone far when the traffic backed up. There must have been an accident with injuries because emergency vehicles were trying to get through. No one was going anywhere. Cars were turning around, and the road's so narrow they made things worse. So Daddy took a side road and we came back. He wants to wait until 6 and this time take 216 to 95. We called Mother. She's worried, of course. Daddy told her no one will be using 216 except the few who live on it, which makes sense: It's not an evacuation route."

"Now I'm worried, too. Promise you'll call when you're on 95."

"That's what Mother said. We'll be fine, honestly. Actually, it was good that we came back. The Merc only had a half tank of gas. We could've run out in the traffic jam, or before we got home. So we filled up at Michael's. By the time we left, there was a line of cars behind us. Then it began to rain and the sky had an eerie light to it. Kind of creepy. That's when I started to feel uneasy, when it hit me that something's really going to happen. Now it's getting darker and there are gusts of wind."

"It's alright. The strange light was Altostratus translucidus, not anything supernatural. You saw the first of Hannah's outer bands moving in, so the sun looks as if it's shining through frosted glass. I bet your dad liked that... I wish I were with you and could hold you close."

"Me too, but tonight we'll hold each other very close. I'm incomplete without you. I won't feel whole until we're together again... Daddy's giving disapproving looks. I'd better go. Did I tell you that I love you?"

"I love you, too. Now I'm getting disapproving looks. I'll just have to show you how much when I see you."

*   *   *

Groping for headlines that came grudgingly to his agitated mind, he lost track of time until the chime of his cellphone jarred him back into his surroundings. His stomach grabbed when he saw the time on his screen was 8 p.m. not 6 and heard not Juliana's voice but her mother's asking if he'd talked to her. She hadn't heard from them and couldn't reach them. The cellular network was down – swamped with calls in and out of the shore area. Texting brought no response.

His brain raced for an explanation to allay the unspoken fears building in both of them. It had to be the storm. Radio waves are weaker at sea level even in good weather; reception was always weak at Quonnie, far from a cell tower. She'd hear from them once they got beyond the overloaded towers. They'd show up any minute. There'd be some innocuous reason; then they'd both feel foolish. She seemed to buy it.

"You're probably right. I'm sitting here with a bottle of wine, getting morose instead of merry. My excuse is, if I don't finish it I'll never get the cork out again. It's plastic, and I must have pulled a stomach muscle getting it out the first time. The pain was excruciating, but the alcohol's helping. When the bottle's empty, I won't feel a thing!"

They agreed to keep their phones free and call when there was news.

As the night wore on, he found himself fighting off dark fears that welled up intermittently. He dismissed them as irrational and tried to focus on his work, but they lay squirming in his subconscious, gnawing at his composure. Breaking his word to stay off the phone, he called Juliana: No signal, no respite from the gloom.

Then the flurry of editorial activity ceased. The first edition was put to bed with time to spare, thanks to the extra hands on a thin Monday paper. Word filtered down from the managing editor: Early call-ins could go at 11. The first flush of relief gave way to high anxiety. Unfettered by toil, his mind was free to comprehend that what had been unthinkable at 8 was now an increasing possibility. He called Alise Palmer. Her calm hello cheered him, momentarily.

"No, I've heard nothing. It's unbelievable down there. I got through to the Rhode Island State Police. They're getting

NIANTIC JEWEL

hundreds of calls from people like me. There's no phone service to the shore. Eight-mile traffic jams coming from it. They said people are giving up and going to emergency shelters, and that's where Ben and Juliana will be. The police have radio contact everywhere. There've been no fatalities, just lots of minor accidents. They told me to sit tight and I'd hear from Ben in the morning. I'm beside myself. I don't know what to do...."

As he listened in dismay, his gaze was fixed on the overhead monitors with their radar maps. The snatches of commentary he half-heard said Hannah's eye would pass over central Long Island soon after midnight – providentially at low tide. She'd lost some punch over the past 4 hours and was now a Category 2 with winds of 98 mph. He knew the improvement didn't warrant the leap of faith he was about to make, but the words spilled out anyway:

"I'm going down. Things aren't as bad as they were. I feel so helpless up here. If they're back at the house. I can drive out again and get word to you. Then there are the cows I promised to watch... I don't want to leave you alone. You've been so good about putting me up, but I have to go. I hope you can understand."

"I really can't. It's a bad idea, Colin. The wind's howling outside, the rain's beating against the windows. And you're going to drive into a hurricane in a sports car?"

"Nothing handles better in wind and rain. It's the aerodynamics. There'll be no traffic. I'll just have to watch out for flooding, and I'll be there before that happens."

*   *   *

It wasn't the screaming blasts of wind buffeting the Jag on I95 that unnerved him, or the sheets of rain he strained to see through, or the pounding of both that made the cabin boom and vibrate like a kettledrum. It was when he got into the pitch-black woods on Route 216, when twigs and leaves started hitting the car, when the explosive cracks and eerie groans of splintering timber made him clench. Then he was sure he was driving straight into hell.

Now and again, he hit a low-lying pocket of calm where the high-pitched roar became the sound of a wailing woman. Without wind resistance in the valleys, the Jag lurched forward, only to be pushed back when it climbed to higher, exposed ground. Within the converging beams of his headlights was a maelstrom of onrushing water and flying vegetation that splatted and pinged against the hood and windshield. The fury made his brain throb until he thought it would burst through his skull. He couldn't tell whether he felt sick or high, but lurking behind the confused sensations was the unmistakable tug of hysteria.

The thud from a chunk of debris hitting the undercarriage cleared his mind. Down the hill he could see the dim haze of streetlights along Route 1 and the blinking orange traffic signal at the intersection with 216. A warm surge of relief coursed through him. He'd make it after all. In a few minutes he'd be at the Palmers'. He imagined Juliana being there to hug him.

NIANTIC JEWEL

CHAPTER 12

BLOOD BROTHER

Strangle my heart, and my brain will still throb;
and should you set fire to my brain,
I still can carry you with my blood.
RAINER MARIA RILKE

All was quiet now. The familiarity of the picture on the wall finally registered. He'd been staring at it vacantly to avoid looking at the IV in his right arm. Whoever selected a print of John Singer Sargent's "The Daughters of Edward Darley Boit" for a Trauma Center room must have a quirky sense of humor, he thought.

The four girls in white pinafores looked like little nurses, and much of the picture was a dark void. In these surroundings, the scene of sweet domesticity also seemed to carry a subliminal contradictory message that didn't inspire confidence in a patient. Then he realized it gave him something to think about: whether to feel calmed or disquieted.

He chose to be amused, and was grinning inanely when two doctors emerged from the curtain dividing the room. The younger one, a soft-spoken resident, had interrogated him about his medical history before the procedure, but he hadn't noticed the shorter man with the dignified bearing of a chief in the comings and goings to the bed behind the curtain. Now they came up to him. The resident smiled and squeezed his hand.

"It's nice to see you in such good spirits Mr. Grosvenor – after all you've been through. This is Dr. Lindsey. Will you share with him how you got here? It's quite a story."

Colin made contact with the kindly eyes and repeated the condensed version he'd given earlier.

"I was on my way home to the farm at Quonochontaug… to sit with the cows during the hurricane. While I was showing my pass at the roadblock, a call came over the police radio about a life or death situation at Westerly Hospital: An 0- blood donor was needed stat. I told the officer I fit the bill, and he led me down here in 10 minutes flat. It seemed as if the wind blew me here."

The older man nodded, betraying no emotion.

"Another half-hour and it probably would have been too late. You're a godsend Mr. Grosvenor. Every blood donation potentially saves a life, but that's really the case tonight. There's every reason to think so, anyway. Our patient over there is in good shape and should make a full recovery. I'm sorry we had to relieve you of so much blood – a little over two units. We could have used more, but one patient in hemhorrhagic shock is enough for one night. The lightheadedness will pass after we finish filling you back up with plasma. Rest here for 45 minutes, then you're free to go home… to your cows. Take it easy for the rest of the day. Make sure you eat well. Fair enough?"

"No problem. But what happened?"

"Car accident. There've been so many injuries tonight that we ran low on some types of blood. More was coming from New London until the van drove into a pileup on I95. The police brought the blood eventually. Meanwhile, our patient was sinking fast and couldn't have hung on that long. There's a limit to what blood expanders and hemostatic agents can do. We rounded up the two O- people on duty, but it wasn't enough to halt the deterioration. There'd been too much exsanguination. So we threw a Hail Mary, and you answered our prayer. You put us over the top… Remember, no heavy lifting for awhile."

He nodded and they left when a perky nurse came over to remove his IV. Now he was fully alert, and curious.

"How does someone lose so much blood? What was the injury?"

"Many reasons. This was a ruptured spleen – massive internal bleeding and a lot more during surgery, including all the O- we

NIANTIC JEWEL

had. Luckily, one of the cars was driven by a vet. He knew there were internal injuries when she collapsed and lost consciousness. It happened close by. Even so, if he hadn't rushed her in... Just a few more minutes and it would have been all over. She'd lost five units. Then you arrived – in the nick of time again... Talk about guardian angels...."

The awful feeling at the word 'she' made his head reel. He gasped for air and tried to sound matter-of-fact even as he heard his voice break.

"Was this near Route 216, up in Quonochontaug?"

"No, no. It was right outside the veterinary clinic farther South on Route 1. Dr. Babcock was called out on an emergency – to sedate a frightened horse at the riding stable. It sensed the hurricane coming and went berserk. Animals can tell... Anyway, it was raining pretty hard and he didn't see the other car coming. He hit the passenger door and the impact pushed her into that thing in the middle...."

"The center console?"

"I guess so. It looked as if everyone was OK thanks to the seatbelts and airbags – not even a scratch. Dr. Babcock was walking her back to his clinic when she dropped."

Relief that it wasn't Juliana mixed with renewed anxiety as he thought of the Palmers, and the cows. It was 3 a.m. and he'd done nothing about either reason for coming down.

He was supposed to rest for another 20 minutes, but the next nurse to pass his bed merely gave a hurried thumbs-up when he announced he was leaving.

The exit signs led him into the Emergency Room's waiting area, where a handful of people sat around looking glum. A couple read magazines while others stared at the walls and floor. This is limbo, he thought: They don't know if they'll be going home thankfully with those they brought in, or despondently alone. One by one, they glanced as he passed, until, deciding he was of no significance, they resumed their vigil. Except for the man bent forward with his head in his hands. It was his size that made Colin do a double take as he went by.

Graham Griffith

The automatic doors slid open and the night air felt good. Hannah was gone, leaving a tangy breeze in her wake. He was glad to be outside again, free from the murmurs of claustrophobia that hospitals induced in him. There was the Jag, splattered with leaves. He stopped to reach for his keys and found himself peering back through the glass doors. From this angle, there was no doubt. A lump formed in his throat. He ran back inside and up to the big man.

"Mr. Palmer?"

The large head jerked up.

"Colin!... How did you find out?...."

"Find out what? Is Juliana with you?"

He perched on the next chair and leaned in close to the tired eyes.

"She's in bad shape, Colin. It's touch and go. Internal bleeding. They operated but didn't have enough of her blood type. Goddamn hurricane. They're doing everything they can. Last I heard, they'd found another donor, but maybe not in time. She might not be able to rally. I'm waiting to hear. God, let her live!"

A tear ran down his cheek. Colin took his hand and felt his own eyes welling with an overload of emotion.

"She's pulled through! I was in her room 5 minutes ago and that's what they said...."

Before he could further explain to the dazed father, a voice interrupted him:

"Mr. Palmer, I've some good news for you at last: I think we can say your daughter's going to be fine. And we were able to save her spleen. She's a very strong young woman! She's awake – although sedated. You can see her for a couple of minutes before we move her to a private room. I'll take you to her."

Dr. Lindsey's face remained expressionless as he recognized Colin.

"Mr. Grosvenor! How did you...?"

"It's not important... I'll wait here."

Ben Palmer got to his feet unsteadily, then turned to Colin:

"I'd like you to come with me. Seeing you will do her a world of good."

NIANTIC JEWEL

They followed the doctor into the Emergency Room, where he stopped at the desk and picked up a red folder.

"Mr. Grosvenor. You know your way from here don't you? I like to give out the good news myself, but I have another surgery. It's a busy night. So if you'll excuse me, could you take Mr. Palmer the rest of the way?"

Hurriedly shaking hands with Ben Palmer, he turned his attention to the folder while he spoke:

"Dr. Moore is with your daughter. He'll be glad to update you. Goodnight sir."

Colin ushered a speechless Ben Palmer away and recounted the night's events as they walked down the corridor to the Trauma Center. He finished as fast as he could because there was something he didn't understand.

"So you didn't take 216 after all?"

"No. There were strong gusts when we left at 6:30. We couldn't get onto 216. It was blocked. A panel truck blew over making the turn and they had equipment there trying to right it. Then I thought we'd head toward Westerly and take the Route 78 bypass to I95. Nearly made it too, until the vet's Range Rover hit us... I can't think about it... And you're the donor. I can't get over it...."

Dr. Moore, the young resident, was leaving the room as they approached. He shook his head in wonder at Colin's story and led them back in. It was darker now with the lights lowered, the mood tranquil instead of tense. The daughters of Edward Darley Boit smiled down in their nurses' uniforms. Behind the curtain, Juliana lay dozing beside a bank of monitoring units and IV packs, whose wires and tubes snaked to her exposed right arm and under the white johnny. The cannula of an oxygen line lay snaked from her nose. Her ashen face made the red hair glow in the subdued light.

The doctor touched her hand and motioned them to the other side of the bed.

"Miss Palmer, you have visitors – but only for a minute or two."

Her eyes opened slowly, followed by a weak smile. Ben Palmer kissed her cheek.

"Everything's going to be alright now, Jewel. You look ten times better than the last time I saw you. How are you feeling?"

"I've felt better... I'm OK! I don't remember anything, but they told me what happened – after I passed out. I'm kind of groggy. Am I dreaming? Is that Colin with you?"

Her father stepped aside to make room.

"Yes, Sweetheart. Colin is here. He came looking for us... and gave blood for you."

It was only a peck on the cheek, but the contact with her skin sent a jolt through him. He heard his voice breaking again.

"I'm so happy you're back with us...."

She pulled her left hand out from under the sheet and pressed it against his face. Her eyes brightened.

"... I wasn't going anywhere, without you... But how did you get here? You're supposed to be in Wellesley, remember?"

As he finished explaining, a roguish thought crossed his mind:

"I should have known it was you behind the curtain when they said the patient was in good shape."

Now the broad smile returned. She drew his face close to hers and kissed him briefly on the lips.

"My Sir Galahad... And you know what? I think it's time you called me Jewel."

The doctor checked her pulse and cleared his throat.

"That's probably enough for now."

*   *   *

It was while Ben Palmer was talking to his wife at last, just as they drove by the buckled sign to Route 1A/Watch Hill, that the chill ran down his spine: Could Juliana's spleen have ruptured just as her mother got the pain in her side opening the wine? He smiled to himself and eavesdropped, wondering if she'd pick up on it.

"... No, I'm just fine I tell you. I'm going back to the farm with Colin. It has a generator... They told us we can see Jewel again after noon... It's still too dark to see what the damage is like. I'll call you after I've checked the house. If there are no lines down on the main road, they'll be able to turn the power back on. We just

NIANTIC JEWEL

don't know yet… I want you here, too. We'll manage somehow… Yes, the Merc will have to be towed… I will. Love you too."

He put the cellphone back in his pocket.

"Alise says to give you a big hug, but I think I'll leave that to her when she gets here."

The cruiser was gone when they turned into Sunset Beach Road and headed for the farm. There was flooding again beside the pond and a carpet of leaves and twigs covered the road, but no branches this time. Colin was thinking of what Joe Stanton said about the last storm clearing out the deadwood when the floodlight in the yard came into view. He let out a whoop.

"Yes! We've got power. We can have a nice cup of tea."

Then he remembered everything else there was to do. A couple of shingles crunched beneath the wheels as they drove into the yard. They got out and peered around. A ghostly-white crust of salt covered everything in sight. More shingles were strewn about. A windrow of pulped leaves lay beside the barn. Ben Palmer pointed to the house.

"Your shutters are still on. You've lost some shingles, but the roof and chimney look good. I wouldn't be surprised if it was just a Category 1 after all."

He went to follow Colin to the barn, then heeded his advice.

"It's not the best time for them to meet a stranger. I'll only be a minute."

Opening the door quietly, he crept inside, unsure what he'd find but not expecting the somnolent scene that emerged in the dimness of the single light he'd left on. The cows were slumbering, except for Angel, who took his arrival to be feeding time and stood up against her pen, bleating and drooling.

While the kettle boiled, he checked the house. Ben Palmer was sitting in the inglenook stroking the cat and listening to the weather radio when he returned.

"What's left of Hannah is up in New Hampshire already. Thank God for fast women! And I never got chance to meet her. I was in the waiting room the whole time, but I could hear her… Did you find anything amiss upstairs?"

"Nothing, just as Old Joe predicted... I hope this water's boiled long enough in case the well's contaminated?"

The big man chortled.

"Damn! You've got to hand it to him. Joe's as tough as this old place of his – doesn't depend on anyone. The rest of us have to wait for power and water to be turned back on, then see what's fallen apart."

Revived by the tea, he wouldn't rest until he'd seen his house. Debris choked the puddled lanes; salt coated the thickets on either side. The driveway bore tangles of vines speared into the ground, where they'd collected everything blown into them until they looked like tumbleweeds. A dim floodlight, its backup battery almost drained, glimmered over the portico. When the headlights picked out the left side of the house, a frame of jagged glass with flapping strands of masking tape was all that remained of the picture window in the living room.

Inside, their storm lanterns showed the room to be a sodden wreck. The heavy furniture was all bizarrely in place, though covered like the saturated carpet and hardwood floor in smashed ornaments, pictures, glassware and mashed vegetation. A 4-foot chunk of deadwood lay amid a pile of shards by the window. Destruction glittered all around. Amazingly, it was a solitary pit of chaos in a home of otherwise undisturbed order and gentility.

Colin tagged behind as they went from room to room. Photographs of Juliana and her brother as children lined the walls of the upstairs landing. A thrill tingled through him when he realized the yellow and cream bedroom they went into first was hers. On the dressing table opposite the door was a picture Juanita had taken of them at the beach, to the left a double bed with a yellow coverlet beneath a huge print of Gustav Klimt's "The Lovers," to the right a wall-to-wall closet. He pictured her sleeping in her hospital bed and felt the ache of longing.

Back downstairs, Ben Palmer pulled out a bottle of Michel Couvreur 12-year-old scotch and two glasses from the liquor cabinet beneath the TV. He brought them to the breakfast island and slumped into a chair.

"I need this. I bet you could use one too. What a night!"

NIANTIC JEWEL

"Oh, no thanks. I'll have some more tea when I get home... I'm sorry about the living room...."

A dismissive sweep of the hand silenced him.

"Juliana's going to be alright. That's all that matters. This is nothing. It's what insurance is for."

"I can help you pick up this afternoon... Do you think I could see her?"

"Of course! We'll all go together. There's nothing to be done here until the insurance agent gives the word, probably not until the adjuster's been around, and that could be days. It'll be upsetting for Alise, but the rest of the house is livable... I think I'll have another drink and stay put. Then I can get a few hours' sleep in my own bed. Go on home! You must be ready to drop."

He drained his glass and, holding out his arms, beckoned Colin over.

"Come here, my boy. I will give you a hug... We never know what's around the next corner. Life is unfair. Good people get hurt and those who don't deserve it get all the luck. Some things happen that shouldn't and some just weren't meant to happen... Come what may I'll always be grateful to you for tonight – we all will."

Colin puzzled over the enigmatic words while driving back to the farm. They'd slipped off a tongue loosened by exhaustion and alcohol, but were they more or less credible because of it? Were they the musings of a weary mind or were the `things not meant to happen' intended to be taken personally? If he were an unsuitable suitor in Ben Palmer's eyes, maybe the blood thing had taken a brief summer romance to a forbidden level of intimacy. In that case, the unfortunate development might require a warning to prepare him for eventual, inevitable disappointment.

Dodging the mangled remains of mailboxes and a screen door in the littered lanes triggered a sickening feeling that maybe Hannah had changed everything; nothing would ever be the same again. He recalled Lloyd Forbes' admonition that he was out of his depth with Juliana. She wouldn't go against her father's wishes and his hopes for her.

Colin could see it happening: After a few harmless flings to test the waters, after she graduated, introductions would be arranged to young hotshots with the appropriate credentials – sons of business associates, drinking companions at the MIT Club, golf partners at the country club, sons of people the Palmers socialized and networked with. The Right People.

She'd be a dutiful daughter and accept the dates. Soon there'd be competition. A foreigner with uncertain prospects wouldn't make much sense anymore. She'd fall in love with someone else, because she had so much love to give. Her parents would be proud of the choice she'd made: the perfect match. He'd lose her forever. She'd forget him, except as part of a tender, distant memory of a blissful summer long ago.

The script played out, leaving him with an empty feeling of loneliness before it occurred to him that he was wallowing in self-pity on the basis of mere inference. It was the same old defeatist attitude, maybe even borderline personality disorder, that made him buckle under stress and engage the flight response to remove himself from his problems. Juliana had spotted it the first time he took her out. No one has to think morose, self-destructive thoughts if they don't want to, he reasoned. That's what free will is for; what kept his alcoholism in its box. Buck up; think positive; get some rest, he told himself.

It seemed like a good idea until he climbed the slope into the farmyard and saw the eastern sky brightening in the rearview mirror. Five a.m. and two hours to milking time. Now he didn't feel like sleeping. Instead he sat on the door stoop drinking tea, watching the orange sun come up and thinking about Juliana. Molly sauntered out to rub against him, asking to be stroked. He felt connected again.

The stark light revealed the full extent of Hannah's wrath: heaps of leaves and twigs everywhere; the glinting film of salt on every surface facing East; shingles missing from the house and barn; windows plastered with leaf pulp. He got up and walked over to the sheep pasture, Molly leading the way. The Cheviots were under the white oak, some grazing amid the litter of stripped leaves but most still huddled together, fast asleep. He started to

NIANTIC JEWEL

count them, then broke off, smiling at the absurd thought that it might put him to sleep.

More debris carpeted the cow pasture. The dock was intact and the Old Queen lay where he'd towed her, halfway to the rubbing rock. He could tell she'd been afloat in the storm surge by the crescent of flotsam that traced the high-water mark. The thin line of tangled reeds, shells and muck curved away from the foot of the big rock, which now tilted 30 degrees from vertical. He pictured how it must have happened: the pond rising 5 feet to the boulder; 90 mph winds pushing the Old Queen away from it; the bow line transferring her weight, eventually dislodging the huge rock in the waterlogged earth.

The quacking of ducks in the farmyard made him realize he hadn't heard Eric crowing when the sun came up, nor had he checked the coop. There was no telling how flighty hens would fare in a hurricane. He opened the door expecting to find a mess of feathers inside. Instead his eyes fell on Eric's prostrate form. His harem clucked mournfully, it seemed to Colin, as he knelt to feel the stiff but still-warm body. Picking it up by the feet, he felt for fractures and looked for blood before coming to the conclusion that Eric had succumbed to a heart attack: Eric the Fierce had died of fright.

Joe Stanton made light of the news when he called as soon as he knew Colin would be back in the house from milking.

"Eat the rascal! That bird was more trouble than he was worth. It's one less mouth to feed. Tell me about the important stuff. You sound pretty calm. I was worried for a while there last night, but when it turned out to be only a Category 1, I knew things would be OK... On the other hand, if you've had enough I can be back this afternoon if you want. "

The prospect sent a chill through Colin. There was nowhere to go until Labor Day; separation from Juliana was unthinkable; she'd blame him for leaving and end it. He tried not to let his frantic emotions show as he politely brushed off the idea and suggested they stay with the original plan. The response made him exhale in relief.

"That's fine by me. My brother's still not 100 percent. And I just remembered your living arrangements. I wouldn't kick you out. Stay as long as you want. But only if you're sure... Sounds like there's a fair amount of work to do though. It would be best to get the Old Queen back in the water as soon as you can. Don't bother with the lobster pots, but if you like riding the tractor, there's a gang of harrows in the shed. They'll clean up the pastures pretty good."

*   *   *

By noon, a few homeowners were already returning when Colin picked his way through the leaf-choked lanes to the Palmers'. Power and water were back. Ben Palmer was arranging for the picture window to be boarded up while his wife put together a bag of things for Juliana. They had talked. Her father and Colin were to wait outside her room while her mother helped her put on makeup.

They took the Prius and, seeing activity at Hoxsie's Nursery, stopped partly on the off chance there were flowers left to buy and partly to view the destruction. The old man and his wife were winding in irrigation lines. He glumly swept his arm past the flattened beds on one side of the dirt track and leveled rows of corn on the other.

"We rescued what we could yesterday. The rest will have to be plowed under. We'll start over with lettuce seedlings from the nursery, but the outside is mostly finished for the season. We'll have to buy in corn. Plenty of tomatoes in the greenhouses, though... It could have been worse. Chief Kenyon stopped by to check on us since we wouldn't leave last night. Said the evacuation plan needs work. The only injuries were in fender benders."

He led them to a jumble of buckets filled with flowers inside a hothouse, then slapped his hand against the doorpost.

"Help yourselves... I thought these would be wrecked, too, but we got lucky. What if that had blown a bit farther?"

NIANTIC JEWEL

He pointed to the open land between the Nursery and Michael's Shell, where there was a new addition to the landscape. The huge canopy had blown off the gas pumps, cleared the store and landed on some scrub pine 60 feet away. Now it sat balanced on the crushed trees like a bench installed for the convenience of passing giants.

They took as many flowers as they could carry. Told where they were going, the old man waved off payment, but Ben Palmer stuffed two 20s into his shirt pocket.

"The Cove couldn't get along without you."

*   *   *

From Juliana's glowing face, it was hard to imagine she'd been at death's door 12 hours before. She remembered everything now, even through the morphine. Colin held one hand and her mother the other while she related the event with the wine bottle and the rest of her night at home. Ben Palmer lamented about the picture window, then noticed Colin's silence.

"Tell Jewel your funny story, my boy – funny strange, not humorous, although maybe it's that, too, since Eric was your nemesis."

At the end, Juliana sighed sympathetically.

"What will you do with him? You're not going to eat him, are you?"

"No, I couldn't stomach that."

A chorus of groans alerted him to the unintended pun. Alise Palmer shook her finger at him.

"You get a D for dreadful. Now here's a pun: I once sent ten puns to all my friends in hopes that at least one would make them laugh. No pun in ten did… Or, two hydrogen atoms meet. One says, `I've lost my electron.' The other asks, `Are you sure?' The first replies, `Yes, I'm positive'… Then there was the Buddhist who refused Novocain for a root canal. Her goal: transcend dental medication… But really, how will you dispose of the body?"

"I'm going to bury him at sunset beside the boulder in the pasture."

Juliana wiggled his hand as the thought occurred to her.

"They say I can go home in a few days. Can you wait until then and we'll do it together? Give him a proper funeral – with all the hens standing around clucking?

He smiled as he visualized the wacky scene.

"I could try packing him in ice on top of the milk tank in the dairy. That would keep him cold. It's always cool in there. We'll do it!... But I do have a funny story I heard at work last night. One of the chaps said there's a scam going on at Dunkin" Donuts. A few days ago when he came out, he found two attractive young women washing his windshield. When he thanked them and offered a tip, they declined and just asked for a ride to any Dunkin' Donuts on his way. They got in the back seat and started undressing. Then one climbed into the front and started kissing him while the other took his wallet. He said he's had his wallet stolen five times already."

Juliana pressed her hand to her side.

"No more you two! It hurts when I laugh. You're supposed to cheer up the patient, not kill her."

A nurse came in to check vitals and remind them it was time to leave.

Alise Palmer dabbed her eyes when they got back in the car.

"I'm sorry. It's all just catching up to me. They're tears of joy, of relief. We were so close to losing her. You saved her life, dear Colin. Words can't express our gratitude, can they Ben?"

Her husband shifted in his seat.

"They can't. It was a wonderful thing you did, a debt that can never be repaid. You're a very special young man – like a son to us. We'll always think the world of you."

Colin felt uneasy again. There seemed to be an implication of `always like a son, never a son-in-law.' He pushed it from his mind.

"I was only returning a favor. Remember, Juliana did save me from drowning. Now we're even – until the next life-threatening experience."

Alise Palmer turned to him smiling, her teary eyes bright once more.

NIANTIC JEWEL

"Don't say that! Once is enough for both of you. Those sympathetic pains really hurt, you know!"

Her husband shook his head.

"Take no notice, Colin, or she'll have you believing in her Indian witchery, too."

Graham Griffith

CHAPTER 13

DREAMGIRL

Dreams are the touchstones of our characters.
HENRY DAVID THOREAU

By Wednesday, life at Quonnie Cove had settled back into its peaceful, late-August routine, even if the landscape remained scarred by violence. Three days of balmy sunshine and ocean breezes shriveled Hannah's residue. New leaf buds began to color denuded vegetation. A small army of contractors tidied up, replanted, replaced and repaired. Families returned, eager to enjoy the precious time left before another school year started.

Colin was at Juliana's bedside noon and night; her parents went mornings and afternoons. When she was alone, she called him to ease the boredom, just to find out what he was doing. During one call, she had him drive to the beach and describe it in detail, so she could be there.

He told her how Hannah had resculpted the cove: An immense deposit of sand had raised the beach 5 feet above the high-tide mark. Knowing that much of it would soon slip back into the ocean, she had him go into the water to take video, and send her the clip. Another, which she went to sleep by, was of a vermilion sunset over the ocean accompanied by the rhythmic drumming of the surf and ending with a declaration of his love for her.

As she regained her strength, she began getting up for longer periods. Vicodin kept her pain-free and in such good spirits that her only concern was whether she could wear a bikini again. He'd tried to keep a straight face when she mentioned it. They were lying on her bed nestled in each other's arms. To illustrate her

NIANTIC JEWEL

point, she pulled up her lavender chemise and bunched the material under her left breast so he could see the dressing.

"Look at this thing! I'm going to have a 6-inch scar across my ribs. I'll die if I have to get something a matron would wear."

He tapped the back of her hand, causing the cupped flesh to jiggle provocatively.

"I wouldn't worry about that! Your endowments cover it up – one of the blessings of having such a womanly figure. You'll forget all about it when the dressing comes off."

*   *   *

Once when they were playing Scrabble at the table by her window, she told him of a dream she'd had.

"It came back to me when you said you wanted to bury Eric by the boulder. We were there in my dream. It wasn't surrounded by pasture, though. Just bracken and brambles. I was lying in your lap while we watched the sunset. Except we were Indians. Men were fishing with spears and nets from dugout canoes on the pond. Women and children were clamming on the mudflats. Some were gathering plants along the banks and cutting reeds at the water's edge.

"You were feeding me oysters and blackberries. We both had really long black hair; mine was over my eyes. Yours got caught in my shell necklaces when you bent over to kiss me for making you a new snakeskin belt for your breechcloth. But the best fun was pricking your arm with a thorn I dipped in a bowl of squid ink to touch up the tattoo of an osprey's head on your right bicep.

"I know it was an osprey because it's Mother's favorite bird; there's a pair here every summer. Could be I did the original tattoo; I don't remember. There was no mistaking it as an osprey. It had the curved beak of a bird of prey and the osprey's broad black cheek patch. You looked very handsome. Your body was bronzed and glistening. So virile."

He tapped his finger to his lips.

"That would be fish oil or bear grease to repel insects and parasites. Plus, it insulated the skin from heat and cold. You probably couldn't smell it because of your own!... It all sounds quite authentic, like a scene from a book that stuck in your mind."

"I suppose so. You'd have liked my outfit: only a knee-length deerskin skirt – and you even took that off. It was such a nice dream.... "

"Just my luck to be there only in spirit... The Narragansett believe the soul is a duality: One part (michachunck) lies in the heart and is the body's animating force; the other (cowwewonck) lives in the brain and is free to wander when the body sleeps. They call it the dream soul or ghost soul. "

She drew his hand to her and kissed it.

"I'm sorry. I was looking forward to Sunday night with you in Wellesley, and my libido wouldn't be denied... At least we really are soul mates now. Our souls mated!"

Rolling his eyes, he took her hand and returned the kiss.

"Try as you might, you can't help being your mother's daughter. I love you anyway. It's so good seeing you get well. I can't be happy unless you are."

"I'm happy to be alive, because of you! Even after my body replaces your blood, I'll still keep its basic components. You're part of me now – body and soul. It feels so good... I'm promoting you from Sir Galahad to Prince Charming because knights don't have jewels and princes do. But you're only allowed one, and that's me. No more Juliana for you. I want Mother and Daddy to get used to it. We were talking about you earlier. They still think you're my summer infatuation; that it's over when fall semester begins. Daddy was so sweet. He wanted to make sure I let you down gently!"

"Do you think the blood thing upsets them; that an anonymous donor would have been better? Viscerally, they might feel as if I've impregnated you...."

"... and they want me to drop you before you do, because you're not right for me?"

His gut clenched at hearing the unspoken thought completed.

"They just want the best for you. That's all I was thinking."

She squeezed his hand and shook it in frustration.

NIANTIC JEWEL

"Sometimes you can be too perceptive for your own good. They're not like that. Granted, Mother had to explain some biology to Daddy – cellular senescence and ovular epistemology – but only because he thought the blood mixing meant that if we stay together we could never have children; you couldn't give him grandchildren because they'd be abominably inbred! And that I ought to break it off before it's too late. You have to remember he's a geek from MIT: His thing is computer science, not life science. Now he understands... They trust me to fall in love with someone who'll make me happy. That's all they care about – so long as they get grandchildren, too!"

"But don't you think they want someone with better prospects – more earning power?

"They don't want me to rush into anything – as if I would – but when the time comes I'll have a career of my own. I don't ever want to be economically dependent on a man or have children with one who doesn't share equally in raising them. It has to be a total partnership. That rules out anyone like Daddy! Not that I'm ungrateful for the sacrifices he's made. They've made my life a lot easier than it would have been.

"Acquiring wealth defined success and provided a purpose in life for males of his generation. It gave them their identity and they didn't stop to think about what it was doing to them. The women they married – except those like Mother – bought into it. What else could they do? They had no identity other than as wives and mothers. And they could only validate themselves as women by having a son. The social dictates crippled them, too. But that's all behind us now. It's a post-feminist world.

"Money doesn't matter to me beyond having enough to live comfortably, beyond the lack of it being a constant worry. You don't hear me asking about the size of your trust fund, do you? I want you to do what makes you happy. How many men are ground down by jobs they hate but can't afford to give up? As Thoreau said in the 1850s: 'The mass of men lead lives of quiet desperation.' It's just as true today."

*   *   *

There was a homecoming dinner with champagne and lobsters at the Palmers' Thursday night. Juliana looked spellbinding in a short sundress of apricot gauze. They were in the dining room for the occasion, and so that she could be in a comfortable chair. With two leaves removed, the cherry table sat four, with Juliana and her father in armchairs at each end and Colin across from her mother.

Her father's eyes glazed over when he made a toast recalling that the last time he brought her home from the hospital she was a tiny newborn. She'd arrived prematurely and looked so delicate he was afraid to hold her. Her mother remembered gardening with her when she was a toddler:

"The rabbits were eating my bedding plants, so I was spreading cayenne pepper around them as a repellent. I told Jewel not to get it on her hands and explained that Peter Rabbit was eating all my flowers and this would keep him away. She looked up at me with those big blue eyes and pleaded, 'Please Mummy, can we plant more flowers so Peter Rabbit can still come?' She was solving problems even then. Such a darling!"

They'd finished eating when the phone rang. Alise Palmer got up to answer it.

"I know who this is, Jewel! He said he'd call again tonight. He wanted to surprise you as soon as you got home."

To Colin's great relief, it was her brother Nathan in London. She squealed in delight and talked excitedly while Colin helped clear the dishes. When the phone passed to her father, and her mother went to make coffee, he knew this was as alone as he'd be with her tonight.

"Close your eyes. I have a surprise for you, too."

He'd found the gold tennis bracelet set with Indian rubies at the Fantastic Umbrella Factory, a cornucopia of retro stores she loved to browse on Route 1A. The oblong box hinted at its contents, provoking a look of wild anticipation when she saw it and began tearing off the red gift-wrap. He leaned in close and murmured:

NIANTIC JEWEL

"You've shown me what true love is… Jewel gives me her love with ruby lips. I give her mine with the ruby jewel of love."

He winced at his turgid declaration, but she gasped as she fingered the stones and slipped the band on her wrist.

"Oh Colin! It's the best present I've ever had. If I cry it's because I'm so happy."

Her eyes grew moist, but instead of wiping them she reached for him and gave him a torrid kiss just as her mother returned.

"My goodness, Jewel! I don't think that's such a good idea for now. You're supposed to be resting. What prompted that outrageous display of affection?"

Juliana waved her wrist ostentatiously.

"Just my Prince being charming… I do believe he's blushing."

Ben Palmer finished talking to his son and peered over.

"You have good taste, Colin. Be warned, she'll find you limitless opportunities to exercise it."

The unforeseen attention set his thumbs twiddling nervously in his lap. He regretted not waiting for a better moment, and yet… What bothered him most was the flush of pride that always seemed to come before a fall. He sought comfort in her beaming face.

"We should bury Eric when you're cleared to come over. Romano from the farmers' co-op got a shock when he saw Eric on the milk tank. He wanted to know if he was supposed to take him, too."

"Absolutely. We'll do it tomorrow. I'll be over around noon."

Her mother looked at Colin and shook her head.

"It's too soon for her to leave the house. Besides, she can't drive for two weeks, And I have no wish to attend a funeral for a bird I never laid eyes on – mutant marvel or not."

Juliana put her hand to her side, trying not to break up.

"Oww! Don't do that, Mother. It hurts to laugh… Just for an hour. It'll do me good to get out. And Colin will drive me."

*   *   *

"Careful, Sweetie! There's a cavity under that rotten plank. The whole thing might cave in and bring the boulder down on you."

Juliana sat cross-legged on the grass watching him dig a grave for Eric beside the cows' rubbing rock. Her hair sparkled in the sunshine creating a golden halo that overpowered the pale green tank top where the tresses brushed her shoulders. Even the Jerseys, hunkered down and lazily chewing their cud on the slope to the pond, had their heads turned toward her. Colin drove his shovel into the small pile of soil and pebbles he'd dug up, and wiped the sweat from his face.

"That'll have to do it. I don't think this pasture's ever been plowed. The slope must be too steep. The ground's so stony I can hardly get the shovel into it."

He walked around the side of the big leaning boulder and pushed against it perfunctorily.

"It would be nice to have it vertical again, but there's probably as much below ground as there is above. It'll take another hurricane to move it… I wonder what this old plank's all about."

Kneeling down, he pulled away a few crumbling chunks and tossed them on the pile.

"You're right. The subsidence opened up a space here. Eric will fit into it nicely. Now he'll be deep enough so the raccoons can't dig him up. I'll fetch him."

When he returned, Juliana was crouched over the hole, peering into her cupped hands.

"Come look at these little things. I saw one glint down there. This is all I could reach. What do you think they are?"

She emptied them into his palm. He rolled the tiny cylinders between his fingers to get the soil off.

"Crikey! They look like purple and white wampum beads. See those holes in the middle plugged with dirt? They're for stringing, and the size is just right: quarter-inch long, eighth-inch diameter. What a find! Maybe there's more."

Grabbing the shovel, she was about to plunge it into the pit when he stopped her.

"Wait! That's too destructive. I'll get a trowel and a bucket. And there's an old potato screen in the shed to sift the soil."

NIANTIC JEWEL

Ten minutes later, they had another handful of beads and two hard green globs, which she cleaned with a hairpin.

"These are metal – maybe copper, but covered in verdigris now... I bet they're mounts for pendant earrings. The beads hung from them... It's not wampum then. Not Indian after all."

The look of disappointment on her face was too much for Colin to bear. He knelt down and kissed her.

"It is wampum, I'm sure. Before it was used as money, it was worn on the body decoratively and as a kind of medicine. Shiny objects, especially seashells from the underwater world, had spiritual significance – what the Algonquian called manitou. It's an impersonal force, a divine power that permeates all creation: animals, mountains, rivers. Originally, only sachems could own wampum. They used it in the ritual exchange of gifts accompanying marriages and tribal alliances, not as money but as symbolically charged objects associated with their cosmology.

"The white beads come from the whelks Busycon canaliculatum and carica, the purple from the quahog Mercenaria mercenaria. They're found mainly along Narragansett Bay and Long Island Sound, where the shoreline configuration and water temperature are just right. That's why the tribes here grew rich and powerful from wampum production. It was traded as far north as the Gaspe Peninsula, west to the Hudson Valley and waterways of the Great Lakes and down the Ohio River south to the Florida Keys.

"Strictly speaking, only the white is wampum; the purple is suckauhock or mohacke, a reference to the Mohawk, the closest of the Iroquois nations who all especially prized it. Purple was worth two or three times as much as white. It was harder to perforate with stone and wood drills dipped in wet sand, and the color carried extra power.

"In the 1620s, the Dutch discovered they could barter wampum for beaver pelts. Trader Isaak de Rasieres told the Pilgrims about it while visiting Plymouth in October 1627, and soon wampum became an official medium of exchange, since coinage was scarce in the colonies.

"By the 1660s, nearly all the beaver were gone. Meanwhile, the Dutch had introduced steel drills and set up wampum factories on

Long Island, glutting the supply. It was demonetized in 1663. Now, the Indians had neither furs nor wampum to trade for European goods and the liquor they were plied with – only land. Soon they lost that, too.

Juliana stood up to brush soil from her blue shorts.

"I thought we gave them glass beads. They're shiny and colorful. Why weren't they better than wampum?"

"They didn't have manitou. Plus it was Murano glass from Venice, which wasn't cheap. The Dutch made their own beads in Amsterdam. Actually, it wasn't the beads themselves that had value; it was what they represented after being strung. They were woven into belts, bracelets, necklaces, brooches, amulets, hair and ear decorations with intricate designs.

"But they weren't just artwork. Some were memory aids with symbolic powers. The pictographs laid out treaties, told stories and passed on oral tradition. It was a kind of writing. The 12-foot-long belt in Metacom's regalia contained abstract figures, flowers, birds and beasts to tell the story of the Wampanoag people.

"All these properties made wampum magical, especially since it came from the water, the underworld realm of Chepi, Hobbomok or Abbomocho. He was the deity they interacted with daily. At night, he appeared in dreams as a serpent, eagle or deer.

"But the greatest spirit was Cautantouwwit or Keihtan. Like God, he was a necessary being – the sole Creator and entirely good. He shaped the land from primordial matter and made the other gods. Then he fashioned a man and a woman from stone. For some reason he didn't like them, so he broke them and made a second pair from a tree, giving trees and people a common origin. He sent the first corn kernels in the beak of a crow. In gratitude, they were never harmed even when they damaged crops. Good souls went to Cautantouwit's house in the Southwest for an afterlife of carnal bliss.

"Chepi, on the other hand, was a constant presence manifested in death, night, the Northeast wind and anything dark (like purple). Bad souls went to his underworld for an afterlife of torture. If you were neither good nor bad, your soul just wandered restlessly forever.

NIANTIC JEWEL

"Because Chepi caused evil, he could also prevent it, so he was ambiguous. He appeared as an eel or snake and was accessible directly in visions or indirectly through powwows (medicine men and women) and manitou (which resided in places, objects, creatures, qualities and phenomena). There was also a giant called Wetucks or Maushop who performed miracles, walked on water and showed people how to do things. Because of the religion's complex unities and dualisms, he may have been another version of Chepi or just a folk hero.

"The English tried to understand Native Americans by applying a European matrix. Often as not this led to misunderstanding and confusion. Sachems weren't kings and manitou weren't gods, but guardian spirits – a bit like patron saints. The three realms of creation had their own demigods: a thunderbird for the sky, a turtle for the earth and a horned serpent for the underworld. These were the most powerful, but Roger Williams was told of about 35 others concerned with all aspects of life from day and night, heavenly bodies, directions, seasons, fire, rain and flood to the home, women, children and crops.

"Indian pantheism was far richer than Christianity, yet so subtle and personal that some early colonists could see no religion at all. There was no creed or communal worship. What were the materialistic Europeans to make of the Qunnekamuck ceremony when hundreds gathered to watch dancers give away or burn their possessions, and the Nickommo feasts at which material wealth was displayed and disposed of with the object of bringing good fortune to both the donor and the community?

"To the Puritans, all who didn't worship their version of God worshipped the Devil – even Anglicans and Catholics. Being a Baptist, Quaker or other 'sectary' would get you hanged, branded, jailed, whipped, fined or banished. In 1646, Massachusetts imposed the death penalty for denying or ridiculing God and fines for practicing rituals and Sabbath-breaking. These were the people who hanged 14 women and 5 men as witches at Salem in 1692-3.

"The Bible was manitou because it magically carried the white man's religion, which to the Indians wasn't false but ran parallel to theirs. Its power was apparent from European goods and

Graham Griffith

technology, but most of all from the terrifying epidemics that even the Puritans believed to be an instrument of God....

"If they're earrings, who knows, maybe there's a treasure trove under here!... Unless you dropped them in that dream you had – when we made love and I missed the whole thing."

She reached down and mussed his hair.

"Stop it! You'll remember the next time, I promise... This is exciting! But if we excavate the hole, what are we going to do with Eric? Pretty soon, there's going to be a foul smell... I didn't say that!"

*   *   *

Eric was buried with fitting solemnity beside the gatepost. Juliana sat on the wall while Colin swung a heavy pick he'd found in the tool shed to pry out the ubiquitous rocks. Molly came out to see what was going on and a couple of cows trudged over, but the hens had refused to leave the shade of the farmyard when Colin tried to shoo them over while getting the pick.

He knelt with the body in his hands, then realized he had nothing to lower it with. The grave was only 2 feet deep, yet wide enough to allow excavation. Even lying prone on his stomach he had to let Eric drop the last 6 inches. Juliana gave a shriek when she saw the corpse bounce off a protruding rock and collapse headfirst into a corner. Stretching his arms, Colin latched onto a clump of feathers, which came away in his hand. His body teetered on the edge of the grave as his toes left the ground and his head dipped into the hole. He was sure he was about to join Eric until Juliana hopped down from the wall and grabbed his feet. She giggled as he got to his knees.

"Are you alright?... You've just proved Jewel's Rule!"

He brushed himself off.

"What's that?"

"A dropped object will always come to rest in the most inaccessible position possible... Isn't that just like Eric? His last hurrah was to try to take you with him. You could have broken your neck. It makes my eulogy all the more apropos."

NIANTIC JEWEL

They stood hand in hand while she read a valediction she'd prepared for the occasion:

"We have gathered here today to express mixed emotions for our feathered fiend Eric as we lay him to rest.

"In some ways, we are thankful for having known him and for the harrowing memories he gave us. Those who played chicken with him always lost. He showed us how to be humble without ever crowing about his own humility, since he had none.

"We can't recall an instance when he endeared himself to us, but if we could it would gladden our hearts for many years. He was unfailingly foul-tempered, his feathers easily ruffled. His generosity was limited only by his ignorance of the word.

"Eric fulfilled his purpose and had a good time doing it. He is survived by numerous wives, who served his every need, like it or not. No one ever called him a hen-pecked husband. He was also the frustrated father of thousands of appetizing blastocysts.

"Let us pray that we never see his like again. Rest in peace, Eric. You sure didn't give us any."

CHAPTER 14

SKULLDUGGERY

The holiest sod of a nation's soil
is the sod where the greatest of her dead lies buried
PATRICK PEARSE

An afternoon shower drove them onto the veranda, where they cuddled in the loveseat, watching a rainbow rise from the dancing surface of the pond. When they went back to the dig, Juliana noticed a glossy ocher patch the rain had exposed halfway down the side adjacent to the boulder. Ignoring the wet grass, she lay on her stomach and poked around with the trowel until bits of the surrounding soil fell away from the hard surface. She reached over to touch it, and recoiled.

"Ugh! It feels like bone, Colin!"

She scrambled gingerly to her feet, fluttering her hands in repulsion.

"I'm sorry. That was creepy. See! It's an animal skull."

He hugged her to him.

"Maybe it's a farm dog or a pet sheep. But why the beads? Let's make sure first. We'll have to widen the hole to get at it – and make sure we don't damage whatever else might be here."

Turning the thigh-deep hole into a trench began as a laborious task of troweling and sifting. Soon it became clear that the side away from the boulder was 3 feet of earth and rocks atop another massive undergound boulder. Colin decided to use the pick to expedite matters. Juliana was headed toward the shovel when he stopped her.

"Sorry. You can't help yet. Your mum would kill me. Go talk to the cows, and when you come back I'll be done."

NIANTIC JEWEL

He piled the dirt into a wall around the outside curve of the trench, leaving one end open with the bigger rocks arranged to make a step down. When it was finished they crouched beside the find, she carefully troweling away the topsoil onto the mesh screen, he sifting it into the bucket beneath. As a bulbous shape emerged, their excitement grew. She traced her fingers over the curvature and gasped:

"It's a human cranium. Here's the eye socket. My Gosh! Why is it here? What should we do?"

Colin looked out across the pond.

"See how it's facing Southwest? It's an Indian burial – a shallow pit covered with planks. They were often near the water – a portal to the underworld. We've disturbed a grave – accidentally it's true, but it's still a serious matter. Should we go on, or report it?

Juliana's eyes lit up.

"It's our secret. Let's keep it that way, for now. We found it; we should see it through."

They worked until milking time. Just as the cows began gathering around the gate, Juliana's cellphone rang. She stood up and stretched her back while she answered it.

"Hi Mother... Sorry. I'm fine. I'm coming. We were burying Eric, and you won't believe what we found...."

Colin put a finger to his lips, and she nodded.

"... I'll tell you when I get home, but you can't breathe a word to anyone... Love you."

She threw up her hands.

"I'll burst if I don't tell them. They'll be cool... Look! It's fully intact. Even the lower jaw's in place – missing some teeth though... With a bit more scraping, I think we can lift it out."

And so they did. Juliana held it in her outstretched hands and marveled.

"This is totally awesome!... You have to take me home now, but can we clean it tonight?"

Her beaming face brought a lump to his throat.

"I don't think your mum will let you out again. She's probably mad at me for not getting you home sooner as it is. You're supposed to be convalescing."

"I guess you're right... But you'll be in Boston tomorrow. I can't wait until Sunday. And it can't stay out here for the raccoons to play with. Why don't I take it home with me? You'll eat with us, then we'll clean it together. There! It's all taken care of. You'd better get a box though. I don't think Mother would appreciate my walking in with a skull in my hands."

"No, just seeing you covered in dirt might give her a heart attack. Go inside and wash up while I let the ladies into the barn."

* * *

Before he went over to the Palmers' two hours later, he covered the dig with plastic sheeting held down with rocks, so the cows couldn't stumble in.

Juliana was at the garden shed in back. She had the skull on a potting bench and was flushing caked soil from the brain cavity with a mini watering hose. He bent forward to kiss her, keeping clear of her muddy rubber apron and messy hands. She pointed to the lower jaw, which took on a honeyed patina as it dried in the sun.

"The mandible detached when I rinsed away the dirt holding it on. It's missing the second bicuspid on the left and the first molar on the right. There's a lot of wear, so it's an adult. The cranium seems too small for a man. That leaves us with a middle-aged woman, and her earrings."

He stooped to study the skull at eye level, running his fingers over the pitted surface.

"You did nice job cleaning it... These red spots must be stained in."

"They are. I didn't want to scrape them. What do you think it is?"

"I don't know... unless it's from the red ocher powder they sprinkled on the body – an aromatic iron oxide that perfumed it before burial, and afterward facilitated entry to Cautantowwit's house."

She wiped her hands on a rag.

NIANTIC JEWEL

"That makes sense... I'll finish up tomorrow... Mother won't have it in the house. It'll be safe in the shed... she'll be safe. She needs a name... I know! Let's call her Gail, because a gale brought her to us."

They talked about her over dinner. Alise Palmer said nothing until she'd finished her swordfish, then shook her head.

"I think you should stop right now, before you dig up the whole skeleton and anything else that's there. Jewel Googled it, and excavating a burial site without a permit is illegal. You have to notify the state Historic Preservation Commission. There could be more artifacts holding information that only archeologists are qualified to recover. It calls for scientific methodology...."

Juliana finished her mother's thought:

"... Measurements, documentation, analysis, electronic equipment, experts swarming all over it. Won't Mr. Stanton love that when he comes home! He should decide whether or not he wants strangers digging up his farm. And if it is an Indian burial, the tribe has an interest. It's sacred ground. But we don't know anything yet. Let's see what else we come up with before certain people let their imaginations run wild... Why the puzzled look, Prince Charming? You agree with me, don't you?"

Colin took a sip of water.

"As usual, you've both summed up the situation admirably. It's getting complicated isn't it?... I'm puzzled because something's not right. For it to be an Indian burial, Gail's legs should be flexed, with the knees up against her face, in the fetal position – to be born again into the afterlife. She had her back to the boulder, facing Southwest, so we should have come across her arms and legs when we dug the trench. Yet there was nothing...."

Ben Palmer scratched his head.

"If you say the slope's never been plowed, then maybe things got pushed around when the boulder tipped. Why would a skull be sitting there by itself?... I think you'd better solve this mystery before it drives us crazy."

*   *   *

When he arrived at the Palmers' after the drive back from Boston the next night, Juliana was waiting at the portico. Seeing her come toward him with a wide smile and her hips swaying in a honeysuckle coverup made him want to scoop her into his arms. Then he remembered the surgery and settled for pressing his lips against hers. She rubbed his chest and gave him a petulant look.

"I'm not that fragile, Sweetie! Did you miss me?"

"Can't you tell? If your mum hadn't let me come over, I'd have you on the phone all night long."

She led him to into the sunken garden, where, secluded in the dappled moonlight, she clasped him to her in a ravenous French kiss, then pushed him to the bench and straddled his legs. The heat of her body inflamed him to seek out her lips again as he held her. But she wanted to talk, and finally held his head against her bosom.

"I had another Indian dream last night – almost as good as the earlier one: I was in a wigwam. The first light of dawn awoke our baby daughter, who was with me on the sleeping platform. She was hungry, so I took her outside to nurse her and perform the morning ceremony as the sun came up. I remember the first two words: 'Wunnegan nippaus – Welcome sun.' Then I thanked the Great Spirit, the Earth Mother and the four directions from which all things come."

Colin lifted his head and kissed her cheek.

"What a good student you are. That book you read years ago is still there in your unconscious. Though it could never describe the morning ritual as beautifully as you just did... Do you know where you were?

"Same place as before – by the boulder. The sun was raising a layer of mist on the pond, but I could see a dozen canoes huddled together in the distance. You'd all been out there most of the night, taking advantage of the full moon. Everyone shared the catch, then split up and made for shore. I spotted you coming when the sun glinted on the birch-bark of the Abenaki canoe you'd traded for with Roger Williams. Nearly all the rest were homemade dugouts and not nearly so fast, even a couple of big ones that held four men.

NIANTIC JEWEL

"We went down to the water to meet you. I looked in the canoe while you pulled it onto the bank. You'd speared a huge sturgeon when they came into the pond at high tide and a cormorant you'd glided up to as it slept on the rocks. I was so proud of you...

"By the time you'd cleaned the sturgeon and hung it on the drying rack, you were super hungry. All you'd had since supper was the pouch of nokake I made up for you – my special recipe of cornmeal, powdered walnuts, dried raspberries and maple sugar. I was a really good cook. For breakfast, we had your favorite chowder of lobster, crab, oysters and bluefish thickened with boiled chestnuts and kelp. I took good care of you. Then just before you had a nap, I took good care of you again...."

"That's not fair! You promised I'd be there the next time we made love... And, you broke a taboo: Mothers didn't have sex for a year while nursing. It was healthier for the babies. They had 12 months of breast milk, since the mother couldn't get pregnant and stop lactating. That's one of the reasons polygyny – multiple wives – was allowed, but not adultery... Did you notice any other wives in the wigwam?"

Tousling his hair, she scoffed:

"In your dreams maybe, not mine. No way am I going to share you because of a silly taboo. I want all of you, all the time. What do you take me for!"

"Just checking. It sounds as if keeping you satisfied will take everything the man you choose has to give."

She ground her hips into his lap.

"You'd better believe it. He'll give me his all, just as you said you wanted. That's why I've chosen you. Agreement is not necessary!... I want to make love right now. It would be so perfect here, under the moon. It would also be just like Mother to sense something amiss, and come out. Plus, I'm still supposed to be taking it easy, and I'm warning you I don't plan on taking that easy...."

He pressed her to him, kneading the firm, warm flesh of her shoulders as their mouths locked. Soon, the screen door inside the portico slapped shut and Alise Palmer's voice wafted into the night:

Graham Griffith

"Jewel, don't be long. The mosquitoes are out."

* * *

They resumed the dig late Sunday morning after brunch at the Palmers'. As before, they crouched side by side in the trench, Juliana troweling soil onto the screen for Colin to sift into the bucket and empty over the wall. His attention turned from a close scrutiny of her moist, parted lips and tanned flesh when he heard the ring of metal striking metal. She caught him staring, and smiled indulgently.

"I love the way you look at me, but you're supposed to be helping. Here, see what this is...."

She handed him a horsehair whisk from the parapet and watched him slowly expose a dull yellow object about 5 inches long.

"Look Jewel, it's shaped like a woman."

She carefully pried the figure loose and cleaned it in her fingers.

"So it is! I think it's a comb. The handle's her head and body, and the five teeth are her dress. It's adorable... but heavy. That's why it must be for grooming. You couldn't wear it in the hair like a peineta... What's it made of? Let it be gold!"

Colin found a paper towel in his back pocket and gently buffed the metal until it shone.

"'Fraid not. It's cast brass, There's some pitting on the teeth; otherwise it's perfect. The salty soil's a natural preservative... Keep digging. I think you're onto something."

Every few minutes saw a new find emerge from the earth: brass and wampum beads, a copper bracelet incised with a serpentine design, and most enigmatic of all, a 2-inch-long tooth etched with the profile of a bird's head. Then, just as they dared to hope they'd hit upon an intact Indian grave complete with its burial trove, they ran out of earth to dig. With the soil cleared away to bare rock, the tall rubbing rock was exposed below ground level inside the trench. Three feet down, it thrust through the same sloping mass of greywacke on which they stood. The two planes formed an enclosure now emptied of its contents.

NIANTIC JEWEL

In frustration, Juliana drummed the point of her trowel on the rock.

"That's it then. What rotten luck. Or should we run the trench around the back side, too?... The rest of the skeleton has to be here somewhere. Unless we're not the first diggers. But then why is there anything left?"

Colin saw the forlorn look and leaned across to steal a lingering kiss.

"This is the lee side of the boulder – the only place where any depth of soil can have accumulated. The ledge slopes up to the higher ground behind. I doubt there's much soil there at all, but let's try it."

He helped her out of the trench so she could watch him dig behind the boulder on the upslope. No matter where he plunged the shovel in, he hit ledge before the 9-inch blade was fully into the ground.

"You know, I think the ledge in back would have been exposed rock when the site was chosen. The ocean has encroached maybe 100 feet over 350 years. This whole slope would have been steeper; higher up from the water; more spectacular. The wind scoured it. Sand and soil were trapped against the rubbing rock – just enough to contain a burial. Then planks and rocks were placed on top... I'm glad this is all there is. Any more would be overwhelming. Labor Day's coming up fast. Realistically, we only have until then to find answers. Now that the dig's finished and we have our haul, such as it is, this is when the fun begins."

She beamed the wide smile that always made him weak at the knees.

"I can't wait to get you out to Wellesley. It's going to be so incredible... But you're right. These last days here will be marvelous too. After you get back from Boston tonight, I'm not going to let you out of my sight until we've exposed Gail's secrets, among other things."

"What other things?"

"Gosh! I must have forgotten to mention it. Mother has department meetings the last half of the week. She'll be at home with Daddy. They'll come down late Friday. I'll be all alone for three days and two long nights."

Pulling him to her, she covered his lips with hers, between kisses murmuring

"And since we need to do a lot of online research and my setup's in my bedroom, we're going to be spending all of our time there. I wouldn't be surprised if it takes a couple of all-nighters."

With dirty hands, it was frustrating not to be able to caress her. Instead he ground his hips into hers, kissing her with the urgency of impatient longing.

"I'm yours to command. I love you so much... But promise you'll leave us time to get some work done."

Without breaking the kiss, she dropped her hands to encircle his butt in a tight grasp that to his uninhibited joy immediately produced the reaction she patently desired. She looked him straight in the eye.

"I guess that depends on how long you plan to keep it up – this single-minded devotion to archeology."

The lowing of the cows at the gate, in seeming disapproval of the questionable display, caused them to laugh. She burrowed her head into his chest and took his hand to lead him back to their finds.

"It's milking time already. Do you mind if I don't help today? I'm sure the ladies over there have seen enough of this hussy for one day. I'd like to take the trove home and clean it. Then tomorrow we'll be ready to take stock of things."

While he covered the dig, she poked about in the kitchen for a bag to hold the artifacts. He was driving her home when it dawned on him:

"Blimey! I'll have to call Joe from work tonight. It's time to tell him, and find out what he wants to do. Won't he be surprised!"

Juliana held aside the hair blowing in her face long enough to caution Colin.

"I hope he's not angry. What if he's known about it for years and considers it sacred... I guess you can blame Hannah, or Eric."

"That's brilliant. I'll mention it matter-of-factly in connection with burying Eric."

NIANTIC JEWEL

He pulled up to the portico and hopped out to open her door and take her hand. Once on her feet, she threw her arms around his neck and covered his lips with a forceful open-mouth kiss.

"Come over early tomorrow, Sweetie. Let's get the research and analysis finished by midweek, then while the cat's away the mice can play."

He rubbed noses with her.

"I'm sure I don't know what you mean, Ms. Palmer."

"No you wouldn't, being English. I'll have to show you. I hope you're a fast study."

*   *   *

Any guidance Colin may have hoped for from Joe Stanton was unforthcoming. The answering machine at his brother's said they'd gone to York Beach for a few days and could be reached at the Candleshop Inn. Making contact would take longer than Colin anticipated, and he let it go.

On his way over to the Palmers' late Monday morning, he was still wondering whether to call the inn. What he had to say could wait until after the old man's vacation. Then again, what if he and Juliana were on a wild goose chase that Joe could halt before they wasted any more time? If that was it, something deep down told him he didn't want to know.

He found Juliana at the patio table. She held the copper bracelet in one hand while scrolling down the screen of her 17-inch MacBook Pro with the other. But it was the short-sleeve lilac henley and cream capris that grabbed his attention. She got up, twirling the bracelet seductively on her index finger and sashayed sensuously over. Standing in front of him, she rotated her bare midriff in rhythm to the spinning band, then stopped abruptly with a provocative thrust of her hips and an enigmatic smile.

"Where've you been, Sweetheart? I've loads to tell you."

She kissed him urgently on the mouth and drew him to a chair beside hers.

"There's coffee inside if you want it."

"Thanks, I'm fine. I'm getting all the buzz I need from your perfume – if those torrid moves weren't stimulant enough. I get my high from you."

He kissed her neck and drank in her fragrance.

"Sorry. I'm powerless over my esthetic instincts... What's the scoop?"

She turned her head and sought out his lips for a probing osculation. There was a sardonic grin on her face when she withdrew. Again she spun the bracelet suggestively on her finger while placing the other hand firmly in his lap.

"Was that esthetic enough for you, Sweetie? How coy we are this morning! None of this is for your intellectual edification. I'm aiming straight for your pleasure centers – because you're going to deserve it after you hear what I have to say. The only instincts I want to arouse are the animal kind of the id. You have to grant I'm a good psychologist. You sure have a buzz on now. You've risen to the occasion splendidly. But enough teasing... You don't mind, do you? I can't help it. I feel so happy when we're together."

"Me too. It's as if we're one. You're always in my dreams...."

"... That's what I have to tell you. I had another Indian dream last night."

"You're kidding! Do I want to hear about it? Our dream souls made love again, and only you got to enjoy it?"

She kissed his hand, then with a sigh cupped it to her chest.

"I'm sorry. I told you I can't do anything about it! Don't worry; you were fantastic again. Forgive me. But that's not the important part. When I cleaned the bracelet and the tooth some more, I made a couple of discoveries. There's a second design element on the bracelet. See!"

He withdrew his hand slowly, his fingers brushing over the turgid nipple beneath the cotton tee as he took the bracelet from her. She shivered momentarily before going on:

"The three snakes are separated by three square-ish shapes that look like axe or tomahawk heads. And the tooth has two stringing holes at the base. It's an amulet. This is where it gets wild. The bracelet belongs to you, the amulet and comb to me!

NIANTIC JEWEL

"They were all in my dream. I remember fingering the amulet on my chest and comparing its bird's head to your osprey tattoo. They were identical. Is that spooky, or what? I originally saw the tattoo in the first dream before we found the amulet!"

He thought about it, then shrugged.

"The mind plays strange tricks, especially in dreams. But you're right. I can't understand it... I just envy you your dream; there's nothing to forgive. Beauty bestows full absolution upon itself... Naturally you'd have another dream after yesterday's excitement. The three finds would be in it, and your healthy libido would find a way to manifest itself. Tell me everything!"

"It was dusk; there was a chill in the air and leaves on the ground. It must have been fall. The last rays of sunlight turned the sky a haunting mauve. We were sitting around a big campfire at a village in the woods. There were wigwams everywhere. You were obviously the sachem and people had gathered to listen to you speak. I was the only woman in the front circle. There was a second row of people sitting cross-legged; everyone else was standing in back.

"You held my hand while telling a story about your cousin, who'd been killed by the Mohegan. His name wasn't mentioned, but I gathered he'd been co-sachem with your father. He'd despaired of getting along with the English and went to Long Island to muster support for driving them out. You recited the speech he gave and said his words were still true today – whenever that was...."

Colin couldn't help breaking in:

"Now that is uncanny. I was reading the same speech again last night. It's famous – one of the most eloquent on record by a Native American. The Narragansett co-sachem Miantonomi gave it to Wyandanch of the Montauk in 1642."

Juliana gripped his hand in anticipation

"You've mentioned those names before, but not the speech. I bet you know it verbatim. How does it go?"

"He says the native peoples must join together `otherwise we shall be all gone shortly, for you know our fathers had plenty of deer and skins, our plains were full of deer, as also our woods,

Graham Griffith

and of turkeys, and our coves full of fish and fowl. But these English having gotten our land, they with scythes cut down the grass, and with axes fell the trees; their cows and horses eat the grass, and their hogs spoil our clam banks, and we shall all be starved.' Is that how it went?"

She let out a squeal and hugged him.

"Yes! Yes! How could it be? No one will believe it – except Mother! What does it mean? What's happening?"

Colin took her hand and patted it to try to calm her.

"The rational explanation is that it was lurking in your unconscious all the time – except that there's more to it than just the speech, it seems. You didn't hear any names of the dead mentioned because to do so was taboo – bad karma. But it's obvious who they were. Miantonomi, who was killed by the Mohegan at the behest of the English in 1643, was co-sachem with his uncle, Canonicus. His eldest son (and Miantonomi's cousin), who succeeded him when he died in 1647, was Mixanno. I was him in your dream, retelling a story so it would pass into the tribe's oral history...."

He paused to catch his breath, but she was impatient to hear more.

"Don't stop. If you were Mixanno, you must know who I was...."

"His wife was Quaiapen!"

A chill went down his spine as he spoke the name. Juliana gulped for air.

"Quaiapen Farm! The Old Queen!... Omigosh! Gail is a woman's skull! Could it be her? We've got to find out. This is amazing. What else do you know about her? Maybe there's a clue somewhere."

He tapped his forehead, as if calling up a file.

"She was a sister of Ninigret. You remember him. She married Mixanno in 1649; they had three children before he died of an unknown cause in 1658. So your dream took place when they would have been blissfully happy... She's mentioned quite a bit in the historical record – just enough to give a tantalizing sketch of what she must have been like.

NIANTIC JEWEL

"None of the other squaw sachems – say Weetamoo of the Pocasset or Awashonks of the Sakonnet – were nearly as powerful. They were sachems of their bands, but Quaiapen was one of six sachems of the whole Narragansett confederacy in addition to leading her own village band and having a fortress, Queen's Fort, in North Kingstown. Some think she succeeded Canonchet after his death in April 1676 as co-sachem with Pessicus. Probably even more so than her brother Ninigret she would have been involved in all the tribe's major decisions.

"Just before Metacom's War broke out in June 1675, the English alleged, not for the first time, that she'd been plotting with the rebel leader. But her reason for visiting him at Mt. Hope may well have been humanitarian, since she was sheltering Wampanoag women and children at her village. The Puritans wanted her arrested and she had to hide out with Ninigret at Weekapaug for a time.

"When they found out and demanded that he turn her over, she went back to her village at Bassokutoquage on Route 102 in North Kingstown. The United Colonies army discovered and burned it in the days preceding the Great Swamp Fight in December. But she had fled to her secret fort nearby, where it seems she spent the next six months undetected.

"When Connecticut and allied Indian forces under Maj. John Talcott came across her band 35 miles away at Nipsachuck Swamp in North Smithfield July 2, 1676, she may have been trying to reach sanctuary in New York state. In his July 4 letter from `Mr. Stanton's at Quonocontaug,' Talcott says she was killed at the swamp, which he spells Nipsaichooke. Others think he meant Nachek or Natick swamp on the Pawtuxet River, 7 miles southwest of Providence. In any case, it was an indiscriminate massacre of 92 women, children and old men and 34 warriors who offered no resistance. An additional 45 women and children who survived were sold into slavery."

Juliana made a grimace of disappointment.

"Rats! So Gail can't be her after all. It would have been so neat. But there's still the dream – the bracelet, the amulet and the comb...."

Graham Griffith

He picked up her thought:

"... and we just might be able to trace the designs through the Internet."

"Yes! Mother had to give me her professor's accesses so I could work on the book. I can get into a whole lot of research databases.... You've got a funny look. What is it?"

"It just struck me. The allied Indians with Talcott were Mohegan, Pequot – and Niantic. In the final months of the conflict, Ninigret found it expedient to contribute a few warriors to the English war effort. They would have been well acquainted with his sister, and stunned to find her killed in a battle so far from home.

"Talcott doesn't say so, but her fate as a leading traitor would have been beheading at the very least. The head would then have been displayed in public. Women weren't exempt; that's what happened to Weetamoo, whose body was also mutilated. Strangely, there's no mention in the record of the treatment accorded Quaiapen's body. And you'd think Talcott would have said something in the letter if he'd ordered her head to be displayed.

"Probably, she was beheaded but women were spared the full traitor's defilement of being hung, drawn and quartered: First the victim was hanged, then cut down while still alive and disemboweled, the intestines being burned in front of him. Beheading and quartering of the body followed. The parts were displayed and left to rot. That final indignity was the worst because denying the body a Christian burial in consecrated ground consigned the soul to damnation.

"Similarly, in the Algonquian religion, remember the cowwewonck I told you about – the dream soul that resides in the head. Well, that's the part of the dual soul that has the afterlife. The head must be buried if someone is to enter Cautantouwit's house and live in eternal happiness. Otherwise the soul will wander restlessly forever.

"What if the Niantic warriors, out of love and respect for Quaiapen, somehow rescued her head and brought it back here to Quonnie, where she was born and raised and spent her happiest

NIANTIC JEWEL

years. They buried it, together with the jewelry she was wearing, on the site of her wigwam looking Southwest over the pond – so that her soul could enter Cautantouwit's house and be reunited with Mixanno's in perpetual bliss."

Juliana sighed.

"I hope so. It's such a lovely ending. And she did live by the pond in my earlier dreams... When you think about it, though, Ninigret's warriors would have had to do something like that. They couldn't go back to him and say, `Oh, by the way, Talcott's men killed your sister up north and displayed her head on a pole. We were there, but didn't know what to do. Sorry about that.' Ninigret would have had them roasted alive."

*   *   *

Between afternoons at the beach and sunset walks, they spent much of the next two days trawling the Internet for clues about what they'd unearthed. Using their two laptops and a search methodology Juliana designed, they pored over hundreds of pages of material that met her program's criteria.

Their enthusiasm was starting to wane when Alise Palmer left for Boston around noon on Wednesday. Colin had just stowed her suitcase in the trunk of her Prius. She hugged Juliana goodbye, then turned to him.

"I'm entrusting her to you, Colin. One request: Don't keep her up late: She shouldn't work or play too hard. You can have fun – in moderation. You're on your honor. I know you won't let me down... It's a marvelous project, but she's still recuperating – as I have to keep reminding her. Maybe she'll listen to you. I know you'll solve the mystery. I can feel it. Gail's a treasure, but I want her off the property as soon as possible!"

He nodded in general agreement, wondering if her parting words contained a veiled warning in addition to imposing an obligation. As if reading his mind, Juliana waited until the Prius backed out of the parking area and started down the driveway before embracing him defiantly for her mother to see, or not, in the rearview mirror.

They walked back inside hand-in-hand, both feeling a rush of anticipation until Juliana stopped at the foot of the stairs.

"It should have occurred to me: We've been looking for 17th-Century Algonquian jewelry with bird and snake designs keyed to their symbolism as the Thunderbird and Chepi. The chances of us linking ours to an individual are minuscule. But maybe these are more like initials... a monogram, a personal logo – like Quonnie Cove's is a gull in a circle."

A light went on in Colin' head.

"... a mark, a signature! That could be it. Sachems couldn't sign their names to English legal documents like land deeds. The next best thing was an ensign – a symbol of their office, a pictograph, a glyph. Canonicus' mark was a bow and arrow, Miantonomi's an upward-pointing arrow, Metacom or Philip signed a P with two dots, Wyandanch drew two stick people and Uncas depicted himself as a strongman... Or the osprey and the serpent and tomahawk could be more general totemic symbols of the clans or families that made up a tribe."

Juliana climbed the wide staircase with renewed energy.

"Now we're getting somewhere. We have to keep thinking outside the box. What do the objects tell us? First, the raw materials: The shell and bone would be locally available; the brass comb and beads are Dutch or English trade items; and the copper originally came from around Lake Superior via the Iroquois. Second, the designs: Snakes, tomahawks and a bird of prey could be clans or guardian spirits... Oh dear! That doesn't help much."

Colin let his gaze wander to the ocean in the distance.

"No, but let's forget the osprey for now. We've been sidetracked by it. That huge tooth says a lot by itself; likewise the pairing of snakes and tomahawks on the bracelet... They're trying to tell us something. Do you see?"

They sat down facing each other at their laptops. Juliana's nose twitched – a bewitching tic she exhibited whenever she was unsure of herself.

"Whatever it is, I'm not getting it. Psychologists think inductively, empirically – evidence based on experience. What

NIANTIC JEWEL

little we have to go on leads nowhere... Go ahead Sherlock! What's your deductive logic, your powers of ratiocination, told you?"

"That no animal around here has teeth as big as that."

"I thought of that! It's a bear's tooth."

"Maybe a 1,500-pound kodiak bear but not our 600-pound native black bear."

She sat back in her chair, contemplating, then raised a fist in triumph.

"Eureka! It's a whale's tooth. The etching should have tipped me off: It's like scrimshaw. Daddy used to take Nate and me fishing when we were little. He loved to tell us stories. I bet you don't know what Quonochontaug means, do you."

"In Narragansett? Oh, let me guess... Lovers' paradise?"

She puckered her lips, then relaxed them into a smile.

"That too, but no. It means 'place of the blackfish' – to anyone in Quonnie, that is. The linguists say a more likely meaning is 'adjacent ponds by the long beach', but neither's certain. The thing is: What are blackfish? Daddy said they're whales. 'They're in the ocean all around us,' he'd say. 'Keep a lookout for them in case one capsizes us.' He said we might catch one. That really scared me, in a fun way. We never did see any, but we believed him because whales were in the field guide he kept in his tackle box – so we could always identify what we caught... They were such happy times...."

Colin felt sorry to break her reverie.

"I wish I'd known you then. My life didn't begin until I met you... It's a lovely fisherman's yarn your dad spun for you. But why would a field guide call a whale a fish? And what does it have to do with our tooth?

She gave him a scolding look.

"If you'll let me finish, I'll tell you... Blackfish can be sea bass, tautogs or any black fish. Most people who know the story assume Quonnie's named for the tautog aka tautaug because there are lots of them here and it's an Indian name. But blackfish can also mean pilot whales. Their native name also has an 'aug' ending. They're a species of dolphin that can grow to 20 feet and weigh 3 tons. They have big teeth for eating squid.

"Even whale-watchers are lucky if they see them nowadays, but they used to pass by off the coast in their thousands long ago – before the whalers almost wiped them out together with the rest of the great cetaceans. Nantucket and New Bedford were early whaling centers – before they became the world capital in the industry's heyday – due to their proximity to the summer feeding grounds of Stellwagen Bank, which runs from Cape Cod to Cape Ann.

"Nowadays, whale-watching cruises go there to see humpbacks, minke, fin and right whales. Daddy took us a couple of times. That's how I learned about them. Pilot whales live in pods of 10 to 30, but one group of 100 is on record. Whales sometimes get sick and disoriented. Strandings are common on Cape Cod. The pod follows its ailing leader into the shallows.

"In pre-Colonial days, ocean levels were lower, the coastline different and pilot whales abundant. What if the configuration of Block Island Sound formed a trap, leading them to strand at Quonnie? That would account for our tooth, and explain the name better than tautog, which are everywhere along the coast... What do you think?"

Colin twirled a finger in his long blond hair until it pulled pleasantly at the roots.

"I like it! They could have been driven ashore too. Quonnie Neck might have been the preferred place to strand them. The Nauset on Cape Cod and the Wampanoag on Martha's Vineyard and Nantucket used to go out in 10-man canoes to hunt and drive in whales that came too close to shore. I imagine the Manisee on Block Island did the same.

"The whales would be returning from the Gulf of Maine to warmer waters at summer's end, just as the Native Americans were stocking up for winter – always a time of semistarvation at best. An animal that size was an important source of food, oil for lighting and cooking, bone for tools, skin for clothing.

"Killing and flensing a whale and drying the blubber in smokehouses was a big job, requiring cooperative effort. So it was directed by the sachem, who was assigned ownership of the creatures and made sure the bounty was distributed fairly...

NIANTIC JEWEL

That's super. It means the amulet was crafted at Quonnie more likely than not... You made that look easy. Now do the same for the bracelet!"

Juliana furled her brow, deep in thought, and looked out to sea. Finally she took a sip of her iced tea and cleared her throat.

"It's really the same problem as the amulet – except there's an extra clue. The bracelet has two linked motifs – the serpent and the tomahawk – not just one – the osprey. To be buried with her – I know it's Quaiapen – they must have personal significance beyond the animals being clan totems. The tomahawk can mediate the snake's potential for evil – imbuing the wearer with its power. But this wasn't your ordinary snake. The Algonquian believed in a great serpent of the underworld. The bracelet neutralized it.

"Likewise the osprey represents the Thunderbird, the serpent's analog in the upper or sky world, whose great wings cause wind, thunder and lightning. It's a supernatural force for good and evil, and you want it on your side. This was a person who wielded power.

"But beyond that, of greater personal significance is that Mixanno wore the bracelet in my dream. He died in 1658 and Quaiapen in 1676. She wore it to remember him by or maybe it was a badge of office – of being co-sachem after him.

"Let's see if we can attribute a mark on a treaty or land deed to either of them. You focus on Mixanno and I'll take Quaiapen."

An hour later, Colin felt a surge of excitement. He swiveled his laptop around so she could see the screen.

"Look Jewel! Here's a 1655 letter from Mixanno in the Massachusetts Archives. He's congratulating John Endicott on being elected governor for a fifth time. It's written for him by Roger Williams and a tomahawk is given as his mark. We've really got something at last – proof that it's Mixanno's bracelet!"

Juliana looked at the mark and sighed sympathetically as she turned the laptop back to him.

"Unfortunately not, my dear. The sub-sachem Coquimaquand used a similar mark when he sold land at Boston Neck in today's Narragansett in 1659, the year after Mixanno died. I came across it in the Rhode Island Historical Society's records. Then I searched for tomahawk marks and, just for fun, bow and arrow marks.

Every Tom, Dick and Harry seems to have used one or the other. They were almost as popular as the ubiquitous X... Sorry to burst your bubble, but a tomahawk mark could belong to almost anyone. Coquimiquand and Quaiapen were neighbors up in North Kingstown, so now there's the possibility that, despite my dream, the bracelet is linked to him. Maybe she took up with him after Mixanno died."

Colin rapped his knuckles on the desk.

"Blimey, you're good. The two of them had adjoining lands. They'd have been a perfect political match. If he's the same sub-sachem the English also knew as Coginaquan, he was very high-born – a nephew of Canonicus, Mixanno's cousin and Quinnapin's father.

Juliana's face brightened.

"He's a complication for us, but on the plus side, the possibility of a connection to him points a bit more toward Gail being Quaiapen... Too bad Mixanno died before more about him could be recorded and that Quaiapen kept her distance from the English."

Colin gulped as a realization came to him.

"Now that you mention it, there is something else to suggest Gail is Quaiapen: There's a Narragansett burial ground known as the West Ferry site at Jamestown. It's thought that one of the graves is Mixanno's. Another contained the headless skeleton of a woman....."

Juliana jumped in on his thought.

"... Quaiapen! So they were buried together – minus her head – after all. But why there?"

"Because Roger Williams said Mixanno summered on Conanicut Island (now Jamestown). Actually, the tribe sold it twice. Williams and Sir Henry Vane of Boston acquired grazing and haying rights from Canonicus, Mixanno's father, in 1638. Twenty years later, Mixanno's two sons disputed the sale and got a group of Newporters to pay for it again.

NIANTIC JEWEL

"The burials fit the timeframe for Mixanno and Quaiapen. He died in 1658; she in 1676. The second sale of the island stipulated that the Indians be gone by 1660, but it's known that some returned after Metacom's War in 1676. Carbon dating plus the type of European goods interred with the dead indicate the cemetery's most active years were between 1630 and 1660.

"As with Quaiapen's skull, the rest of her remains would have been buried secretly.

"The Mixanno idea was put forward by anthropologist William S. Simmons, who excavated the site in 1966-7 and wrote about it in 'Cautantowwit's House.' He based his hunch on the fact that one grave stood out from the 57 others in the wealth of goods it contained: a flintlock musket, a storage trunk, a kettle, knives, wampum to name a few. It had to be a sachem's grave, and Mixanno lived there.

"Although some of the burials were disturbed during a partial dig in 1936, the headless woman's was not, leading Simmons to assert she was beheaded.

"Of course, only we know she's very likely Quaiapen. There's another hint that her body was brought there to be with Mixanno: Unlike the prized possessions that accompanied the vast majority of her neighboring souls into the afterlife, this woman was given nothing to take with her. That would be in line with how Quaiapen met her death in a massacre and what happened to her remains."

Juliana patted his arm in a gesture of encouragement.

"Well done connecting the dots! We're almost there. But why weren't the head and body reunited if Quaiapen's people recovered them? Why wasn't she buried beside Mixanno rather than in her own grave?"

He couldn't help but smile at her dogged skepticism.

"Chaos, that's why! What's done is done! What I mean is, after the beheading the head and body went their separate ways. It's maddening that Major Talcott didn't tell us more when he wrote about Quaiapen's death. I imagine it was a chaotic scene long after the actual massacre.

"If Ninigret's men ended up with the head and brought it to Quonnie, maybe some of her own people from North Kingstown escaped the massacre and retrieved the body. They'd want to bury it with Mixanno. Neither group knew what the other possessed. And they had to keep it secret or else the English would seize and further desecrate the remains.

"A couple of reasons could explain the two graves. Although we open graves to inter family members together, the Narragansett may have had a taboo against it. Or, considering the size of the graveyard and that at least 18 years had elapsed between burials, maybe Mixanno's exact whereabouts were unknown. After all, they didn't have headstones, just rock markers."

Juliana's body tensed and she gasped at the realization:

"Now that Quaiapen's headless grave's been rediscovered and her skull unearthed to us, her spirit wants it reunited with her body and her husband at Jamestown...."

Colin picked up her train of thought.

"... Her spirit's been wandering all these years, unable to enter Cautantowwit's house because she's not complete. Once they're together again, and she's next to Mixanno, they can spend eternity in carnal bliss.... That's why she revealed herself to you in your dreams."

Juliana cut in:

".... We're her intermediaries. She exposed her skull to us and started us on this treasure hunt. We have to finish it for her. If we're right, we still need more than just circumstantial links to them both."

*   *   *

They broke off the search at 4 and hurried over to the farm to find the Jerseys grumbling impatiently at the pasture gate. Two pairs of hands made the chores go faster, and by 6 they were swimming at the secluded nook off the Cove where he'd first laid eyes on her.

NIANTIC JEWEL

Scanning dozens of pages in the archives of four states had left them bug-eyed. Colin floated on his back, away from the rocks, tipping his head to let the saltwater soothe his eyelids. Juliana was out in deep water, swimming lengths as part of her daily regimen.

Back on the sand, stretched out with his hands clasped behind his neck, he watched her wade out of the shallows. A tingle went through him as he comprehended that she didn't mind his staring and even seemed to dwell on the act of drying off with the towel he'd tossed to her. Finally she lay down beside him, resting her head on his chest so that when she spoke the sound vibrated through his ribcage.

"It's not fair. I found four squaw sachems' marks. You'd think one could be Quaiapen's, but no... Weetamoo of the Pocasset, Awashonks of the Sakonnet, Quashawam of the Montauk and the Pawtucket queen without a name who took over when her husband Nanepashemet was killed by Tarrantine raiders from Maine in 1619. She befriended the English, especially the trader Edward Gibbons, and on her death in 1667 left his eldest son Jotham a vast amount of land.

"The Narragansett had two female sachems after Quaiapen: Ninigret's daughter Weunquesh who succeeded him in 1679, and Queen Esther, who was crowned in 1769 at Coronation Rock on Route 1A. But they would have been buried at the Royal Indian or Fort Neck burial grounds and their remains removed during excavations at both sites between 1859 and 1912.

"And, I found three other squaw sachems who didn't leave marks. In fact they left nothing but their names: Askamapoo of Nantucket and Addomas and Wunnatukquannumou of Martha's Vineyard.

"It's infuriating that Quaiapen helped negotiate at least two treaties with the colonists and yet had proxies sign for her. Fascinating too. You could infer that, as you said of her brother Ninigret, she was contemptuous of English coercion. He acquiesced only until the heat was off; she didn't personally sign anything, so she couldn't be held accountable the way he was....

"... Not that it helped her in the end. She might have been better off staying at her fort – in the Queen's Chamber. You probably

Graham Griffith

know there's a legend about a secret underground chamber. It's supposed to be 100 feet outside the western perimeter. But nobody's been able to find it. Can we go look for it?"

He started to laugh but their position made him sputter for air instead, and he had to prop himself up on his elbow.

"People have been searching for it for hundreds of years. At this point, I think we can say it doesn't exist. Maybe there was one and it caved in before people started looking for it... We could try to find Crying Rocks though. It's right here in Charlestown and it's haunted!"

She rolled over on her back and gazed up at him, wide-eyed.

"Now that sounds scary! Do we have to go there at night?"

"Not on your life. It's deep in the woods on the reservation. We'll need to get permission at the tribal administration offices."

"And directions, I hope. Remember when we went looking for the Narragansett Indian Church and the Royal Indian Burial Ground last month? You'd think they'd be easy to find, being on the National Register of Historic Places, but they're deep in the woods, too. Thank goodness you called ahead and the Tribal Police offered to take us. That was fun, riding forest trails in their SUV."

"I doubt if they know where Crying Rocks is. It's more folkloric than historic. Another book by William S. Simmons, "Spirit of the New England Tribes," quotes Rev. Harold Mars in 1983 as saying the rocks are about a mile west of the church and north of the old schoolhouse site on the edge of Indian Cedar Swamp. He was the tribe's minister for many years so he related the legend as a negative memorate – an apparently supernatural happening with a logical explanation – but who knows for sure? Most legends have at least a grain of truth."

Juliana yawned and rose slowly to her feet.

"That would make a nice outing to come down for some warm afternoon in foliage season, but for now just tell me the legend... The sun's so warm, I'll go to sleep if we stay here much longer, and I'm getting hungry. I'm in the mood for the Hitching Post's clam plate, and you can have the fish and chips."

NIANTIC JEWEL

He took the hand she offered and pulled himself up while pondering how much easier life was when decisions were made for him, and comforted by the prospect of his favorite meal at the venerable diner-cum-takeout stand on Route 1.

"Alright, but we have to eat in the car so we can watch the people parade... Anyway, you wanted to know the legend. It was being told in the early 18th Century. Possibly, it's very ancient. The Crying Rocks are a formation of huge glacial boulders. They were described in 1761 by Rev. Ezra Stiles, the foremost intellectual in the Colonies who was a Congregational pastor in Newport 1755-77 and president of Yale 1778-95. He called them Bastard Rocks.

"The story goes that Narragansett babies with birth defects were abandoned there to die. You could hear them wailing if you passed by at night. Maybe you still can. Rev. Mars said the crying is caused by the wind funneling between the rocks."

Juliana clutched his arm as they stepped from the beach onto the boardwalk.

"That is a good ghost story! Most primitive cultures sanction selective infanticide... It's horrible, but makes sense, particularly in New England. Winter was an instrument of natural selection allowing survival of only the fittest. I suppose babies born out of wedlock were added to the toll after contact with Christianity."

Colin opened the car door for her.

"There'd be more of them after that, but the Narragansett had a pretty strict moral code themselves. Probably the fruit of adulterous or incestuous unions was doomed – and don't forget that incest included the whole clan not just the nuclear family... No one knows what criteria the Narragansett used: Were birthmarks taboo as they were for the Hawaiians?

"In any case, there was nothing to agonize over. It was all preordained by the custom of millennia. Crying Rocks has manitou derived from Chepi. Remember him? – the ghost descended from souls unworthy of admission to Cautantouwwit's house. He was feared because he punished bad behavior, made rain and cured and created illness. Chepi appeared in cold, dark and windy places, but in daily life he acted through the powwows, who were his 'priests.'

"The English who took the trouble to get to know the Narragansett were struck by their love of children. They were indulgent parents compared to the disciplinarian Puritans. Putting their babies out to die must have been devastating for them. Presumably, the manitou of Crying Rocks perfected the little souls, so they could enter Cautantouwwit's house to live in everlasting joy."

CHAPTER 15

SOUL-SEARCHING

I felt that there were invisible lines stretched
between my spirit and the spirits of others.
HELEN KELLER

Twilight settled over the pond in a velvet embrace as they passed by on their way back to the Palmers'. The sun's disc had already dipped below the wooded hills beyond Route 1, casting an iridescent mauve light on the underside of a long band of cirrus clouds.

Colin felt the tension of conflicted emotions. Nightfall was likely to change their relationship forever. Juliana had made it clear she wanted to seize the opportunity of her parents' absence to consummate their love at last. His pulse quickened at the prospect of becoming one with her, and yet... Alise Palmer's parting words bound him to forgo his heart's desire: "I'm entrusting her to you... I know you won't let me down." Just the idea made his stomach spasm with the bitter taste of betrayal that would turn the sacred into the profane.

He waited until they'd parked before drawing her hand to his lips and kissing it.

"I want you so much. But your mum's outmaneuvered us, hasn't she? It's as if she read your mind!"

Juliana gave a growl of exasperation mixed with amused resignation and slapped the dashboard with her free hand. She leaned across to peck his cheek.

Graham Griffith

"I know. Thanks so much for seeing it. I've been wondering what to do all evening. Curses! She doesn't have the right. I'm an adult... We could go to your house, or the beach."

He squeezed her thigh where the short saffron caftan had ridden up. The flesh felt warm and supple.

"Yes, but it really wouldn't change anything, would it? I don't know how I'd face her. She'd know. We're in check... Anyway, she's only thinking of you. They don't want you throwing yourself away on a summer fling with a ne'er-do-well."

She reached for the back of his head and drew him to her.

"I wish you wouldn't talk like that. They'll get used to the idea of us. We'll show them. I'll make you famous. You'll reinvent yourself. I'll inspire you to be the next Samuel Eliot Morison. But you'll be a famous recluse, like Thomas Pynchon or J. D. Salinger. I'm not sharing you. I want you for myself. I want you beside me all the time. You're mine. I love you."

"I love you too. I want to be with you forever. I'll inspire you to be the next Camille Paglia. Maybe it's too soon anyway – for such a total commitment."

She looked deep into his eyes, into his very soul.

"Not for me, but I can wait a while longer."

Their lips met in a long, voracious kiss that lasted until they were both breathless. Suddenly, he gripped her hand and led her back up to her room.

"Why didn't I think of it before! It's been here all along."

"What has?"

He reached for a book in the backpack under the desk.

"Mixanno's doppelganger. It came to me when you said reinvent."

"Whoa! You mean he had a double – a ghostly astral body?... You're talking supernatural now. Let's get real, Sweetie."

"No! Not a ghost, though it might have been part of their cosmology."

He leafed through his copy of Samuel Drake's 1833 "Book of the Indians of North America."

"Remember my mentioning that sachems changed their names quite a bit?"

NIANTIC JEWEL

"Yes… sometimes taking a forebear's name."

"Well, this book shows that they also changed their marks, their pictographic signatures – maybe to reflect a name-change, which in turn could have been their way of reinventing themselves…."

She picked up his drift as she came around the desk and leaned over him to look at the book.

"…. To become a better person worthy of entry to Cautantouwit's house; to make a new beginning on earth; to create a new persona and the prestige to go with it… Like your eschewing journalism for something better… Oops! You know what I mean."

"I think so… But look at these marks. It's the March 24, 1637, deed by which five Narragansett sachems convey Rhode Island (aka Aquidneck) and most islands in the bay to William Coddington et al for eight fathoms of white wampum each. The inhabitants were to receive 10 coats and 20 hoes to vacate by winter.

"Mixanno's mark isn't a tomahawk but the same serpentine squiggle that's on the bracelet. Canonicus' and Miantonomi's marks aren't bows and arrows but stalks of corn… And here's a 1668 deed marked by Metacom with an N not a P; a letter written for him by his interpreter to Plymouth's governor gives his mark as a trumpet."

Juliana gave a low whistle, so close to his cheek that he inhaled the earthy sweetness of her breath.

"So we've traced two marks to Mixanno, both of which are on the bracelet… I don't think it's a snake though. Now that I've seen it in the book, it looks more like a ripple. There's no head. D'you see?"

"You're right. It's water, either a river or the ocean. His family lived near both in the main village of the Narragansett. It was a sprawled out town really because it must have held more than 1,000 people. Yet its location is a mystery. More likely it was several adjacent villages each containing its own clan. The word Narragansett means 'people of the small point,' which is supposed to allude to an island in Point Judith Pond.

"The tribe was certainly concentrated in the area, so the villages were probably beside the Pettaquamscutt River – within 3 miles north or south of Pettaquamscutt Rock, the 60-foot-high landmark where Roger Williams and others did business with the sachems. Mixanno's father Canonicus lived on a plain opposite Williams' trading post at Wickford Point. That seems too far north for the main village complex, but as paramount sachem he may have needed to be away from the hurly-burly. His nephew and co-sachem Miantonomi lived on Boston Neck at the head of the Pettaquamscutt River, closer to the center of things."

Juliana went back to her laptop with a downcast look.

"But now that there's no snake representing evil for the tomahawk to conquer, the figures lose their purpose – they're just pretty decorations! That weakens the bracelet's significance if it has no spiritual meaning. The symbolism gave it a luster of authenticity...."

He held up his hand to stop her.

"Actually, this is far more interesting. The tomahawk is still an instrument of good triumphing over evil. But the water is heavily charged with manitou, the divine power observable in anything marvelous, beautiful or dangerous. Water exhibits all three qualities.

"It's a portal to the underworld, leading to the Cosmic Axis at the center of the earth. Guardian spirits dwelt in watery places. This was one reason, apart from being harder to find them, why Native Americans fled to swamps to escape the English: They were closer to their otherworldly protectors.

"Then there's the reflection phenomenon. Anything shiny that reflected an image was magical – thus the manitou of water, wampum shells, polished stones and European looking glasses and reflective metals. A person's reflection was taken to be the visible image of their michachunk, that part of the dual soul that is the body's animating force. Anytime you got to see it, you were communing with the spirit world."

A disarming smile of approval flashed across her face.

"Well done! The bracelet protects from the underworld and the tooth from the overworld. That's a comprehensive insurance

NIANTIC JEWEL

policy!... Still, it's only conjecture. And to be honest, the link to Mixanno isn't indisputable."

She brought her hands together in prayer and stared at the ceiling.

"Please, Cautantouwit, show me a connection between Quaiapen and the amulet – before these dreams drive me crazy."

*   *   *

Shallow swells broke ashore with glinting spray as they walked hand in hand along Little Beach on their way to the farm late Thursday morning. Sanderlings scurried ahead stabbing for morsels on the wet margin of the ebb tide. Overhead, a gull's raspy cawing drew attention to platinum bands of cirrocumulus advancing into the cerulean sky and the clear outline of Block Island across the Sound.

Colin stopped to look at the island, inhaling deeply as he did.

Mindful of his every move, Juliana leaned backward against him and followed his gaze.

"There's perfect visibility. That means it's going to rain. What do you want to bet?"

"Not so fast, Ms. Palmer! I was checking the wind direction. You need to know that."

"Sooo...?

"You win! It's from the Northeast. We've missed the best part of the day trolling the Internet for nothing. Now it's going to cloud over and rain later on, if the wind holds steady. After lunch let's have a long siesta on the veranda until milking time."

She turned and, clasping her hands behind his neck, reached up to kiss him.

"You're getting discouraged, I can tell. No way was it a wasted morning. We spent it together, didn't we? That's enough happiness for me... And getting nowhere helped me decide on something I've wanted to do for ages."

"Which is..."

"... to find out if Grandma's story about our having a Native American ancestor, Daughter of the Moon, is true – by getting a DNA test. You can order a kit online and mail in swabs of saliva. A few days later, you get a report of how certain genes compare to those associated with the tribe or to a geographic area. I've already got the kit, but I guess I've been scared to go ahead and do it."

He took her hand and started walking. After a couple of steps he kicked off his right sandal, sending it somersaulting into the air and ejecting the periwinkle that had lodged against his instep. Then without breaking stride he stepped back into the sandal as it landed straight on its sole.

"Isn't it expensive?"

"Not if I charge it!... Well, yes – $200. I can manage half, and maybe I can cajole Daddy into coming up with the rest... Just think of what it will mean if...."

She left the thought hanging, as if afraid to give it life. He had no such qualms.

"... if your genetic inheritance can shape your dreams. It would be as if your Native American ancestors were trying to contact you across time. We already know you and your mum can communicate telepathically... I think you should do it. I'll stake you for the rest. It's hardly the kind of investment your dad would jump at, yet it would hurt him to refuse you. Why put him through the grief of that dilemma?"

"You're a sweetie, but I don't know... I'll have to think about it...."

He quickly changed the subject, distracting her for good measure by stroking her bare back between the straps of the purple blouson tank top she had on over ivory cutoffs.

"Anyway, how does it work? How reliable is it?"

"There are labs that specialize in genealogy, including Native American ancestry. They can test autosomal (i.e. non-sex) chromosomes, which we inherit from both parents, or mitochondrial DNA, which comes only from the mother. I want the mtDNA test because it traces the maternal lineage back in time.

NIANTIC JEWEL

"The key is haplogroup X, a cluster of similar haplotypes that share a common ancestor with a single nucleotide polymorphism (SNP) mutation. It's one of five haplogroups found in Native Americans. In Algonquians it comprises 25 percent of mtDNA types.

"Until fairly recently, that was as much as the test could pinpoint for someone like me: a few genes shared with the hundreds of Algonquian tribes. Then, genetic markers were found that narrowed the field down to New England and then to southern New England. Now it's pretty accurate for specific tribes... Race you to the top."

They'd reached the path through the dunes and were plodding through the deep sand up the slope from the beach. He dug in, straining to match her effort, but after a few strides he was left with only the appealing rear view of her rippling thigh muscles. Atop the dune, she knelt to lend him a hand until he could collapse on top of her. Taking full advantage, he showered her face with kisses then rubbed noses and surrendered himself to her mesmerizing eyes.

"You're amazing. A Blockhead observing us would have to say the female is the stronger and smarter of the species. No wonder I can't decide if it's your body or your mind I love the most. Explain that DNA stuff again so a mere male can understand it."

With a swivel of her hips, she rolled him off her and sat up. An impish smile crossed her face.

"Maybe it's Quaiapen's genes... But no, the Blockhead would be wrong. I can beat you only in those areas in which I've trained or studied and you haven't – and vice versa. We can't generalize about gender or the human mind. Predisposition isn't predestination. Psychology can change the course of biology. Take Mitochondrial Eve for example...."

"Riiight. Wasn't she the first woman?

"In a way. She's the matrilineal most recent common ancestor for all currently living humans. Her mtDNA has been passed down through the female line for 140,000 years. Every bit of mtDNA in every person is derived from hers. Conversely, her male counterpart, Y-chromosomal Adam is only 60,000 years old.

Graham Griffith

"She must have had a special transcribable quality, or combination of qualia, that transcended her biology alone. After all, there was unremitting competition from all sorts of mutations that didn't survive. Yet her unique mtDNA did.

"Her phenotype, being the anatomical and psychological traits that result from heredity and environment, was more important than her genotype, being the purely hereditary factors in her DNA."

Colin stood up and pulled Juliana to her feet, taking delight in brushing the sand off her body before they set out along the dune path.

"So the Bible, the Torah and the Koran all have the Adam & Eve story backward: Eve came first and Adam was made from her... I still don't get these haplo thingamabobs. What are they all about?

"Mmmh... I'm afraid it's rather dense molecular biology. Let's start at the beginning. I'm sure you know the main role of DNA/deoxyribonucleic acid is long-term storage of information in a code that contains instructions for making cell components. In the cell nucleus, DNA is organized into chromosomes, which carry genes in a double helix formation. The DNA itself comprises nucleic acids whose basic units are pairs of nucleotides. It's the order or sequence of the nucleotides in the double helix within a gene that specifies its structure and role...."

Emerging from the dunes, they crossed Sunset Beach Road and climbed over the wall by the white oak into the sheep pasture. Out of habit, Colin stopped to count the 20 Cheviots as they lay ruminating under the tree. Juliana waited for him to finish, then tugged him gently by the hand.

"... Sorry about the genetic science, but that's what DNA testing is after all... I said there are two kinds of DNA: autosomal and mitochondrial. Unlike the former, which is part of the cell nucleus, mtDNA comes from organelles outside the nucleus. These are structures that convert food into energy to power the cell.

"Either of two paired genes located at the same position on both members of a pair of chromosomes is an allele. A person's genotype for a gene is the set of alleles it has. The haplotype, i.e.

NIANTIC JEWEL

the haploid genotype, is the combination of alleles at multiple linked loci that are transmitted together on a chromosome. For purposes of genetic testing, it's an individual collection of short tandem repeat allele mutations within a genetic segment.

"The mutations or alterations thus become genetic markers that can be observed. These point to the regions and tribal populations where a person's DNA is most common. If I'm really lucky, the markers will show Daughter of the Moon's tribal affiliation and where she lived. It depends how extensive the lab's data bank is for southern New England... Pretty neat huh?"

As they neared the gate to the farmyard, Molly walked along the top of the wall to meet them, purring loudly and slowly undulating her tail in a feline felicitation. Juliana scooped her off the gatepost and cooed baby talk while cradling her in her arms.

"I'm going to do it, Molly. My mind's made up. I'll put it in the mailbox tonight."

Colin groaned melodramatically.

"Curses! That means no French kissing until you've swabbed your cheek."

*   *   *

In the kitchen, Juliana deposited Molly in the inglenook. Colin put on the kettle for a cup of tea, then opened the refrigerator.

"What do you feel like for lunch? There's not much here. We could share a gut buster from Michael's?"

"I can't wait that long. Let me surprise you."

She started taking cans and jars from the shelves until she had all the ingredients for a tuna melt. Fifteen minutes later Colin gave a satisfied burp.

"Excuse me! That was soo good. Why is it that what you make is always the best I've ever tasted?"

She swallowed the last mouthful and sipped her tea.

"I thought you'd approve. It's Mother's recipe. The vinegar and Dijon make the difference. I had to do without the diced celery, but you don't really need it."

Afterward, they walked down to the dock where the Old Queen rode the incoming tide on her mooring. They sat on the edge, the great pond stretched out in front of them, splashing their bare feet in the water and watching the boats come and go through the breachway.

Soon, Colin swiveled around to rest his back against a piling and Juliana slid between his legs with her head against his shoulder. She took his hands and wrapped them around her waist.

"The sun's so warm, I could doze off in a flash. Tell me an Indian story and maybe we'll have a dream together."

He caressed her shimmering hair with his cheek and drank in her fragrance. High above the boat channel, he noticed one of the ospreys patrolling the current for a meal. It brought Quaiapen back to mind, and when he spoke his voice was tinged with frustration.

"Look at the osprey circling over the breachway. Maybe it's Quaiapen's spirit playing tricks with us – within sight but out of reach. If only there were more stories to tell about her, there'd be more clues. Oh well... I'll tell you the story of Canonchet's greatest victory."

Juliana pressed against him in anticipation.

"He succeeded Quaiapen's husband Mixanno as great sachem, right?"

"Very good! That was on Mixanno's death in 1658. But until Metacom's War in 1675, Canonchet took a back seat to his uncle and co-sachem Pessicus. Their advisors were the sachems Quinnapin, Pomham, Ninigret and... Quaiapen.

"In the lead-up to the war, Pessicus and Ninigret took the pragmatic view that the English were powerful enough to take what they wanted – i.e. Narragansett land – and that by putting themselves at their mercy the tribe would at least retain enough land to live on. Of the other four sachems, Quinnapin, Pomham and particularly Canonchet preferred death in war to dishonor in peace; Quaiapen hoped neutrality would avoid the worst of both extremes.

"After the Great Swamp massacre of Dec. 19, 1675, Ninigret continued his successful policy of English-leaning neutrality until

NIANTIC JEWEL

being forced squarely into the Puritan camp in late March. Quaiapen courageously adopted an Indian-leaning neutrality by avoiding direct involvement in the conflict while providing refuge and humanitarian aid to native people.

"Pessicus sent peace overtures to the United Colonies well into January 1676. They were rejected but bought him time to get those women, children and old men who escaped the Great Swamp slaughter to safety in the New Hampshire forests, where he soon joined them. He was killed `20 miles above the Piscataqua [River]' by Mohawk raiders the following year.

"The departure of Pessicus in late January left Canonchet, aided by Quinnapin and Pomham, at the head of about 2,000 warriors eager for revenge against the English. Skillfully evading the United Colonies army, Canonchet left Narragansett Country to link up in Central Massachusetts with the Wampanoag and Nipmuck, who had already been fighting the English for seven months.

"Although the Narragansett didn't know it, their escape inflicted a kind of defeat on the English – an ordeal that became known as the Hungry March. Fourteen hundred soldiers pursued Canonchet west as far as Marlborough, Mass., where they ran out of food. They ate their horses to alleviate starvation on the 25-mile trek back to Boston, but still endured frostbite, exhaustion and despair.

"Once at the Nipmuck stronghold of Quaboag (Brookfield), Canonchet became the uprising's tactical leader. Metacom was at Schaghticoke near Albany trying to recruit allies and obtain guns and powder. And none of the Nipmuck sachems alone could equal Canonchet's numbers. So it fell to him to carry out Metacom's strategic plan of capturing and holding towns in the Connecticut River Valley as a prelude to bringing Boston, Hartford and New Haven to their knees.

"In the following weeks, he masterminded attacks against several settlements. But the harsh winter, lack of food and rampant disease took a terrible toll on the Native Americans. Metacom's return to Massachusetts and his refusal to take counsel from the other sachems led to growing dissatisfaction with his leadership. By mid-March whole bands were deserting him, either to seek whatever peace terms they could get or to carry on the struggle in their own way.

"Canonchet apparently agreed with Metacom's strategy of concentrating attacks in the Connecticut River Valley, or maybe he just accepted there was no going back: that it was kill or be killed. The April fish runs and the vital food source they represented brought hostilities to a temporary halt. Peace advocates on both sides used the lull to open talks.

"There was an unofficial ceasefire while hundreds of Indians fished openly at falls on the river and the English tried to negotiate the release of scores of captive settlers. Any hopes of peace were dashed with the massacre of Turner's Falls on May 19.

"By then, Canonchet was dead. He left the valley early in March to retrieve the tribe's seed corn from Narragansett Country, intending to return and plant it on abandoned English fields beside the river. His 200-300 surviving warriors also planned to pillage and burn along the way. On March 12 they destroyed Clark's Garrison at Plymouth. Four days later, they torched what was left of Warwick. Old Rehoboth was attacked March 28; 45 homes, 21 barns, 2 corn mills and a sawmill were destroyed. The next day, 100 structures were burned in Providence including the home of Roger Williams.

"The appearance of warriors on the outskirts of the largely abandoned town a few days earlier led the 73-year-old Williams to go out and speak to them. He told them what they had no doubt heard from Pessicus and Ninigret months before: Their cause was hopeless. No matter how many English they killed, others would replace them until there were no Narragansett left. Probably, he spoke to Canonchet himself because he was told he would not be harmed in recognition of past friendship.

"In between these events, on Sunday, March 26, occurred Canonchet's finest hour: Peirce's Fight. Acting on reports of Indians at the Pawtucket Falls a few miles north Providence, Capt. Michael Peirce of Scituate led 63 Plymouth militiamen and 20 allied Cape Cod Indians in search of the enemy. Marching out from Taunton on Saturday, they made contact with the

NIANTIC JEWEL

Narragansett in several skirmishes before returning 13 miles to the garrison for the night.

"Picking up the hunt on Sunday, Peirce saw some apparently wounded warriors fleeing over a rise. He took the bait and pursued them straight into an ambush in which 55 English and 10 allied Indians died. The remaining 9 English were captured and later executed. The 10 Cape Indians who escaped reported they were faced by 500 Narragansett and when they tried to retreat their way was blocked by 400 more. Exaggerating the enemy's strength, then as now, makes military disasters more excusable.

"After the victory, the Narragansett split into raiding parties. Canonchet's was spotted a week later along the Pawtucket River by Mohegan scouts attached to a Connecticut force that included two of Thomas Stanton's sons. He was outmaneuvered and captured without a fight when he dropped his flintlock into the river. Taken to Stonington and told he would be put to death, he...."

Juliana tilted her head back to look at him.

"... gave that heroic speech: `I like it well; I shall die before my heart is soft, or have said anything unworthy of myself.' Am I right?"

Colin's head spun momentarily.

"You beat me to it. That is what he said, word for word. But I don't recall telling you about it before. Do you remember when that was?"

She giggled knowingly.

"It didn't happen, Sweetheart. I knew what you were going to say; what you were thinking. Don't ask me how – but you know I'd never remember something like that verbatim. Don't worry! It only happens between Mother and me once in a blue moon. Your thoughts are safe – most of the time. Isn't that exciting, though? I feel closer to you. D'you think it could have been the blood transfusion that did it?"

He didn't want to deal with the unnerving implications.

"Maybe you came across it browsing one of my books. You know you like to do that. And it is a memorable declaration... Anyway, before his capture, Canonchet was able to send large amounts of plundered corn for the women and children with Pessicus in New Hampshire. The other raiding parties carrying it north burned and looted at Bridgewater, Hingham, Weymouth, Braintree, Sudbury, Marlborough, Chelmsford, Billerica, Woburn and Andover as they passed by.

"The loss of Canonchet dealt a death blow to Native American resistance. As word spread, the will to continue fighting ebbed away and the surrenders began. The steady trickle became a flood after June 19 when the Bay State issued a declaration of amnesty. Under its terms, those who surrendered had their lives spared but were to be sold as slaves. Metacom was hunted down and killed Aug. 12. When mopping up operations ended in October, there were about 200 Narragansett left from a prewar population of 5-7,000.

"A few remained in Rhode Island either in servitude or safe with Ninigret if they had relatives among the Niantic. The rest were in slavery elsewhere or had fled to Canada or New York. In a year, the English had killed or dispersed more than 95% of the tribe – a genocide by the United Nations definition: the deliberate destruction of a racial, political or cultural group."

*   *   *

Juliana said nothing, then pushed down on his thighs and rose to her feet. Turning to him, she offered her outstretched hands to help him up.

"I've had enough sun. It's time for some shade. Let's go swing on the veranda… I need cheering up. That story makes me sad. I don't know what you see in history. It's so depressing. Doesn't it make you ashamed to be English? It was your people who did that."

He took her help and let her lead him off the dock.

"I couldn't be ashamed if I thought of them as my people, could I. That kind of chauvinism would assume they couldn't do anything shameful. A superpatriot must psychologically rationalize his country's evil actions."

She bumped her shoulder against him for effect.

NIANTIC JEWEL

"Don't get cute with me, Sweetie. You know what I mean. Surely your country means something to you. If you want to talk psychology, your motherland anchors your identity. Without it you can never be fully actualized as a person. Hegel said we must love the state to be happy."

"Crikey! I can't think of anything worse. Hitler and Stalin showed us where that leads. I don't deny my country, but I don't have to like it or dislike it. I can be objective. I prefer being a citizen of the world, in which case I can neither take indirect credit for the good nor bear collective responsibility for the bad done by the nation I nominally belong to. It's irrational to bear allegiance to a country right or wrong. If you ask them, most people would say they love their country, but if we love our fellow man, how can we love one country more or less than another?

"A nation's just a society of individuals with a shared culture – or, now that we live in a global village, a shared multiculture. I think we say we love our country because it's the only one we know. We can't love a country we don't know, and the primitive brain registers every unknown as a threat.

"Nationalism is something to be transcended. It brings out the worst in people – a false sense of superiority, a license to run roughshod over everyone else, Manifest Destiny and the dangerous notion that God's on our side.

"It's the same self-righteous extremism the Puritans lived by, and in the end it killed them. Like all bigots, fanatics, zealots and revolutionaries, they devoured themselves eventually."

When they reached the rubbing rock and the excavation's green plastic cover, she stopped and turned to look out over the pond.

"It's more of your weird theory of natural justice, isn't it? The same rationale you use to say that we shouldn't hold people accountable or punish them because they'll inevitably punish themselves worse then we ever could.

"But where does that leave right and wrong? You'd have people get away with murder. Those responsible for the genocide of Native Americans may be dead and unreachable, but we dishonor the victims if we don't condemn the guilty. Isn't it intellectual cowardice to say everything's relative to the Zeitgeist?

Graham Griffith

"You're falling back on cultural/moral relativism/skepticism – whatever you want to label it – rooted in the idea that the English Puritans, and the Americans who continued the genocide almost into the 20th Century, can't be judged because they believed they were doing God's work.

He threw up his hands with a cry of frustration.

"You backed me into a corner while I wasn't paying attention, and now you've skewered me. Your mum would be proud... I wanted to say – ponderous as it is – that these normative values which the weight of popular assent imbues with critical mass so that they become 'truths we hold to be self-evident,' aren't eligible candidates for right because there is no objective truth – only the subjective truth we feel inside us. That's what punishes us, prevents the mentally ill from being culpable and precludes us from judging the past."

She pulled him to her as they walked, laying her head against his shoulder.

"I'll meet you halfway. I love my country in so far as it's the only one I've lived in. And I need a country to love in the same way as I need a family. They're components of the actualized person. On the other hand, my love is conditional – unlike a superpatriot's.

"And since much of what I love about my country has to do with its founding principles – like separation of church and state, freedom of conscience, my right to practice any religion or none – I abhor those who would impose their belief in a Supreme Being on me by institutionalizing it in the state and even outlawing my disobedience.

"What would Roger Williams have thought of state-appointed chaplains, prayers at government assemblies, the Pledge of Allegiance (with or without mention of God) and 'In God We Trust' as the official national motto? He would have gone back to England, wouldn't he?"

Colin cupped his arm around her waist.

"I doubt it. He was fleeing a church state after all. Incredibly, Britain's still a church state, although it's considered poor form to mention it, being inextricably entwined with the monarchy, the aristocracy and all things peculiarly British. But the taxpayers still support the Church of England just as colonial taxpayers were forced to support the Bay State's Puritan/Congregational church until 1782.

"Secular republics have largely replaced church states and monarchies, but they're no guarantee of freedom of conscience. Take flag-burning. We'd agree it's a particularly tasteless form of protest, but bad taste is an effective attention-getter. You'd think countries like Britain, the US and Japan for which the flag is a highly charged emotional symbol might ban flag-burning but their protection of free speech trumps an insult to the nation. Not so in France and Germany, which we think of as being more tolerant.

"It goes to show that the majority can be just as tyrannical as the dictator or the oligarchy – even if they're merely protecting national pride from insolence and disrespect. An idea that achieves the critical mass to become customary and accepted shouldn't be immune from future rejection. We've seen that the Homeland Security Act can protect our freedoms or do just the opposite. Genocide and slavery are still with us, and not just in primitive societies. Germany entered the 1930s being highly civilized; Serbia in the '90s. Deep down, we'll always be human animals."

*   *   *

They climbed the front steps to the veranda and sat in the swing chair, not moving at first until Juliana pushed off with her feet to set it in motion. He put his arm around her and she cuddled close, her voice resonating against his chest.

"It would be nice if there was only progress and no regress: that evils once banished stay that way. Then there'd be no more wars. But few things in life are immutable; the rest are subject to review. You only have to look at Roe v. Wade. It's been under siege ever since the ruling in 1973. Ditto gay marriage, equal rights, nondiscrimination. Abstract tenets must be authenticated by real-life experience superimposed on the matrix of time. Civilization is

Graham Griffith

time conforming to Darwinian evolution, and democracy is a magical time machine, a mechanism for converting past utility into future progress."

She had them swinging so energetically that her outstretched feet grazed the old balustrade, causing it to creak ominously.

"Sorry. I was getting carried away... How can you suspend your judgment about war. Its obscenities confound civilization. It's mass insanity. Pure unrestrained testosterone. There'll come a day when most of the world's leaders are women. They'll rescind the state's monopoly on violence. War is outlawed. No one wants to be a soldier so there are no armies. Then if the militarists decided to have a war, no one would come."

He patted her on the back.

"May we live long enough to see it... Yet if someone's out to kill my family, it's kill or be killed. I justify my violence as self-defense. But all judgments about war are subjective. They're not eligible to be statements of right or truth. They're merely expressions of emotion. The outcome has meaning only to the participants. In the greater scheme of things, good triumphs eventually because it benefits the species more than any short-term success of evil.

"The life force that powers evolution doesn't care about me or my loved ones. We're only vehicles for our genes after all. Our lifespans are insignificant. The sole imperative is survival of the fittest in the sense of best adapted. The blueprint we see all around us in Nature is coldly, mindlessly amoral. What sets us apart is the accident of the human mind which reaches its highest expression in cognitive love – an emotional state unknown by other animals. Because of it, we know right, since it emanates from love. And our conscience knows that we know.

"There's an incident in Metacom's War that's all about judging. It's after the tide has turned in summer 1676. English-led Mohegan are being allowed to torture to death a captured Narragansett warrior. Others will be executed humanely or sold as slaves, but this one has boasted of killing 19 Englishmen and a Mohegan. His suffering will be an act of revenge. The English soldiers look on.

NIANTIC JEWEL

"The Puritans used torture to extract information and confessions or as punishment, particularly against Quakers. Ears were cut off and tongues pierced with hot pokers. Torture for sadistic pleasure was a temporal and spiritual sin, despite the tolerated excesses of racists like Samuel Moseley, the Boston captain who had a captive squaw torn apart by dogs.

"It was different for the Algonquian. Their ritualized battles, lacking tactics, resulted in few casualties. In the Northeast, only the Iroquois waged total European-style war. Until the advent of the fur trade, land was rarely a cause of hostilities. Whereas Europeans fought for territorial dominion and sovereign authority over the vanquished, Indian victors achieved a symbolic ascendancy marked by modest payments of tribute.

"Rather, `mourning war' was the rule. The hardships of existence produced high mortality and low reproductive rates among clans. The customary means of maintaining a viable population was the taking and adoption of captives, especially women, the earth mothers who grew or gathered most of the food.

"Surplus male prisoners were executed by a tomahawk blow to the back of the head. A select few who'd shown courage in battle were singled out for torture, not out of savage cruelty but in a complex ceremonial that served social, cultural and personal needs.

"First, it honored bravery, the most prized of the manly virtues. The prisoner was expected to endure his ordeal willingly, as an opportunity to display his stoicism, sometimes in silence, sometimes shouting in defiance at his tormentors and dancing during the agony.

"Second, it initiated a spiritual journey creating admiration in this world and rewards in the next both for the victim and the dead clan member in whose name the captive undertakes his ordeal.

"Third, the spectacle takes place inside a circle of onlookers who each mourn the deceased while joined in collective catharsis centered on the sacrificial victim's agony and ecstasy. Sometimes, morsels of the warrior's flesh were consumed passing on his bravery to the living. You can see the parallel to Christ's crucifixion, resurrection and Holy Communion, complete with transubstantiation.

"I won't go into the gory details. They were part of the ever-popular literature of atrocity. In Metacom's War, as in all others, both sides committed cruelty. Naturally, the English described only Indian brutality in the standard propaganda ploy of portraying the enemy as subhuman and the Christian soldiers as saints. In fact, this particular episode was chronicled by a minister, Rev. William Hubbard of Ipswich, Mass.

"The point is...."

Juliana put a hand on his thigh.

"... Let me guess: You're pleading special circumstances for the torturers? The madness of war?"

"No. It's not about them. As you correctly suspect, they're exempted by cultural relativism, although even that's redundant by my way of thinking. It's about the soldiers. Even if, for various reasons, they're reluctant voyeurs, their civilized standards have been compromised. By being there, willingly or not, whether disgusted by or wallowing in the depravity, they're no better than the 'uncivilized' participants. They're all defiled by a loss of innocence.

"So the civilized soldiers can't be judged because they're only human – poor souls striving to live honorably while shackled to human fallibility. Free will is license to err. They can look at the Indian and say 'There go I but for the grace of God and the accident of birth.' One fallible being can't judge another. We can be asked to account for our actions, but not punished for them. That's our private prerogative, the burden of our human bondage. Otherwise we're self-righteous hypocrites."

Throwing her head back, she gave him a loud raspberry.

"You're going overboard again. You've already abolished the military. Now you're scrapping the police and the judiciary. Life in your state of nature really would be 'nasty, brutish and short.' Bet you don't know which English philosopher said that!"

"Prince Charles? Monty Python?"

"Stop it! You know it's Thomas Hobbes. Not a favorite, I guess."

NIANTIC JEWEL

"No, he didn't see much goodness in people. Then again, he was a contemporary of the Puritans, who thought everyone was basically evil; born in a state of sin. His idea of a social contract by which I surrender my all to the state as the alternative to a violent death living free but terrified in a state of nature is no bargain is it?

"I'm not saying abolish the whole military establishment – just 90 percent. Megalomaniacs must be stopped preemptively by common consent when all else fails. That's best done by assiduous intelligence-gathering and special forces operations before problems escalate into crises.

"Responsibility would lie with a loose world government. There wouldn't be nations with presidents as we know them exercising sovereignty over territory. Rather, peoples with the same language and heritage would form compacts based on tolerance and freedom for all. They'd pledge peaceful coexistence with their neighbors, without governments, without leaders, without borders...."

She wanted to tease him to see how his utopia would bear up.

"... Without order. It sounds like anarchy and chaos. You should call it the antistate."

He affected a groan of mild disappointment.

"I thought you'd like having no more war... You're right though. It is the antithesis of a state – antiestablishment, antiauthoritarian, antihierarchical – but it's hardly the state of nature or anarchy. It evolves from the bottom up in a series of premises about the natural rights of man. There's no social contract because rights are inalienable. They can't be reassigned to an unnatural construct.

"It all emanates from the institution of town meeting. Cities don't exist anymore. Once a municipality's population reaches 100,000, it splits in two. Things only get done if there's a consensus of 80 percent. Dissenters don't have to obey the majority; they're answerable only to their consciences. There are no taxes. People have to be self-sufficient.

"There are few town services. What revenues are needed come from monopolies on recreational drugs, pharmaceuticals and gambling. High school graduation requires six months of community service. There's a volunteer fire department and a system of neighborhood watches replacing the police department. Elected guardians of right, not judges, hear complaints and responses. Lawyers aren't necessary.

"The justice system, criminal and civil, is supplanted by the doctrine of exclusionary consanguinity, meaning that I can't judge my fellow man. So crimes don't exist; neither do criminals. After hearing both sides to a complaint, the guardian determines whether there's a compensable victim. If not, that's the end of it. No victim, no foul.

"If there is a victim, the respondent must make him or her whole again through restitution. Everyone makes mistakes. We should be able to apologize for them, make amends and move on. Confession is good for the soul. Our penal system discourages that by exacting retribution for mistakes. The way things are, it's better to lie and hope a lawyer can get us off.

"In cases involving violence – emotional as well as physical – behavioral treatment is called for, either as an outpatient at a health center or for serious conditions as an inpatient at a psychiatric hospital. There are no prisons, since their emphasis on punishment turns sinners into sociopaths.

"The only grounds for confinement are mental disorder or failure to compensate a victim."

Juliana put her feet down to stop the swing.

"That's thirsty work. I feel like an iced tea. Want one?

"No thanks. Help yourself."

She went inside but continued talking, louder now.

"Don't you think you're being naïve? It sounds like no-fault auto insurance run amok. I mean it's shamelessly idealistic to expect people to cooperate with the system when it's not in their interests... Say we're arguing and I punch you in the mouth so hard you need dental work. The guardian says I have to pay you $700. I say I don't have it and would rather get attitude adjustment in a residential treatment center. I've beaten your system haven't I?"

NIANTIC JEWEL

He turned sideways on the swing so she could hear him through the open window.

"Actually, you've made things worse. I was hoping for an in-kind arrangement based on sexual favors, but... instead you'll just have to work it off at the treatment center, maybe by cleaning bathrooms, while getting professional help with anger management and social skills. Or, you could continue being noncooperative and remain a guest there for as long as you wish."

The screen door opened and she returned, glass in hand. Then leaning over him, she pushed off her left shoulder strap and inquired demurely

"Tell me more about that in-kind proposition."

CHAPTER 16

GHOSTLY UTTERANCES

And so it was that later
as the miller told his tale
that her face, at first just ghostly,
turned a whiter shade of pale.
PROCOL HAREM

The old Western Electric phone in the hallway rang as Colin sat down to breakfast shortly after 8 Friday morning. Picking up the handset, he felt a thrill of anticipation. He'd hear Juliana's voice and find out what she'd planned for them today. She liked to have a coordinated schedule. It wasn't that she couldn't be spontaneous; she just didn't care for surprises, or anything beyond her control.

He was happy to go along with whatever she wanted to do as long as they were together. They were both organized people. She said it was a mark of their compatibility. Her need to manage their time as if they were one was, he thought, the perfect antidote to what had been his self-centered existence, and he looked forward to her daily call from the moment he awoke.

He could tell something was amiss by the urgency in her voice.

"Can you come over right away? I had another Indian dream last night. It really shook me up."

Hearing her distress brought back painful memories of Moira and Tara's visit.

"Of course, darling. What happened?"

"I'd rather tell you when you're with me."

NIANTIC JEWEL

"I'll be there right away. Don't worry. It's those Indian stories I told you. I shouldn't have made them so graphic... They surfaced in your unconscious mind as frightening dreams I bet."

He bolted down his breakfast and rushed over to the Palmers'. Juliana called him inside through the screen door. She was sitting at the breakfast bar, drawing on a notepad. They kissed and hugged. Then he kissed her again, unable to resist the dazzling sight of her in an indigo halter dress patterned with amber circles, her hair glinting in the sharp light of the early morning sun.

Pulling up a stool beside her, he looked at the bird's head she was drawing.

"See! It's the osprey again – pointing right, just like the tattoo and the amulet."

"Tell me about the dream."

"We didn't make love this time. That's what scares me. It wasn't a happy dream like the others. More like bittersweet. You held me in your arms and we kissed a lot. That part was really good. But I was crying when you left. I can still feel the sadness."

"Was this dream beside the pond again?"

"No. That's the strange thing. It was a lovely night with a full moon. We were sitting on a bench in the garden of a big house near a wharf. It was a seaport town. The harbor was filled with ghostly sailing ships. You were carving the osprey's head into the center slat on the back of the bench. We wore English clothes. Yours were very elegant."

"It doesn't sound like Mixanno and Quaiapen then. Did you feel as if you were her?"

"Well... yes and no. I was me and you were you. Except you had red hair, come to think of it, and mine was black. I was definitely Indian and you were... white. You called me Hannah. We were young lovers, just like before, but don't ask me your name. I don't remember what was said. We were too busy spooning. Then you went back to the house. I was in tears, and woke up with a start – still hurting. It was so painful."

"I'm so sorry, Jewel. I feel responsible."

She leaned over and tenderly brushed her lips against his.

Graham Griffith

"That's sweet of you. I'm over it now that you're here... Here's the thing, though. The place was familiar – the house and garden; the view of the harbor. I've been there, I'm sure. I've been racking my brains, and I just can't put my finger on it. It's so maddening."

"Could we have gone there on one of our trips?"

"I'm not sure. You know how somewhere can feel like home in a dream and yet be a totally strange place?"

"Curses... Maybe something will come to you if you take your mind off it."

She toyed with her drawing for a few seconds, then put a hand on his knee and giggled.

"You timed your arrival perfectly. Mother called just before you came – and asked if you were here. Imagine if you had been!"

"Did she want to talk to me?"

"No, of course not. She just slipped it in offhandedly. I had to laugh. I should have told her you were walking around naked, but she might have believed it. I said she should be ashamed of herself. Then she claimed she was just asking if you'd come over for breakfast."

"So she really was concerned about your virtue. That's interesting. And fortunate that we read through her inscrutability."

"I guess so. I'm still steamed about her minding my business.... Anyway, they won't be here until late. They're stopping to eat at the Stephen Patrick Tavern at Haversham. Daddy likes their manhattans."

*   *   *

They spent the morning at the beach, reading and cooling off in the ocean, then went back to the farm for lunch and to take Joe Stanton's regular Friday call, which came punctually at noon. He was eager to share his plans for coming home now that his brother was fully recovered and Labor Day was only 10 days away.

The arrangements were made: Joe would return the following Friday afternoon, and Colin would leave shortly after. It all seemed so sudden, so final that he was taken by surprise, until

NIANTIC JEWEL

realizing he should have anticipated the conversation. This had been the plan all along. Still, the impact put him at a loss for words. He paused to recall the story about burying Eric – the lead-up he'd rehearsed to relating the discovery.

The old man listened in what Colin took to be shocked silence as he poured out the unlikely tale including their efforts to link the find to Quaiapen, but omitting Juliana's dreams. He decided there was a limit to how much Joe could suspend his disbelief. As it was, there was a long whistle from the other end of the line when he finished.

"Well I'll be damned. You found her."

Without knowing why, Colin suddenly felt guilty, and began to apologize.

"I'm sorry. I'm responsible for all this. We hoped that maybe you've known about it for years. I almost called you at York Beach to get your advice. I hope it doesn't create a problem for you. We disturbed a burial and we take it very seriously... D'you think it could be Quaiapen?"

"Sure it is. Who else would it be? Why d'you think the farm's named for her? Legend has it that she lived on the site. Over the years, I've gathered Stanton stories and snippets of information about her. It's all stuffed into a manila envelope in the rolltop desk."

"So there's family lore that has her buried here?"

"A big helping of folklore and a dollop of make-believe. The way my father told it to me and his father to him, Queen Quaiapen was buried here with all her regalia and a fortune in wampum. It was supposed to be an elaborate royal burial, but what you say about her losing her head and it being buried secretly makes more sense.

"Otherwise the treasure trove would have been found long ago. My own theory has always been that as the farm grew out of the original trading post and pastures were cleared, the grave was plowed up by a long-departed Stanton who kept quiet about it so he could profit from the contents."

Colin breathed a sigh of relief.

"Thanks for understanding our predicament... Do the inscriptions on the bracelet and amulet ring any bells with you?"

"Sorry, I can't help you there... Leave it with me though. The sachem's a friend and distant relative. He needs to know about this. It's a matter for the tribe. I'll ask when I talk to him."

Colin felt a frisson of panic course through him. The little circle of cognoscente was about to expand exponentially.

"What do you think will happen? Will the police get involved? By not reporting the find and then doing what we did to it, I think we violated NAGPRA, the Native American Graves Protection and Repatriation Act of 1990... We just thought you should be the first to know. Nobody else is in on it, except Juliana's parents, and they're sworn to secrecy. We figured that since it's your land, and she's been in your care...."

The old man tried to calm Colin's anxious voice.

"... Easy, m'boy. You did good. Thank God you didn't call anyone! It's no one's business but mine and the tribe's. There won't be any more digging here, mark my words. For one thing the cows wouldn't give a drop of milk, and I can't afford that!... The way I see it, the tribe'll hold a private ceremony at Jamestown to rebury the Old Queen and her things next to her husband. Finally, she'll rest in peace... I hate to lose her, but everything changed once the storm churned up her hiding place. "

He gave an audible gasp as a thought occurred to him.

"Strange that the Old Queen should be unearthed by the Old Queen: If I hadn't had you attach that mooring line to the rubbing rock, the boat wouldn't have moved it and disturbed the ground so you could find her."

Colin put his hand over the mouthpiece and repeated the words, then looked Juliana in the eye.

"Stranger still so that you could find her. You did you know."

He spoke into the phone again:

"One more thing, Joe. This sounds as if it has nothing to do with anything, but is it possible that Quaiapen lived among the English as a young woman, and went by the name of Hannah?"

"I doubt it very much. She despised the English... Why do you ask?"

NIANTIC JEWEL

"Oh, an Indian woman by that name popped up in our research. After her marriage, Quaiapen lived near the Smiths' trading post at Wickford, where English ships were always coming and going... It was a long shot."

"Tell you what. Try the envelope in the desk, the one bulging out of its pigeonhole on the left. My mother started the collection. She got interested in the Stanton-Quaiapen connection and infected me with it. I can't say we made much headway, even though she hand-copied extracts from the Charlestown and Westerly town records. But you never know; you might find something...."

As Colin listened, he took Juliana's hand and led her from the hallway into the kitchen, as far as the phone cord would reach. Then pointing to the desk, he repeated where to find the envelope. Her fingers went straight to it, and soon she was spreading the voluminous contents on the kitchen table.

Impatient to join her among the jumble of faded papers, dog-eared newspaper clippings and sepia photographs, he could only roll his eyes and look on while the old man blithely retold the same family stories Colin had heard more than once before during their weekly chats. He stifled the urge to plead a bad connection and politely waited out his captor, then thanked him and wished him a safe journey.

Juliana pushed out a chair for him. There was the mischievous sparkle in her eyes of a child in a candy store.

"There's some marvelous old photos of the farm and the Stantons here, and all sorts of records: mimeographed tax rolls, land deeds, births, marriages and deaths... Dive in!"

The temptation to be voyeurs to generations of family life was too strong to resist. The more mundane the item – Ephraim's school report of 1876; Abigail's marriage to Gamaliel Hazard in 1901 – the keener the vicarious thrill. And so it went until Colin noticed the cows starting to graze their way closer to the pasture gate as milking time approached.

He got up to stretch his back, then stood behind Juliana and massaged her shoulders. She purred blissfully and began unfolding a browned sheet of paper so fragile that one of the

275

creases tore as she opened it to reveal a Stanton family tree executed in an ornate copperplate script.

"Oh look, Colin! The penmanship's exquisite. It must be really old, but it's unfinished. There are gaps everywhere. You can't tell who's who."

He circled her waist with his hands and pressed close to get a better look.

"Whoever created it was enthusiastic to begin with. They put a lot of time into it. But it got out of hand almost from the start. See how it begins with the first Thomas Stanton, born in Towcester, Northamptonshire, England, on Thursday, Oct. 3, 1616. He marries Anne Lord at Hartford in 1637 and they have 10 children. Then the gaps appear. By just the second generation it's become impossible to keep track of everyone.

"Anyway, Joe doesn't claim to be descended from Quaiapen, just that she lived here. By that he means April to September. The Niantic spent fall and winter in the wooded valleys a few miles inland; the coast is too cold and windy in winter. And, folklore aside, it's a good bet that the sachem's family occupied the prime waterfront real estate. That would be here, on the high ground between the two great salt ponds."

Juliana slowly rubbed her head against his in a gesture of resignation. She was about to fold the paper back up when her eye caught a pencil-written note at the foot of the page. As she read it, she gripped his hand.

"Gosh! This mentions Quaiapen. Someone added it later. The handwriting's different from the tree. Listen to this: `(1) Quaiapen's sons Scuttup, Quequaquenuet [alias Gideon], daughter (2) Quinemiquet all died young. Her issue (3) Wotowssunkotous a squaw sachem. A daughter (4) Wepitano in bond to Capt. Updike. (5) Mercy, sister Lydia also at Cocumscussoc? (6) Hannah in service to Mr. Nichols Jr? Issue unknown.'… What does it mean?"

*   *   *

NIANTIC JEWEL

Colin pondered the notation, reading and rereading the enigmatic words until suddenly the apparently unrelated phrases coalesced into a unified whole.

"It's an attempt to trace Quaiapen's line! The numerals are female descendants by generation, making Hannah her great-great-great granddaughter. The question marks express uncertainty by the writer – Joe's mother I imagine. It's accurate at least to Wotowssunkotous. There's no historical record of Wepitano, but Capt. Lodowick Updike and his wife Abigail, who was also his first cousin, inherited Richard Smith Jr.'s vast estate at Cocumscussoc when he died childless in 1692."

Juliana's face lit up in recognition:

"Didn't we visit a place called Smith's Castle outside Wickford? It was in such a lovely setting down by the water... Wasn't it the English base for the Great Swamp Fight – with a communal grave?"

"Jolly good, Jewel! Richard Sr., the first permanent English settler in Narragansett Country, founded a trading post there about 1637. Roger Williams opened one nearby in 1645 but sold it for £51 to Smith six years later to raise money for his trip to England to obtain Rhode Island's charter.

"Along with Gov. John Winthrop Jr. of Connecticut, Maj. Humphrey Atherton and other Boston land speculators, the Smiths organized the Atherton Company in 1659. The Narragansett Proprietors as they became known bought vast tracts of fertile land in Exeter and North Kingstown and tried to swindle the tribe out of the rest, but Rhode Island and the crown wouldn't recognize the deeds.

"When Richard Smith Sr. died in 1666, he'd renamed the area Wickford, and his premises were the center of social and political life for miles around. The buildings were burned in Metacom's War, but within a year, Smith's Castle, one of the largest homes in New England, rose on the site.

"Later, as great plantations owned by the aristocractic Narragansett Planters and worked by African slaves and bondaged Native Americans changed the natural landscape

Graham Griffith

forever, the Updike family developed its 3,000 acres into one of the largest plantations in 18th-Century New England."

Juliana looked up at him.

"As I remember, Smith's Castle is near Queen's Fort. Quaiapen was royalty, so why were her great granddaughter Wepitano and her daughters Mercy and Lydia 'in bond' there?"

"The type of bondage isn't clear. This is around the turn of the 18th Century, so it couldn't have been the perpetual bondage or hereditary peonage inflicted on Narragansett women and children right after Metacom's War. The genocide may have stopped in Rhode Island, but the English tried to make Native Americans disappear by other means. It could be that Wepitano was indentured as a child to save her from destitution, to make her 'white.' The traditional Indian way of life vanished after the war; the Narragansett became paupers unless they served the English.

"Wepitano probably became free on her 18th birthday but stayed on at the plantation, where she married and raised children including Mercy and Lydia, who also worked for the Updikes. Then Mercy's child Hannah entered service with Mr. Nichols – and the line stops. Of course, it's likely there were other children in these generations, equally Quaiapen's descendants, who are lost to history... When we visited Smith's Castle, we sat on a bench in the 18th-Century garden overlooking the cove. You said how serene it all was. Could that be where your dream took place?"

Juliana smiled weakly.

"Not really, although it's hard to imagine it as a bustling trading post. In my dream there was a harbor full of ships – a big new port with commercial wharves fronting a town... What about Nichols?"

"I'm drawing a blank. And the laptops are at your house. Anyway, it's not much to go on. I think we're going to have to settle for what we've got: tantalizing bits of purely circumstantial evidence. It was fun while it lasted, and Joe seems delighted. But I want to spend my last week here totally immersed in you. No Quaiapen, no Internet, just the two of us. She's taken you away from me. I want to reclaim you."

NIANTIC JEWEL

Frowning, she drew his hand to her and kissed it.

"Keep it up and you'll make a wanton woman of me. What was it Tennyson wrote? 'Man is the hunter; woman is his game.' Don't give up the hunt for Quaiapen. I have this feeling that we're so close... What if Hannah was the last of the line and Quaiapen's spirit moved through her.

"Don't you see? Hurricane Hannah caused Mr. Stanton's Old Queen to lead us to Quaiapen's head where her dream soul lay trapped until we freed it. She was brought here and hurriedly buried in secrecy. She can't enter Cautantowwit's house until she's whole again and the tribe performs the full funeral rites. We were holding a funeral – for Eric – when we found her...."

Colin had a sudden flash of insight

"... When you found her, Jewel. And she's been communicating with you in your dreams. Stone the crows! What made you mention Nichols almost in the same breath as 'wanton woman' and that hunter quote from Tennyson?"

"It seemed appropriate."

"Appropriate? A bit of a stretch I'd say. Quaiapen gave them to you. 'Nichols, wanton, hunter....

Juliana shivered and grasped Colin's arm as he went on:

"You said the dream was at a 'big new port.' Newport. On our trip there we sat on another bench in an 18th-Century garden overlooking a harbor. It was at the Nichols-Wanton-Hunter House, aka Hunter House... Do you remember it – the 1740s Georgian Colonial we stopped by downtown on the way to the Bellevue Avenue mansions. Was that the garden in the dream?"

She wheeled around in her chair and clutched him to her, the words spilling out excitedly.

"Holy smoke! Yes! Yes! I knew I'd been there. The one stuffed with Townsend-Goddard furniture worth millions. It's been driving me crazy. Thank you Sweetheart... This is for saving my sanity."

With that she sprang up and, holding his face in both hands, devoured him in a sizzling French kiss that lasted until he had to break for air.

"Cripes! Was that you or Quaiapen or Hannah?

Graham Griffith

She ran her fingers through his hair, pushing back the forelock that had fallen over his eyes.

"Maybe it was Grannie's Daughter of the Moon. I'm sure she's involved in all this… And if I was Hannah in the dream, who were you? And when was this? Then there's the bench. I didn't notice anything special about it – just the garden and the view of the harbor. How about you?"

Colin recalled the smocked jade blouse and sheer cotton skirt she'd worn, and her perfume.

"Sorry. I remember only being mesmerized by you, as usual… But first, let's figure out the backdrop for the dream.

"Jonathan Nichols Jr. bought the land in 1748 and built a single-chimney dwelling. Nine years later, he sold it to Col. Joseph Wanton Jr., heir to a Quaker shipping fortune, who enlarged it into the present structure. This was when Newport was a commercial and political powerhouse rivaling Boston, New York and Philadelphia.

"It was rich from the Triangle Trade: Dozens of Rhode Island distillers produced rum, which along with iron, flour and tar, were shipped to West Africa where they were bartered for slaves to be sold in Caribbean ports in exchange for sugar and molasses. There was also a lucrative trade with Britain, exporting timber, fish and cheese and importing manufactured goods.

"Much of the foreign trade was, in effect, smuggling. American ship owners largely ignored the Navigation Acts that gave Britain a monopoly in commodities such as sugar. The few customs officers were poorly paid and easily bribed, so that duties on cargoes were rarely paid.

"Merchants grew rich at the expense of the crown, which spent vast sums over the years defending Americans and their trade from the French, Dutch and Spanish while receiving in return a fraction of the imposts that paid for the security.

"In fact, the frequent European conflicts were a goldmine for Newport ship owners. They received letters of marque from the crown to prey on enemy shipping as privateers. The lure of booty endured even in peacetime with some freelance captains simply

NIANTIC JEWEL

continuing as pirates and buccaneers during the lulls in legal privateering.

"But as the war debts piled up, Parliament imposed new levies and made it harder to evade them. The merchant class – the bourgeoisie – all along the Atlantic Seaboard resisted by organizing politically against the motherland under the slogan 'no taxation without representation.' The rest is the American Revolution, which was an economic disaster for Newport.

"Like most of the town's real estate, the house was a wreck when lawyer/politician/diplomat William Hunter bought it for $5,000 in 1805. It remained in the family until 1863, then had several owners ending in 1945 with its final rescue and restoration by the Preservation Society of Newport County."

Juliana began returning the jumble of papers to their envelope.

"So the Updikes and Nicholses were part of the local social elite. That's probably how Hannah went to Newport. Nichols needed a servant girl, saw her at Smith's Castle and arranged for her to join his household. She must have been thrilled to leave the sleepy plantation for the excitement of the colony's capital... But then, who were you in your fine clothes? It's infuriating the way every new twist raises more questions. We must go back there and see if there's anything more we can find out."

Graham Griffith

CHAPTER 17

STAR-CROSSED LOVERS

A wail in the wind is all I hear;
A voice of woe for a lover's loss.
WILLIAM ELLERY CHANNING

Colin was tipping the wheelbarrow filled with aromatic cow muck and straw onto the midden behind the barn when he saw the Mini Cooper coming up the farm track. He returned the barrow to its place in the tractor shed and waited in front as Juliana drove into the farmyard tooting her horn. She pulled up beside him and hopped out waving a piece of paper as she fell into his arms squealing with excitement and showering his face with kisses.

"I'm part Indian! An email came this morning with my data profile. Isn't it just wild?"

He hugged her tight.

"I'm so happy for you, Jewel. Your grandma was right about Daughter of the Moon."

"Yes. And she was probably Niantic. Look at the results."

She showed him the printout and flipped a couple of pages to a chart.

"The haplogroup X analysis strongly suggests southern New England Algonquian. There's not much data inside that parameter, but the markers are consistent with what Niantic DNA should look like. Ironically, it's statistically identifiable, capable of being extrapolated in the absence of an archetype, because of certain allele values common among Narragansett, Wampanoag

NIANTIC JEWEL

and Nipmuc and uncommon among Pequot and Mohegan, the area's other Algonquian tribes."

Colin felt a quiver run down his spine.

"Blinking heck! That fits the facts. The former three tribes fought the English in Metacom's War and were almost obliterated; the latter two plus the Niantic fought on the English side and emerged intact. A lucky few of the defeated survivors who had kinship ties with the Niantic were allowed to join them here in Charlestown after the war, a mercy for which sachem Ninigret must have had to plead. The less fortunate were sold into slavery or fled to New York and Canada.

"Before long, the hybrid tribe was being called Narragansett by the English, possibly because the two peoples were so close prewar that Ninigret was also a top Narragansett sachem and the Niantic were often called Southern Narragansett. But with a core of Niantic, it follows that they'd leave their mark genetically on the new entity, if only implicitly.... "

Juliana nodded her head eagerly.

"... And don't forget the dreams. The first two took place a few yards from where we're standing... We still don't know if it's Quaiapen's head, but I'm positive something will turn up at Hunter House."

He took her in his arms and kissed her ardently.

"I don't care if it doesn't. I've got my Niantic Jewel."

*   *   *

They were driving onto the Newport Bridge Monday afternoon when Juliana took his hand as she always did when crossing large spans. The gephyrophobia (fear of bridges) and related acrophobia (fear of heights) had been with her since childhood, although for 10 years now the panic attacks they'd formerly induced had given way to manageable pangs of unease.

He glanced at her with a reassuring smile. He loved the way her hair came alive in the slipstream with the top down. Jags were made to frame beautiful women, he thought as he ogled her scallop-necked cotton cardigan the color of butter and the little

Graham Griffith

pleated skirt with a rose print, separated by 2 inches of honeyed midriff.

This is an epiphany, he told himself. Imprint it clearly and forever: an enchanted moment of youth that time can never steal.

Greedily, he transferred more details from the bird's-eye view to the mental picture, each one intensifying his euphoria: the sun-drenched blue of the clear sky above and gleaming water below; sailboats dotting the bay, here and there a flamboyant spinnaker billowing for attention; the harbor tightly packed with vessels from pleasure cruisers and racing yachts of all sizes to 3-masted schooners and floating palaces; the colorful wharves teeming with humanity blessed to be there. And just visible near the Goat Island Causeway the balustraded gambrel roof of Hunter House.

The empty parking space in front of the exquisite Georgian Colonial on Washington Street might have been reserved for them. They entered by the visitors' side gate to find five middle-aged women standing at the foot of the backdoor steps, chatting amiably while they waited for the next tour. Colin glanced over the re-created 18th-Century garden sloping gently down to the harbor. And even as its beauty touched him he wondered what they were doing there; how walking through it could possibly lead to anything.

That was when he felt Juliana tug at his hand.

"Look! There are two of them."

At first, he saw nothing unusual about the elderly couple, tucked between a planting of lilacs and the railing to the steps, partially obscured by the five women. He needed a double take before realizing it wasn't the couple who held Juliana's interest but the wooden bench they sat on, one of a pair beside the steps.

She walked over to the empty bench and examined the gleaming brass plate on the backboard, then shook her head.

"This was the bench we sat on when we were here. My heart leapt for a moment, but the plate just names the donors."

They headed into the garden, walking down to the seawall to take in the harbor view before wandering back via the pergola. Telling the story later to her parents, Juliana maintained she was admiring the grapevine creeping over the latticework when she

NIANTIC JEWEL

stumbled into the slat-backed bench and would have fallen over it if Colin hadn't caught her. He didn't recall it exactly that way, but there was no doubt they were left speechless by the eagle's-head medallion on the broad center slat.

Juliana knelt on the seat and ran her fingers over the finely carved profile. There were tears in her eyes when she finally spoke.

"Oh Colin! It's just as it was in the dream. Hannah was the last of Quaiapen's line. This is the proof we needed. We did it! We found Quaiapen's head."

She fell into his arms and they hugged. When she'd composed herself, Colin took cellphone photos all the while trying to think of some rationale for the carving. He stroked one of the arms, enjoying the slippery feel of varnish on plain wood.

"It would be nice to have a few more answers... This bench isn't 18th Century. It's modern. Note the deep relief of the carving. There's not much weathering, but enough to warrant a new coat of varnish."

Juliana traced the outline of the circular border with a finger

"It's lovely. But you're right. In my dream, Hannah's lover carved an osprey, just like Mixanno's tattoo. It looks as if this one was copied from an eagle. The beak's too hooked for an osprey. Still, this links the osprey emblem to Quaiapen.... "

Colin couldn't help interjecting

"... It's her signet. If we'd been able to find her mark on a document, I bet this would have been it. Her own guardian spirit. She tattooed one on Mixanno for protection, or as a claim on him like a wedding ring. If it were a clan symbol we'd expect to come across it in connection with her brother Ninigret and his heirs as chief sachem of the Narragansett... But I wish we knew how Hannah's lover fits in."

Juliana looked up the garden to the house, from which a tour group was emerging.

"Quick! There's the tour guide. Let's buttonhole him before he goes back inside."

Graham Griffith

They explained somewhat disingenuously to the friendly docent that their return visit was to explore the garden. Juliana remarked that the pergola provided a haven of tranquillity.

"I was intrigued by the carving on the bench. Does it have any significance beyond being a handsome decoration?"

A sparkle came to the guide's eye.

"Interesting you should mention that. As well as being the docent, I live here as the custodian, minding the collection – all the priceless treasures, particularly the Townsend-Goddard furniture. Every piece has an illustrious story to tell, yet to me the humble pergola bench's is the most romantic.

He motioned to the pair either side of the steps.

"They're out here summer and winter. These were donated a few years ago, but the pergola bench replaces an identical one that came with the property when the Preservation Society bought it in 1945. Eventually it rotted out – eagle and all. I was new here when it was removed and the present one installed.

"The next day, a curator from the Society came by with a woodworker, who carved a new eagle. It seemed a bit odd, so I asked the curator about it. He told me that from 1917 to '45, Hunter House was a convent affiliated with St. Joseph's Church a few blocks away. Among the conveyancing documents was a letter from the mother superior requesting that the bench remain where it was and words to the effect that 'any replacement shall faithfully reproduce the medallion, in accordance with tradition.'

"Now the curator's curiosity was piqued, but the mother superior had passed on. However, through the church, he found an old nun who had lived at the convent and knew the tradition of perpetuating the medallion, and the legend behind it.

"In colonial days, when the first owner, merchant prince Jonathan Nichols Jr., lived here, this stretch of harbor front was a Golden Mile. The wharves were packed with oceangoing ships and piled with goods. From here, Nichols ran his shipping empire.

"As fate would have it, he had no children. Instead he brought into the business a nephew who lived here with his uncle and aunt between voyages to West Africa and the West Indies. It was

NIANTIC JEWEL

the infamous Triangle Trade you learned about in school, dealing Newport rum for African slaves.

"He was one of the most eligible bachelors in town, surely destined to marry a beautiful Newport heiress. That is until he fell in love with another member of the Nichols household – a Narragansett Indian servant girl. Given the chasm of race and class dividing them, it had to be a secret romance of stolen moments, of ceaseless intriguing to contrive time alone together.

"Naturally, a garden at nighttime is the perfect rendezvous. And so it was here that their love bloomed, and on the bench they used that the young man carved an eagle's head for his Indian maiden. In her religion the eagle symbolized spiritual protection. Thus the bench became a sacred place.

"Alas, happiness was to elude them. The young man's ship had barely set sail on his last voyage when it ran into a sudden storm off Block Island and was drawn onto the rocks by the island's notorious wreckers who lit false beacons to lure vessels to their doom. He drowned along with everyone else on board.

"But the legend doesn't end there. A few weeks later, his grieving lover discovered she was bearing his child. Her master and mistress soon found out the truth. They sent her away to spend the pregnancy on the tribal reservation in Charlestown. Sadly, she died giving birth to a white baby girl with red hair.

"The Nicholses took the baby into their house to be raised as an English gentlewoman. But in 1756, soon after becoming deputy governor of Rhode Island, Nichols died at age 44. His widow then sold the house to Col. Joseph Wanton Jr. and moved out, taking her ward with her. And that's the last anyone knows of the lovechild.

"As for the tradition of perpetuating the bench and its medallion, the nuns say it and the legend were passed on to them by the Storers, the Boston family who summered here from 1881 until donating the property to St. Joseph's in 1917...."

"... that's the story anyway. And now, if you'll excuse me, it's time for the next tour."

They thanked him and he turned to step away, but Juliana caught his arm.

Graham Griffith

"You didn't mention their names. Does Hannah ring a bell?"

The guide shook his head.

"Their names are lost to us, I'm sorry to say… Who's Hannah?"

"Someone we're researching from that era. You won't have come across her, except maybe in your wildest dreams."

*   *   *

Alise Palmer was with them at the beach late Tuesday morning. Juliana had on a salmon bikini that from a distance looked like bare untanned flesh. As usual, she was stretched out on a towel while Colin and her mother were in chairs in the shade of an umbrella.

There was no escaping the bittersweet feeling of summer's Last Hurrah being underway. Many families had already left to prepare for schools opening. They would return for the long holiday weekend, but until Friday there were wide expanses of unoccupied sand. The 70-degree water invited relaxed bathing rather than the thrills and spills of crowded wave-riding that the weekend would bring.

Juliana stopped writing in her notebook and spoke to her mother.

"I think I'll follow Colin back on Friday and help him move into his new apartment."

Alise Palmer lifted her eyes from her magazine.

"And stay in Wellesley?"

"Of course, Mother! Where else would I sleep?"

"I'm sure I don't know, dear. I'm just your mother…."

Colin felt the discomforting presence of electrical potential generated by mother-daughter friction. He didn't like squirming between two poles, getting zapped like a bug.

"Jewel, don't forget Joe Stanton. We don't know when he'll get here on Friday. It could be late. And you have to hand over Quaiapen and the rest of the trove."

Juliana responded by palming sand over his feet.

"Oh c'mon. I was just toying. OK, I'll play it by ear… I've been writing up my notes on yesterday. It shows how shaky oral

288

NIANTIC JEWEL

history is, the way the osprey became an eagle. It's really a hawk, of course. Although they did give it a sweet romantic twist... I still can't believe how the three dreams came true. It seems impossible – unless you're open to magic and metaphysics...."

Her mother interrupted.

"You don't have to convince anyone. Joe Stanton believes it's Quaiapen because legend connects her to the farm. Ditto for the tribe. We three know her spirit has been working through Jewel to get her properly reinterred so she can be at peace again. The dreams place her and Mixanno at the burial site and tie the amulet, comb and bracelet to them. Your real-world research links them to the amulet and bracelet. The facts speak for themselves."

Her confidence encouraged Colin to put words to what had been only formless ideas since yesterday.

"You two haven't said anything about it, but you must be thinking what I'm thinking: Incredible as it may seem, you're both related to Quaiapen through Hannah. You have some of her genes. How else could she get into Jewel's head? Her DNA test strongly suggests she's Niantic. And we know Daughter of the Moon existed... It explains the extrasensory communication between you."

Juliana rose onto her elbows to make eye contact.

"It did occur to me, but there's a problem. Hannah's lovechild was white with red hair. She was raised to be English. Her Indian half was repressed. Now look at Daughter of the Moon. She didn't repress her part-Indian side. Mother's hair is black, as was Granny's. Mine is red. There's no link between Hannah and Daughter of the Moon. Red hair isn't a connection. From 4 to 8% of Anglos have it at any given time, but the allele is present in all Anglos and can express itself randomly."

Alise Palmer returned the magazine to her beach bag and pulled out another.

"By the same token, there isn't not a connection. I've been doing some Googling of my own... Hannah's child and Daughter of the Moon have to be separated by 100 years – three generations. That's a lot of Anglo genetic material entering the mix. Probably no additional Native American genes were added, since Rhode

Graham Griffith

Island forbade Indian-white marriage until 1881. Daughter of the Moon celebrated her Indian heritage, but she lived as a white. And for a white to have Indian genes was highly unusual.

"Conversely, for an Indian to have white genes was less uncommon, since unofficial liaisons occurred not infrequently in the 18th Century. Indian men had a high mortality rate from the occupations they were forced into: the military, whaling, heavy manual labor. So Indian women had to find mates among poor whites and free and enslaved blacks. Plus there was coerced sex between white masters and bondaged Indian women. But the children of all these relationships were raised as Indians, not whites or blacks.

"Put another way, the chances of Lovechild having her father's fair skin and red hair are extremely low. Darker skin and dark hair genes are normally dominant. But in genetics, nothing's for sure.

"So I say Daughter of the Moon is probably the only white woman who could have been Lovechild's descendant. Jewel's hair color is indeed inherited from Lover Boy. And our female mental power is a Native American singularity."

Colin sighed and scratched his head.

"Blimey! Here I am, a newspaperman who's never had a scoop. I come across maybe the biggest story of the century. It's got everything – proof of an afterlife, dreams literally come true, a queen's skull with buried treasure, a beautiful heroine with magical powers. And I haven't the slightest intention of writing it."

Juliana got up and gazed out to sea.

"We're not going to tell anyone. Try it on Daddy and see the reaction. He'd laugh at Mother and me. He'd send you packing, Sweetie…."

With an exuberant jeté leap, she came and knelt beside him, murmuring in his ear

"… Before I barely know you."

*   *   *

NIANTIC JEWEL

Every passing hour left a sweet ache where his bliss had been. He clung greedily to their time together over that last couple of days, hoping to slow it down, to prolong his rapture in case it was about to end. When he abandoned that senseless effort he told himself linear time faded away but their love was measured in psychological time, which is eternal. Sometimes she'd catch his worried look, hug him close and make everything alright.

Briefly, they settled back into their pre-Quaiapen routine: tennis, beach, lunch at the Palmers, excursions from their enchanted cocoon, a late swim, dinner out, intimate evenings on the veranda, moonlight strolls. Thursday night, they went skinny-dipping for the last time at Little Beach. Afterward, they lay together in the shadow of the dunes, lulled into serenity by the hypnotic effect of moonlight dancing on water.

She lifted his hand from her breast and kissed the palm.

"Tell me an Indian story. While we're still Quaiapen and Mixanno. Before we go back to Boston and become ourselves again."

He kissed her face until something came to him.

"The happiest time of the year, the fat time, begins just about now. That's the Green Corn Moon up there. As it grows full, the Three Sisters – corn, beans and squash – begin to ripen. September brings the Harvest Moon. But for now there's green corn to feast on. It's just ripe enough to be edible. And all the more delicious because it's the first fresh corn in a year for the ninnimissinuok, as the Algonquian peoples called themselves. It was the occasion for a festival lasting several days and nights, with religious ceremonies, music, feasting and dancing in arbors built of branches and adorned with vegetation.

"The Narragansett were admired by neighboring tribes for their devotion to ritual and ensuing good character. Their preeminence was attributed to the spirits' smiling on their piety. How else to explain all those great leaders – Canonicus, Miantonomi, Pessicus, Quinnapin, Canonchet, Ninigret, Mixanno and Quaiapen?"

Juliana sat up and began toweling her hair dry.

"I'd give anything to know what Quaiapen and Mixanno looked like. Wouldn't you?"

"Not really. I see them just as they were in your dreams: you and me with black hair. Pictures can be misleading. The only surviving likeness of a 17th-Century New England Indian painted from life was misidentified until a few years ago and is still a mystery.

"It's an oil portrait by an unknown artist dated c.1681. The slender, unimposing youth shown was variously thought to be Ninigret himself or his son Ninigret II. However, it's 65 years too late to be the young Ninigret. And there were no portraitists around when he was young. Then again, someone other than Ninigret II is indicated by considering where the picture came from: Robert Winthrop donated it to the Rhode Island School of Design's Museum of Art.

"Family lore says his ancestor Connecticut Gov. John Winthrop Jr. (1606-76) had his life saved by an Indian boy named David, a servant in his household. The time frame seems better for the subject being David than for it being Ninigret II. He succeeded his half-sister Weunquesh as sachem in 1686, but taking into account the tribe's distressed state after Metacom's War, who would want to paint his portrait? And he wouldn't have commissioned it himself.

"Also, there's a fourth nominee: Robin Cassacinamon, the Pequot sachem and Winthrop associate. If it's him, the painting's accepted date of c.1681 is too late. He was born c.1620 and died in 1692-93, making him around 61 when it was painted. Like David, he was also a Winthrop servant as a boy. It's a good bet that whoever it is had ties to the Winthrops and that they commissioned the work in Boston.

"To add to the mystery, the teenager is portrayed with what looks like the regalia of office: a six-strand wampum headband resembling a crown, a wampum ear loop, a large amulet and three smaller ones in a wampum neckpiece, a short staff in his right hand and an unidentifiable object in the waist of his loincloth where a dagger would be.

"That strengthens the argument for Robin. Suppose the painting actually dates to just after the 1637-38 Pequot War. The defeated sachem Sassacus and the rest of the leadership are wiped out.

NIANTIC JEWEL

Surviving Pequots are dispersed throughout Connecticut or have been given as booty to the Mohegan sachem Uncas and to Ninigret.

"But slowly they're coming together again. John Winthrop Jr. dislikes Uncas, his neighbor, who seeks to wield power over all the Pequots. The solution: Install Robin with English backing as leader of the revived tribe. Have his portrait painted looking regal and show it around to drum up support. If that was Winthrop's plan, it worked.

"Connecticut eventually ordered Uncas to release his Pequots. Ninigret's had already left to settle at Pawcatuck. They became the Eastern Pequot tribal nation. Robin's band lived first next to the Puritan settlement of Naumeag (New London) founded by Winthrop in 1646. Then in 1650, Winthrop returned conquered Pequot land he owned at nearby Noank. White settlement forced them to move again in 1666 when the colony created the Mashantucket reservation. That evolved into the Mashantucket Pequot tribal nation.... "

Colin rose to his knees and brushed sand from his body.

"We could go see the portrait in Boston sometime. If you'd like."

"I thought you said it was at RISD in Providence."

"That's the original. There's an 1838 copy by Charles Osgood of Salem at the Massachusetts Historical Society on Boylston Street."

CHAPTER 18

COUNTER PROPOSAL

Are we not formed, as notes of music are,
For one another, though dissimilar?
PERCY BYSSHE SHELLEY

They dressed and walked back hand-in-hand along the path through the dunes. Juliana was leading the way when she turned to Colin and wrapped her arms around his neck.

"I have to say it. I tried not to think about it just now, feeling your nude body beside me. Cuddling is almost as good. But I need you in the worst way. I want you so much. Can we make it happen this weekend – at your new place? I love you. I want to unite with you in conjugal love. Do you feel the same way?"

He suppressed the urge to chuckle.

"Yes, of course. More than anything. It would have happened by now if the Fates hadn't conspired against us. I think they were trying to tell us something...."

She looked deep into his eyes.

"… That Mother knows exactly what I'm thinking?"

"Maybe that too. She does seem to cover the bases before we get there, except for the night of the crash. But I meant something else...."

He was cut short by the sizzle of a lightning bolt as night turned to day for a millisecond, followed by a deafening thunderclap. Almost immediately, large raindrops began to fall and the wind picked up. The moon and stars disappeared while more thunder and lightning cut through the night.

NIANTIC JEWEL

They ran for the shelter of the old white oak just ahead of them in the sheep pasture across Sunset Beach Road. Under the tree, the sheep were bleating their annoyance at being awakened when Colin and Juliana scrambled over the stone wall to arrive in their midst soaking wet, gasping for breath and laughing like lunatics.

Colin leaned his back against the massive trunk, circling Juliana's waist with his arms, while they waited for the downpour to abate. He looked around at the sheep. Few seemed to care about the intruders, but he found one whose gaze he met.

"Cheerio sheep. You'll have your owner back tomorrow. Actually, I doubt you give one whit who takes care of you. I bet you like to toy with the border collie though. Anyway, thanks for being no trouble."

Juliana rubbed the back of her head against chest.

"Aw, that's sweet. I want to say goodbye to Angel."

"She'll still be here next summer, but fully grown by then. I'm sure you'll be able – we'll be able – to come see her. That's what I was getting to when the rain started. Come to think of it, whether consciously or instinctively, your mum is on the right track...."

"... Because she doesn't want me to Do It? Am I hearing right? Don't you want me?"

The rain stopped and they began walking, arms around each other's waists, over the pasture to the farm. He struggled for words.

"I love you. You're so precious to me. I want to spend the rest of my life with you. But you've only known me six weeks. You have to finish your education. That's at least a year. Maybe more. You might not think of me the same way a year from now. Maybe sooner...."

She interrupted with a trembling voice.

"Don't say that. It makes me feel the way I did that afternoon seeing you with Moira and Tara."

"I just mean that your mum doesn't know how much in love we are. She can't feel it like we do. Your folks can only relate to their own summer flings that didn't last. They think it's too early for you to be choosing a life partner. That you'll do better by waiting a while. That it would be a mistake for you to commit body and soul until you've had time to be sure. And that's basically the same reason why each of us has been waiting isn't it? Until we met each other and found the person we've been waiting for?"

She exhaled deeply in frustration.

"You don't see my point. If I'm OK with it, why shouldn't you be? I'm the woman, with more to lose – more to regret – if it doesn't work out, aren't I? It's not as if you're taking advantage of me."

Now it was his turn to feel frustration.

"That's the conventional wisdom. But I'm not interested in how many girls I bed before I marry. Finding a soul mate isn't a trophy hunt. Both of us want a spiritually richer relationship than the hit-and-miss paradigm of sexual release and instant gratification that limits the spiritual bond when true love finally arrives. Traditional playing the field creates mistakes and disappointments for women in particular, but also for men if we're honest with ourselves and put self-degrading machismo aside."

"Really! I don't recall you raising any objections when opportunity knocked. Where were your principles, your self-denial, then when sensual pleasure beckoned?"

He stopped and found her lips with his for a lingering kiss.

"I almost forget. Every thunderstorm is the anniversary of our first kiss. I'm going to celebrate it like this forever."

"I like that... but careful you don't get carried away."

"You're brutal! OK, there's one caveat: The first time we went out, I said how I think a man is more a slave to his sex drive than a woman is to hers...."

"... I remember. Because his genetic programming is to impregnate at will while hers is to secure prime genes for her progeny. So it's alright for me to seduce you, but not the other way around?"

"No, of course not. For premarital celibacy to work, both partners have to feel the same way. And I thought we did. If you end up marrying someone else, you'd look back on me with sadness and remorse – if you don't erase me from your memory entirely. I couldn't stand that. We've been so happy."

NIANTIC JEWEL

"It's true that Quonnie's an enchanted summer place. Not the real world. Not Boston in winter. But you're being your usual defeatist self. I said I'd cure you of that, and I will. Our love will grow and spread and deepen. Not die. I've made my choice. I want to be with you – always and forever."

They locked in another long embrace that left him aroused and conflicted. He stroked her hair.

"You're so beautiful... You're truly irresistible. I'll do anything for you. I want to make you happy. That's all I care about. I love you with all my heart."

As he closed the pasture gate behind them, the moon reappeared, beaming silver linings onto the rain clouds scudding away to the eastern horizon. Blissful feelings welled up in him at her affirmation, and when he looked at her she glowed with happiness.

Before driving her home, he put the top up on the Jag, more so they could park awhile unseen at the Palmers' than because of the cool of the night. The air smelled recharged and pure through the open windows while the seat warmers sent heat rising through their bodies. She waited until he cut the engine before speaking.

"Being with you puts me in such a romantic mood. Our last night in Quonnie's been perfect. Now I want to make sure it never ends...."

She took his hand, and with it a gulp of breath.

"We've both declared ourselves... That we love each other and want to be together forever. You're right that it's not that simple. That we'll have to wait at least a year before... We'll meet new people. Mother and Daddy have friends and colleagues with sons around my age. We socialize. Sometimes I can't avoid going on dates without giving offense – though nothing ever comes of them... It would be a huge help to know if you want to marry me – sometime."

Colin swallowed so hard he felt his Adam's apple catch in his larynx. Her eyes were limpid pools of vulnerability. He took her hand and kissed it.

"Will you marry me?"

"Yes. Yes. I thought you'd never ask."

Graham Griffith

She was smiling radiantly as she drew him to her and sought out his lips for a crushing embrace. He felt he was being devoured. It was ecstasy like he'd never known. For all he knew, it could have been two or 10 minutes later when she disengaged and drummed her fingers on his chest.

"We can't get engaged officially yet. I mean we are engaged. We know that. But we can't announce it. Not right now. It wouldn't go over well. It's our secret."

"Of course. I understand. It may never go over well. But time changes all things."

She settled back in her seat.

"I've told you, you're wrong about them. Mother would marry you herself if she could. They both want me to have a career. I want a career. It's all about the degrees... Anyway, do you think Daddy's going to deem any man worthy? Don't worry. What you did by giving me your blood will be awfully hard to beat. He knows I wouldn't be here if it weren't for you."

Colin shook his head, then squeezed her hand.

"He also knows I could have been any bloke – in the right place at the right time. It's OK. I'm not marrying your dad. I'm deliriously happy. As long as we're together, nothing else matters. Our love can survive anything."

She initiated another long French kiss, then opened her door. Once out, she leaned back in to declare in a sultry voice

"... And being informally engaged changes everything. Now that we're committed to each other, we can give ourselves completely. We can be one. There's no reason to withhold anything... It's time to think about birth control... Goodnight Sweetie. You've made me the happiest woman alive... I love you."

"I love you too."

He drove back to the farm in ecstatic disbelief and went to sleep playing over and over in his mind everything that had happened.

*   *   *

When Juliana called him during breakfast as usual, she seemed just as ebullient as when he'd left her. For the first time, the short

NIANTIC JEWEL

distance between them caused him heartache. He couldn't wait to see her. Impossible as he would have thought it, he loved her more deeply than ever. His yearning had burgeoned overnight now that he could afford himself the warm glow of knowing she wanted him as much as he wanted her.

She arrived looking spectacular in a steel-blue linen romper that caressed her alluring contours. They came together hungrily until satiating for a while the need to immerse themselves in each other. She'd found a scrolled wire basket and some blue velvet to hold Quaiapen's head and the trove with fitting dignity. He looked it over approvingly and put it on the kitchen table.

"You haven't had any more dreams, have you?

She patted the polished amber cranium.

"Nothing that I recall anyway. I think the Old Queen's at peace again. She's finished her soul journeying. I only hope Mixanno's found serenity, too."

They finished loading his things into the Jag. She wanted a last walk around, saying goodbyes to Molly and the livestock. A last stroll down to the dock, where they sat and cuddled, watching the swans teach the three brown cygnets how to pluck submerged vegetation beside the cattail beds. The pond was quiet in the lull before the big weekend. A great blue heron disturbed by clammers in the mudflats slowly gained height on its 6-foot wingspan. And high above, the osprey wheeled to catch an updraft in its never-ending search for fish.

There was a dreamlike quality to it all, which Juliana picked up on. She pointed to the bird of prey.

"They live for up to 25 years and mate for life. The swans are monogamous, too, but they only live for seven years. I think they must feel love the same as we do."

Colin nuzzled her bare shoulder and kissed it.

"Your skin always tastes so nice. The scent of your body is sheer heaven. You're a goddess and I adore you. I want to lose myself in holy communion with you.... "

He reluctantly broke off his absorption in her.

"Ospreys and swans as lovebirds. Attachment, devotion, lust, deep affection. They share with us those elements of love; those hard-wired potentials driven by evolution. I can't see their love being as rich as human love though. Otherwise they'd have advanced beyond their narrow niches in Nature."

But he couldn't keep his mind off her for long.

"I'd like to give you a ring. Something really nice that's not a diamond. That would be too obvious. We could pick it out together."

She turned to him, her face beaming.

"You don't have to ask me twice. And I know just where to get it. DePrisco's in Wellesley is like a second home. I can show you off...."

The barking of a dog proclaimed the approach of Joe Stanton's old red Chevy pickup along the farm track. They ran to meet it in the farmyard. Old Joe had on the same faded blue bib overalls and red and black checked shirt he was wearing six weeks ago when he left. Colin introduced Juliana and they went inside to hand over Quaiapen, telling the undemonstrative but teary-eyed old man only as much as they thought he'd believe.

They went back outside to view the excavation. Colin pointed out Eric's grave before making a final swing around the rest of the livestock. Then it was time to go. Colin was expecting a handshake and a thank-you. He was unprepared for the outpouring of gratitude and the bear hug that followed.

*   *   *

Back at the Palmers, on the patio with Juliana's parents, they chuckled good-naturedly over the half-gallon can of maple syrup and crock of White Mountain honey that was Joe Stanton's parting gift.

Ben Palmer was in a mischievous mood.

"You came away ahead of the game, Colin. If Joe were a true Rhode Island Yankee he would've handed you a bill. How many hours a day did you work?"

"Three I suppose."

The big man started reckoning in his head....

NIANTIC JEWEL

"So that's 3 times 7, times 6 weeks, times $15 an hour. And a waterfront property like that rents for $3,000 a week, high season... You owe Joe $28,110. You can leave the check with me and I'll see he gets it."

When the laughter quieted, Colin reached as if to pull out his wallet.

"Don't forget eggs and milk... It's a bargain. I met the woman of my dreams."

Juliana lifted his hand and kissed it.

"And I met the man of mine."

There was a pregnant pause until Alise Palmer caught her husband's eye.

"Colin's driving back to Boston. Jewel's going to follow and help him move into his new digs."

She turned to Colin.

"We'll miss you, dear. It won't be the same without you. But we'll see you soon in Wellesley I hope... Are you sure everything's ready for you? You're welcome to stay at our house if it's not."

He thanked her and stood up to leave.

"I checked this morning. The key's with the super... You've both been so good to me. I don't know how to thank you. It's been the most wonderful summer of my life."

Alise Palmer stood and hugged him.

"We should be thanking you, dear boy... It's been an extraordinary summer. And now that Jewel's made a full recovery, I wish it could last forever. But we say that about every Quonnie summer. Not that we have this much excitement every summer. Nor shall we ever again, I dare say."

Ben Palmer held his arms outstretched daring Colin to lean down for the inevitable bear hug.

"You're a limey radical and a feminist sympathizer to boot. You've allowed the sisters of militancy here to co-opt you to their egalitarian agenda. Not to mention their predilection for supernatural mumbo-jumbo. But you're alright. Your heart's in the right place. And you helped save Jewel's life. So Godspeed."

His playful mood wasn't lost on Colin. It seemed a good time to take a gamble, but when the words came out they seemed strangely disembodied, as if he wished he could distance himself from them if he'd overstepped himself.

"I think the doctors deserve all the credit. But since they don't practice in Boston would you mind if I set up some appointments with her – for checkups?"

Juliana and her mother grinned while Ben Palmer let Colin dangle awhile before responding.

"A doctor willing to make house calls, huh! I'll let Jewel decide if she wants that. After her experience with the Morton boy, never let it be said that I encouraged unwanted attentions. It's a Quonnie rule you know: All bets are off after Labor Day – affirmations of eternal love notwithstanding. There's a real world to be faced out there, and we'd better have what it takes... I suppose I have no objection, as long as you don't play Doctor!"

Juliana blushed and scolded her father.

"Daddy! It's none of your business. I'm an adult. And Colin's an English gentlemen. Not an immature American schmuck. You're identifying with your own dissolute youth."

"No, I'm identifying with my investment in your education. Boys and books don't mix. That's why you're at Wellesley."

He sensed Colin was becoming mildly uncomfortable.

"Don't mind me, Colin. My daughter has brains and beauty. The world's her oyster. She can be anything she wants. But like me she's an epicurean, a connoisseur of the good things in life, especially the sensual pleasures. That's why I have martinis with lunch and manhattans with dinner. I wouldn't be a good father if I weren't fiercely protective of my daughter's best interests, especially when her emotions prevent her from doing it herself."

Alise Palmer, now also feeling a twinge of discomfort, interrupted.

"We can tell, Ben. Thank goodness you're a happy drunk, if not always a tactful one... Listening to you, Colin could easily get the wrong idea. Jewel's right. It's none of our business. If they want to see each other back in Boston, they have my blessing."

She gave him a kiss and a hug as she whispered in his ear:

NIANTIC JEWEL

"Get some nice furniture. It's important to a woman."

He paused to wonder what she meant until Juliana took him by the arm.

"C'mon Sweetie. I'll see you to the car while the going's good. Before Daddy drops any more gems of wisdom on you."

Once beside the Jag, he lifted her off her feet in a tender embrace.

"Thanks for defending me. Your dad was just having fun."

"He's not usually that insensitive. Are you sure you didn't mind?"

"Positive. I asked for it by egging him on."

"It would serve him right if you stayed with me in Wellesley tonight."

"I think you more or less gave your mum your word that we wouldn't."

"I could stay at your place then...."

"... In a bare apartment with little more than a mattress? You deserve something more romantic. I should have it furnished by midweek, and you can stay in comfort. I want it to be our sacred space."

It was then that the meaning of Alise Palmer's prescient words struck him.

He got in the car, buckled up and turned the key.

"Take your time. Remember to turn after the light on Morrissey Boulevard. Your TomTom will tell you. Call when you pass the yacht club and I'll run down to the corner."

They joined together in a long and languid French kiss that left him delirious. She mussed his hair as she stepped back.

"This is the beginning of the rest of our lives."

THE END

Made in the USA
Middletown, DE
15 December 2018